13 $\frac{50}{}$

THE HISTORICAL ROAD OF EASTERN ORTHODOXY

Alexander Schmemann

Translated by
Lydia W. Kesich

ST VLADIMIR'S SEMINARY PRESS
CRESTWOOD, NY 10707–1699
1992

By the same author

For the Life of the World (1963)
Ultimate Questions: An Anthology of Russian Religious Thought (1965)
Introduction to Liturgical Theology (1966)
Great Lent (1969)
Of Water and the Spirit: A Liturgical Study of Baptism (1974)
Liturgy and Life (1974)
Church, World, Mission (1978)
The Eucharist (1988)
Liturgy and Tradition (1990)
Celebration of Faith (1991)

Library of Congress Cataloging-in-Publication Data

Schmemann, Alexander, (1921–1983)
  The Historical Road of Eastern Orthodoxy.

  Translation of Istoricheskii put' pravoslaviia.
  Reprint of the 1963 ed. translated from the Russian by Lydia W.
Kesich and published by Holt, Rinehart and Winston, New York.
  Bibliography: p.
  1. Orthodox Eastern Church—History. I. Title.
BX290.S373   1977   281.9   77-123074
ISBN 0–913836–47–8

This edition first published in the United States of America in 1977
by St. Vladimir's Seminary Press, Crestwood, New York.

ISBN 0–913836–47–8

FOREWORD

This book is not a scholarly investigation into the history of the Orthodox Church nor a mere manual. It is a reflection on the long historical pilgrimage of Orthodoxy, an attempt to discern in our past that which is essential and permanent and that which is secondary, mere past. I have always been amazed by the absence within the Orthodox Church of historical reflection aimed at the whole Church, at the Church as a totality. Our historical memory seems to be fragmented into local and national memories, just as—alas—is our Church life itself. Yet without the restoration of a common and truly "catholic" memory, without a common understanding of our common past, we shall not recover that catholicity, that universality of Orthodox life and experience which we confess and proclaim to be the very essence of our Tradition.

Written at first in Russian and for Orthodox readers, this book may also serve as a general introduction to the Orthodox Church and her history for Western Christians. The twentieth century has witnessed a rediscovery of the Christian East by the Christian West. Today few people in the West would say, in the words of Harnack, that "the Orthodox Church is in her entire structure alien to the Gospel and represents a perversion of the Christian religion, its reduction to the level of pagan antiquity...." On the contrary, Western Christians are seeking and often find in her spiritual and theological tradition, her religious art and her liturgy, the forgotten elements of their own background—forgotten standards, now recognized as necessary, for the measurement of Christianity. Nevertheless, despite the encounter of these two religious realms and the ever-deepening intercourse between them, and in spite of the recognition by all Christians of their common destiny in the contemporary world, knowledge—and therefore also understanding of Orthodoxy—is still far from complete in the West. Our past has not yet been integrated into the Western "memory." To the majority of Western Christians, Orthodoxy is still marginal, exotic, oriental.

It is my sincere hope that in reading this book Western Christians may realize that our past is also their past, or rather our common past, that essential "term of reference" without which no mutual understanding is possible. As the "Eastern" isolation of Orthodoxy is coming to an end, as it becomes more and more implanted in the West, it becomes urgent that its history be known and understood. The present always depends on the degree to which we have "digested" the past; it is my hope that this book may be of some help in this essential process.

ALEXANDER SCHMEMANN

July, 1977

CONTENTS

vii

the historical road of eastern orthodoxy

1 THE BEGINNING OF THE CHURCH

Acts of the Apostles

The Book of the Acts of the Apostles is the cornerstone of Church history. Written by the evangelist Luke as the sequel to his own Gospel, it tells us of the Church's first years, of the initial events in her life.* It describes the first Christian community in Jerusalem and its persecution by the Judean authorities, the preaching of the apostles—especially that of St. Paul—and finally the spread of Christianity from Jerusalem to Rome. The historical value of this account has often been challenged; indeed, at first sight it may seem remote from the modern conception of the functions and methods of history. There are many "blank pages" in Acts, many things passed over in silence. Sometimes it is more like a commentary than a simple narrative of events. But in reading it we need to remember that, just as the content of the Gospels is not exhausted by the description of the life of Christ, so Acts was not intended to be merely a historical chronicle.

This account, later a book in the New Testament, was

* Since pronominal references to the Church in the major languages other than English are usually feminine, a compromise was effected in the style of this work, with the Church as "she" in its earliest period, and "it" starting with its growing incarnation and institutionalization. Cf. "The Church and the Greco-Roman World," pp. 25 and following. (Editor's Note.)

3

written at a time when the Church, after emerging from
the first stage of her development and establishing herself
in many major centers of the Roman Empire, was already
fully conscious of her mission and was beginning to crystallize in writing her earliest experiences. St. Luke, more
than all other New Testament writers, may be called a historian in our sense of the word; nevertheless, he did not
focus his attention on history alone, or on history as such.
His theme is the Church, as the culmination of the New
Testament, as the fulfillment in the world—that is, in human society and in history—of the work Christ has accomplished. The subject of Acts is not simply the history of
the Church, but her essential nature and living image as
they were revealed in the very first years of her existence.
The book also contains the first doctrine of the Church,
with the facts of her life as illustrations; it therefore includes only facts that are of service to this teaching and
vital to its understanding. All succeeding generations of
Christians have interpreted this book doctrinally, for they
have seen in the community at Jerusalem, in the apostles'
preaching, and in the life and teaching of St. Paul the pattern that set the standard of Church life for all time, and
the inspiring beginning that laid the foundations of the
Church's entire subsequent history.

Acts begins its account with events which, for the historian, are still only on the threshold of Church history: the
Ascension and Pentecost. But in St. Luke's perspective the
Church is based on these events; they are what gives meaning to her existence, which the succeeding chapters of Acts
portray.

A small group of disciples—fishermen ("simple men,
without learning" as St. Luke describes them), women, a
few relatives and friends of the Master—here in its entirety
was the "little flock" left behind after Jesus of Nazareth.
What is it that will make them fearless preachers and lead
them to the ends of the world? It is the descent of the Holy
Spirit, the mysterious transformation after which all that

Jesus did and taught will become their own strength. Thereafter He Himself will act through His disciples and in them
His presence on earth will continue.

But what is the content of this witness? Before beginning
the actual history of the Church, we should recall to mind—
in very general terms, of course—that Gospel, or "good
news," which is the basis of Church life and Christian
preaching to the world. In the days of His earthly ministry
Jesus proclaimed the kingdom of God to men. And the
meaning of His preaching and His works was this: that His
coming is also the beginning of this kingdom, that the Son
of God has come to reveal the kingdom to men and bestow
it upon them. Although they have been torn away from
God by sin, have been subject to evil and death, and have
lost their true life, through faith in Christ men may again
come to know the one true God and His love for the world;
in union with Him they may inherit the new, eternal life
for which they were created. Jesus taught that the world
does not accept the kingdom of God, because the world
"lieth in evil" and has loved the darkness more than the
light. The Son of God, therefore, has brought to men not
only true doctrine and knowledge of the kingdom, but also
salvation. He has conquered evil and sin, which ruled over
mankind.

By His whole life He showed us the type of the perfect
man, that is, of a man utterly obedient to God. The authority and power by which He forgave sins, healed the
sick, and raised the dead existed only through this love and
obedience. In His own Person He revealed the kingdom as
complete union with God, as the power of love and sacrifice
for God and men. He was delivered up to a shameful death
and abandoned by all, yet remained the image incarnate of
complete self-surrender, perfect love, and absolute humility.
By this surrender of self, love has triumphed over hate, and
life has conquered death, for God raised Christ from the
dead. The evil of the world and the forces of disintegration
that rule it have proved powerless, and in one Man they

have been overcome. In one Man the kingdom of God—of love, goodness, and eternal life—has penetrated the realm of sin and death.

Christ did not win this victory for Himself, but for all men—to save them all and lead them into that kingdom which He brought into being. Therefore, at the very outset of His work, He chose twelve witnesses—men who were with Him continually, who heard His teachings and beheld His works, who were to be witnesses of His death, resurrection, and glorification. And when, by way of death on the Cross, He entered upon His glory, He entrusted His kingdom to them, promising that after His glorification He would bestow His power upon them, so that what He alone had done they all might do. With His power they would be able not only to tell men about Him, but also to lead them to Him and make them partakers of His kingdom.

Such was His promise, and on Pentecost it was fulfilled. On that day the little band of disciples received the power to witness, not only to the Master's life and miracles, but also to the fact that He is the Savior, King, and Lord of the world. For the disciples it is in the Church that His life continues; His dominion and power become realities through their hands, and His life becomes the new life of all who believe in Him. The coming of the Holy Spirit means all of this—out of the little flock it makes the Church.

Pentecost took place in Jerusalem. The apostles were Galileans, inhabitants of the northern part of Palestine, and we are told by St. Mark and St. Matthew that it was in Galilee that they first saw the risen Lord. But in Acts, St. Luke emphasizes the Savior's words as He instructed them not to leave Jerusalem, and the fact is important for an understanding of Church history. Jerusalem was the focal point of all the religious and national expectations of the Jews, and the heart of all Old Testament history. Steeped in the golden legend of Solomon's glory, in the past the city had witnessed the political flowering of Israel.

Now, in a time of captivity, she recognized even more clearly her role as the mystical center of Israel, the Holy Zion where, on the yet hidden "day of the Lord," the Messiah must appear to save His people and restore His kingdom. In the visions of the prophets this messianic kingdom had been transformed from a narrowly national, political restoration into the religious renewal of the world and the triumph of truth and justice. They had envisioned the Messiah Himself as the Savior of mankind from sin and death. And so on Pentecost St. Peter answered the questions of the perplexed crowd in the words of the prophet Joel: "And it shall come to pass in the last days, saith God, I will pour out of my Spirit upon all flesh" (Acts 2:17), and he professed his faith that the "great and notable day of the Lord," which every Jew awaited and believed in, had already come. This meant that for Christians the Messiah was here and all the promises and expectations of the Old Testament had been fulfilled; the messianic kingdom had arrived. It meant also that the glory of the Lord promised to Jerusalem had come down upon her and that the Old Testament history of salvation had culminated in the Church.

Such was the meaning of the first chapters of Acts, the prologue to Church history. The unbeliever may doubt their historicity. But even he must admit that at no time have Christians failed to believe in this divine origin of the Church, and unless this belief is kept in mind it is virtually impossible to understand the whole subsequent development of her history.

Community in Jerusalem—The First Church

A small sect within Judaism—viewed superficially, this is a possible definition of the Christian status in Jerusalem during the very early years. There were many similar sects and religious factions in the Jewish world of that era. It

was a period of religious and political excitement, of a
heightening of the hopes and expectations connected with
Israel's national destiny and the biblical prophecies of the
ultimate triumph of the chosen people. The time of the
final revolt against the hated Roman rule was approaching;
the destruction of Jerusalem was near at hand. "Lord, wilt
thou at this time restore again the kingdom to Israel?"
(Acts 1:6.) The question the disciples addressed to their
departing Master burned deep in Jewish hearts. But for the
Christians (and at first almost all of them were Jews) their
own faith was the answer, for the confession of Jesus as the
Christ was central to it, and in bringing their own kindred
to the Messiah they saw their first goal, for He had come to
"the lost sheep of the house of Israel." If He had been
crucified by the rulers of the people, Israel could still repent
and turn to her Savior. "For the promise is unto you, and to
your children" (Acts 2:39); these words of Peter's first
address to the Jews were the basis of all the early preaching.
For the first Christian generation, which was by birth almost completely Jewish, the conversion of Israel seemed
the fulfillment of Christ's covenant. He had charged His
disciples to begin preaching about Him in Jerusalem and
Judea, and we are told in Acts that a great many Jews were
converted at the very beginning. Later there was to be a
final and total break with Judaism, but before that event
the Church lived believing in the possible conversion of
Israel.

The explanation for this belief is a fact which seems
strange to us now: the first community in Jerusalem not
only did not separate itself from Judaism, but even preserved Jewish religious forms intact in its own life. The
apostles observed the appointed hours of prayer and all the
ritual injunctions concerning food; when St. Paul came to
Jerusalem, he agreed without objection to a request by St.
James and the presbyters that he perform the ceremony of
ritual purification, in order that "all may know . . . that
thou thyself also walkest orderly, and keepest the law"
(Acts 21:24). The Temple at Jerusalem remained for

Christians a place of prayer, instruction, and preaching. Even when the initial link with it was broken and Christian worship began to develop independently, that worship retained—and always will retain—the stamp of its Jewish origins. The fundamental principles of Orthodox worship were determined almost entirely by the Temple and the synagogue.

Although we do not at first see any sharp break with Judaism, this does not mean, as some historians once thought, that Christianity began to experience its own radical newness only later, after entering the Greco-Roman world; that only then, under the influence of that world, did it create its "original" pattern of life and organization. The fact is, this sense that a radical change had taken place in world history and human life was the most basic and outstanding trait of the early Christian community as described in Acts and St. Paul's epistles. But we must understand that for the Christians of Jerusalem the preservation of the Jewish religious tradition and mode of life was not a mere survival of the past from which they were released as they grew in understanding of their own faith. On the contrary, they observed the tradition because for them it all bore witness to the truth of their faith. Christ Himself had declared His work to be the fulfillment of the Scriptures: "Thus it is written . . . thus it behoved . . ." (Luke 24:46). "You pore over the scriptures . . . it is of these I speak as bearing witness to me" (John 5:39). The old accustomed words and ancient rites were now radiant with new light, and in them Christians were always discovering new points to confirm the truth and plenitude of the New Testament. St. Matthew's Gospel, written in the Judeo-Christian milieu, was later to express this fundamental Christian belief in the Old Testament as prophecy and doctrine about Christ.

Just as the prophecies have come true and the Church is the culmination of the Old Testament, she also, while preserving Old Testament doctrine, incarnates in her life the "new thing" revealed in Christ: the society that Christians compose, which, despite all its links with the traditional religion, is quite distinct from it. The New Testament Scriptures, already set down in Greek, called it *ekklesia*—the Church. In the social and political life of the Greco-Roman world this word signified an official citizens' assembly with legislative powers, called together to decide on public questions and express their sovereign will. But in the Greek translation of the Old Testament—the so-called Septuagint, made in Alexandria during several centuries before the Christian era—this term acquired a religious meaning, that of the company of God's people, the chosen people whom God Himself has summoned to His service. Thus the application of the word to the Christian community in the New Testament indicates that even from the beginning this community knew itself to be a divine institution called to a special ministry. It was not to be merely a religious brotherhood or spiritual society, but the Church, the visible company of those who have been called to declare God's will and carry out His work. "But ye are a chosen generation, a royal priesthood, an holy nation, a peculiar people; that ye should show forth the praises of him who hath called you out of darkness into his marvellous light: which in time past were not a people, but are now the people of God" (I Peter 2:9 f.)—here is the definition of the Church we find in Peter's first epistle.

So new and so holy was this company that joining it is already defined in the Gospels as a new birth, accomplished through a symbolic act. This is baptism, the liturgical immersion in water of the new Christian which commemorates and symbolizes Christ's death and resurrection. On the day of Pentecost those who believed in St. Peter's preaching asked him what they must do. "Repent," Peter said to them, "and be baptized every one of you in the name of Jesus Christ, for the remission of sins, and ye shall receive the gift of the Holy Ghost" (Acts 2:38). The early Church lived by the experience of baptism, men were brought to it by the call of the Gospel preachings; the community's liturgical life was bound up with baptism, and the symbols and allegories of the earliest Christian paintings on the walls of the catacombs testify again and again to the tremendous power of regeneration the first Christians experienced in the baptismal water.[1]

Baptism ushers men into the new life which is still "hid with Christ in God," and into the kingdom of God, which in this world is as yet only the kingdom of the age to come. In early Christian experience the Church was the anticipation of the future by faith; she was the mysterious growth of the seed that had been cast upon the earth and was now hidden in it. "Maranatha . . . the Lord cometh"—with this triumphant liturgical cry Christians express both their expectation that Christ will come again in glory and their faith that He is implicitly present among them now.

But if this new life begins with baptism, the central act of the community, in which it professed its essential nature as Christ's kingdom, was the breaking of bread. On the night before His Passion, Christ Himself commanded His followers to continue this act. It was a meal in common, modeled after the supper Christ had eaten with His disciples. At this meal the Eucharist, or thanksgiving to God for Christ's sacrifice, was offered up, after which all who were present divided the bread and wine among them and through it became partakers of the Body and Blood of Christ, that is, of the life of Christ Himself. All the records of the time which have come down to us testify that then, as always, Christians believed that in the breaking of bread they were united with Christ Himself.

The breaking of bread took place from house to house, at gatherings of the community separate from its attendance at the Temple. And the special day of the Eucharist was the first day of the week, the day following the Sabbath, on which, according to the apostles' testimony, Christ had risen. Christians call this day the "Lord's day." Here was perhaps the most vigorous expression of the early Church's awareness of herself as an absolutely new beginning which was leading Christians beyond the framework of the tradi-

[1] Cf. V. V. Weidle, *Baptism of Art* (Westminster, England, 1950).

tional religion. During the three centuries that preceded
Constantine, the Christian holy day was not a day of rest
but an ordinary working day. It was not the "seventh" day,
which men since ancient times had reckoned as the final
day of the week; it was the following day. In this conscious
departure from the earlier emphasis of the week, the Church
bears witness to the fact that her own life, as it flows
onward in this world, is a foretaste of that eternal day which
dawned on the morning of the first victory over death.
"For ye are dead," said the Apostle Paul, "and your life is
hid with Christ in God. When Christ, who is our life, shall
appear, then shall ye also appear with him in glory" (Col.
3:3 f.). At that time these words were understood literally:
into our familiar, everyday world and natural human existence had come a great and growing light—the dazzling
radiance of another world, of eternal life.

Thus the little Judean sect, almost unnoticed by the
world when it first emerged, felt itself to be the salt of the
earth and the light of the world—the source of the new
light, called to enlighten men and save them.

Early Church Organization

This community has often been contrasted with the "organized" Church of a later age, as though early Christians
had been a kind of fluid, ecstatic brotherhood living on
inspiration, with no authority except the "breath of the
Spirit." In fact, however, from the beginning the very concept of a Church included the idea of an organized
society, and nothing was more foreign to the early Christian
outlook than any kind of opposition between spirit and
form, or between freedom and organization. Human society, they believed, was now filled with the Spirit of God
and was thereby a vehicle of the divine life, so that everything human in society becomes a channel for things
divine, while everything spiritual is made incarnate in the

life of mankind. When Paul called the Church the Body
of Christ he had simply found words to describe something
Christians had experienced from the very beginning—the
sense of the Church as one body made up of the many
people united by the new life—in the language of a later
day, the life of grace. "For by one Spirit are we all baptized
into one body" (I Cor. 12:13).

The idea of an organism presupposes a structure essentially hierarchical in character. In the very first descriptions
of the Church we see a definite ruling body invested with
power and authority. This was the Twelve, the original
group of disciples whom Christ Himself had chosen. "It is
not ye who have chosen Me, but I have chosen you." This
election by the Savior and not by men was the source of
their unique and incontestable authority, and it was through
them that the Lord's dominion was exercised in His
Church. They had witnessed His earthly life; when they
preached about Him they were telling of what they themselves had heard, seen, and felt. At Pentecost, they were
filled with the Holy Spirit and granted the power to give a
reliable account of their witness and to practice it in this
world. They were also granted the power to teach, to "bind
and loose," to make decisions—in a word, to be the archi-
tects of the Church. To enter the Church, therefore, meant
to believe in their teachings; the community itself "continued stedfastly in the apostles' doctrine and fellowship"
(Acts 2:42).

The significance of the Twelve as the cornerstone of the
Church was so indisputable to the first community in Jerusalem that its first act, even before Pentecost, was to complete their number, replacing Judas who had shown himself
a traitor. This twelfth man had to be one of the early
disciples. "Of these men which have companied with us
all the time that the Lord Jesus went in and out among us,
beginning from the baptism of John, unto that same day
that he was taken up from us, must one be ordained to be
a witness with us of his resurrection" (Acts 1:21 f.). This

choosing was thought of as an election by the Lord Himself: "And they prayed, and said, Thou, Lord, which
knowest the hearts of all men, show whether of these two
thou hast chosen, that he may take part of this ministry
and apostleship, from which Judas by transgression fell
. . . and the lot fell upon Matthias; and he was numbered
with the eleven apostles" (Acts 1:24–26).

The author of Acts singles out Peter as the leader of the
apostles, the spokesman of their unanimity. It is Peter who
proposes filling the gap in their number and who explains
the meaning of Pentecost to the bewildered crowd in a
sermon. He it is, also, who replies to the accusations of the
Judean rulers and pronounces judgment upon Ananias and
Sapphira, whose evil cunning had disturbed the solidarity
that prevailed in the life of the first Church. In a later age
the position of Peter in the early community and among
the apostles became a bone of contention, and eventually
this controversy separated the Christian West from Eastern
Orthodoxy. But in Acts he always speaks in the name of all
the apostles and expresses only the common consensus
of their witness. In Eastern tradition he has always remained the "supreme" apostle. But this primacy has been
understood as a gift of grace to be the voice of apostolic
unanimity—not in terms of any special power over the
apostles or the Church.[2]

The apostles governed the Church, but their basic ministry was the "ministry of the Word," the preaching of
Christ. Therefore, when the number of disciples multiplied
and the cares of ruling the community increased, they proposed that special persons be chosen for this administrative
work, so that the Twelve would be able to give themselves
"continually to prayer, and to the ministry of the word.
And the saying pleased the whole multitude," and they
chose seven men, "whom they set before the apostles: and
when they had prayed, they laid their hands on them"
(Acts 6:4–6). In the selection of these seven, Luke gives

[2] Cf. Afanassiev, Schmemann, Meyendorff, Koulomzine, *The Primacy of
Peter in Orthodox Thought* (London, 1963).

us the fundamental principles upon which the Church's hierarchy and its later development are based. If the apostles had been chosen by Christ Himself, these new ministers had been chosen by the Church, but at the apostles' initiative and with their approval. Moreover, after the election of the seven, each was ordained by the apostles through the laying on of hands. It was the apostles who decided the conditions for selection; those chosen must be "men of honest report, full of the Holy Ghost and wisdom" (Acts 6:3). Thus all ministry in the Church, indeed her entire hierarchic structure, is rooted in her apostolic beginnings; this means that she is rooted in Christ Himself, since the apostles were His witnesses. The Church chooses her own ministers, but it is God Himself, through the hands of the apostles, who bestows upon them the special gift of the Spirit to perform their ministry.

But although their preaching and teaching was the link between all the churches, each Church through its local hierarchy also received the apostolic gifts and doctrine in full measure. In the community at Jerusalem, the model upon which all the other churches were based, even at a very early stage St. James and the presbyters exercised authority along with the apostles. The apostles moved on, but everywhere local hierarchies remained to continue their work, preserve their witness, hand on their gifts, and—in harmony with all the other communities—to realize in this world the unity of the Church as the one, indivisible people of God which is everywhere assembled together to proclaim the new life. In this way we are given from the outset an example and definition of what later became known as "apostolic succession."

Life of Christians

But what, one may now ask, was the positive ideal of life held by this community? For the early Church, unity in love was the ultimate value; it was the supreme purpose

of life that Christ Himself had revealed to men. The
Church was the restoration of the unity that had been
broken and torn asunder by sin; those who were baptized,
who were living in union with Christ and sharing in His
life through the breaking of bread, were reunited with God,
and in God they also found unity with one another.

This unity was demonstrated above all in the active love
through which each Christian was conscious that he belonged to all the brethren, and conversely, that they all
belonged to him. The unity of Christians with one another
is now, alas, only symbolized by their communion in divine
service; in the early Church the liturgy was the crowning
point of a real unity, a continual communion in everyday
life; moreover, the liturgy was then unthinkable apart from
that communion. In early Christian writings no other word
is so often repeated as "brother," and Christians of that
age filled the idea of brotherhood with vital meaning, which
showed clearly in their unity of thought: "And the multitude of them that believed were of one heart and of one
soul . . ." (Acts 4:32).

Brotherhood also meant active mutual support among
Christians "of all for all"—a care which was both material
and spiritual. "And all that believed were together, and
had all things in common; and sold their possessions and
goods, and parted them to all men, as every man had need"
(Acts 2:44 f.). The very smallness of the Christian community in Jerusalem made it possible to put unity of life
into practice in a radical way through sharing their property. This phenomenon, inaccurately described as "primitive Christian communism," was not the product of any
specifically Christian economic or social theory, but a manifestation of love. Its meaning lies not in community of
property as such, but in the evidence it gives us of the new
life that manifested itself among them, entirely transforming the old. In the Pauline epistles we find the summons:
"Every man according as he purposeth in his heart, so let
him give" (II Cor. 9:7)—a remark which points to the

survival of private property in other Christian communities. But the utter devotion of the Jerusalem community —the brotherhood of "beggars" as St. Paul called them— remains forever in the mind of Christendom as an ineffaceable example and legacy, the ideal of an authentic regeneration of all human relationships through love.

The early Church has often been described as indifferent to this world and as existing in a continual tense expectancy of the End. But the new life also involved a new attitude toward the world; since for Christians this love is not an internal affair of the Church, but, on the contrary, the essence of her witness in the world. "By this shall all men know that ye are my disciples, if ye love one another" (John 13:35). If we read the New Testament with care we discover a complete doctrine concerning the world and how Christians should relate to it and live in it. The Sermon on the Mount, the Beatitudes, the figure of the merciful, succoring Christ are proclaimed to the world by the Church and will remain the world's ideal even when men reject the Church. And when Christians have sought the basic standards by which to determine their relationship to the state, to the family, to work—indeed, to all aspects of human life—have they not always searched the epistles of St. Paul? The expectation of the End, the prayers for the coming of Christ—everything which it is now the fashion to call eschatological—cannot, without doing violence to historical truth, be divorced from this positive ideal. The kingdom to come for which Christians pray is for them inseparable from judgment, and their judgment will reflect the precise extent to which they have embodied their faith in their own lives, i.e., in the world. "Inasmuch as ye have done it unto one of the least of these . . ." (Matt. 25:40). Through Christ the kingdom of God has entered human life in order to regenerate it.

Here, then, is the image of the Church bequeathed to us by the records of her earliest days. Does this mean that she had no failings or weaknesses then? Of course not. The

author of Acts mentions many of them, and in the Pauline
epistles whole chapters will be devoted to exposing and
scoring these sins. But as we begin the history of the
Church, in which such sins and weaknesses will too often
be painfully obvious, we also need to keep in mind that
"icon of the Church"—that image and realization of the
first experience of true life in the Church—to which Christians will always have recourse when they seek to cure their
spiritual ailments and overcome their sins.

Break with Judaism

The conflict with the Judean religious authorities, the
next main topic in Acts, introduces us to the second phase
of Church history in the apostolic age. By providing the
impetus for the expansion of the new faith beyond the
limits of Jewry, it brought the Church out onto the broad
highroad of history.

This conflict had been brewing since the very beginning.
The members of the Sanhedrin twice ordered the arrest
of the heads of the Church, but on both occasions set them
free after questioning. After all, the Christians were not
breaking the Mosaic law; their sole offense was that they
preached "the name of Jesus" and the resurrection of the
dead. But the doctrine of resurrection had its adherents,
particularly among the Pharisees. Gamaliel, a leading
Pharisee, spoke out in favor of avoiding conflict: "If this
counsel or this work be of men, it will come to nought:
but if it be of God, ye cannot overthrow it" (Acts 5:38 f.).
The author of Acts constantly emphasizes that the Jews
have no objection they can raise against Christian teaching,
since it is itself based on the Scriptures and testifies to the
fulfillment of the Law and the Prophets.

But difficulties developed none the less, to which the
interrogation and stoning of Stephen gave explosive mo-
mentum under the zeal of Saul. "And at that time there

was a great persecution against the church which was at
Jerusalem; and they were all scattered abroad throughout
the regions of Judea and Samaria, except the apostles. . . .
Therefore they that were scattered abroad went every where
preaching the word" (Acts 8:1,4). Up to that time the
Church had stayed in Jerusalem. We have already seen that
the Church, by virtue of her very purpose, at the beginning
had to reveal herself as a united, visible company—the
messianic community gathered together around the Twelve
in the Holy City in order to testify to the advent of the
promised kingdom of God. Now she would have to accept
as her lot all the heat and dust of her long—and very
human and earthly—journey through history, a journey
that began with the expulsion of Christians from Jerusalem
by force. The Christians of Jerusalem, who were Jews by
birth, naturally looked upon the Church as primarily the
crowning point of their own Jewish tradition; they did not
yet comprehend her universal, pan-human mission. Indeed,
the question as to whether or not pagans should be received into the Church was to be one of her first acute
growing pains.

The Apostle Paul

The preaching to the Samaritans, St. Philip's conversion
of the Ethiopian nobleman, and the conversion of the
Roman Cornelius were still exceptional cases; even missionaries who went further afield—to Cyprus, Antioch, and
Rome—at first preached only to Jews, though other converts
began at Antioch, and no doubt elsewhere, to share the
Good News of Christ with pagans.

The life work of St. Paul, which won for him the title
of Apostle to the Gentiles, brought to completion the
formative period of the Church. Since Acts was written
by his traveling companion and "beloved physician," and
since Paul's letters to the various Christian communities

both describe his spiritual experience and expound his understanding of doctrine, we have more information about him than about any other apostle. An orthodox Jew born at Tarsus in the Diaspora, his religious consciousness was completely conditioned by the insatiable Old Testament thirst for the living God, but he also breathed freely in the atmosphere of the Greco-Roman world. He received his religious education in Jerusalem from Gamaliel, the intellectual spokesman of the Pharisees; his consequent natural enmity to Christianity already revealed the wholehearted ardor with which he applied his religious ideals to life.

In the turning point of his life on the road to Damascus, which Paul always described as a call to him "not of men, neither by a man" (Gal. 1:1) but by Christ Himself, he heard the voice of the Master and was converted to Him completely and with finality. Books have been written to explain the conversion scientifically as the result of psychological or neurological factors, or even of the epilepsy from which he is alleged to have suffered. But it is clear that we are dealing with a mystery which science, even with the aid of its most delicate instruments, cannot fully explain. What is important is that every word spoken by Paul that has come down to us shows how his whole being and consciousness were rooted in the person of Christ, and attests his conviction that he had received a special revelation of the Christ. That is why the Church, despite the abundance of opposition and misunderstanding encountered by Paul during his life, does not hesitate to acknowledge him as an apostle equal to the Twelve, and to number him among those whose witness is a cornerstone of the Church.

After his baptism Paul spent three years in Damascus. He then went to Jerusalem, which he was always to regard as the elder Church, the focal point of Christianity. Driven out by the hatred of the Jews, he journeyed back north to Antioch, which was, after Jerusalem, the second most important center of Christianity, and there rose to a leading position as a preacher in the Christian congregation. His lifelong devotion to the "ministry of the Word" led to the founding of a whole network of churches in Asia Minor, Greece, and possibly also in the western part of the Roman Empire.

From the very outset of his ministry Paul was confronted with the whole problem of the position within the Church of converts from paganism, a problem destined to affect the entire future of the Church. Christianity had taken root in the chief centers of the Roman Empire—Antioch, Alexandria, and Rome—even before he began to preach. As yet, however, the controversy over it remained an intra-Judaic dispute. Thus the Roman historian Suetonius states that the Emperor Claudius banished all Jews from Rome in the year 49 A.D. because the question of "a certain Christ" had provoked outbreaks of disorder among them. Paul, too, began his preaching in Asia Minor by addressing the local Jews. On arriving in a given city, he would go into the local synagogue and, basing his sermon on the Scriptures read there every Sabbath, would begin to preach about Christ. With only a few exceptions, the Jews rejected him and he would then turn to the Gentiles. Paul never doubted that "the word of God should first have been spoken to you . . ." (Acts 13:46)—i.e., to the Jews. The Jewish rejection of Christ was a "continual sorrow" to him. "For I could wish that myself were accursed from Christ for my brethren, my kinsmen according to the flesh" (Rom. 9:2 f.). But he was equally certain that the Gospels had been addressed to the whole earth for salvation "unto the ends of the world" (Rom. 10:18).

Soon it was no longer a question of individual conversions or exceptional cases; now there were whole Christian communities of Gentiles. Did the ritual prescriptions of the Old Testament, which had remained in force among the Judeo-Christians of Jerusalem, apply to these people? St. Paul answered this question with a flat "No!" Nor did he see the problem in terms of the best method of converting Gentiles; he believed this was an issue involving

the very essence of the Christian Good News. First in his
Epistle to the Galatians, written in the heat of controversy,
and later in a more academic manner in his Epistle to the
Romans, he developed his doctrine concerning the relation
between law and grace and the freedom of Christians from
the law. He was not in the least inclined to deny the importance of the Old Testament. "The law is holy, and
the commandment holy and just and good" (Rom. 7:12).
But the law simply defined evil and sin, it gave no power
of salvation from sin. Even when a man knows what is
good and what evil, he is often powerless to crush the latter.
"For the good that I would I do not: but the evil which I
would not, that I do" (Rom. 7:19). Man is the slave of
sin and he cannot free himself from his servitude. If the
setting up of a law or norm—the knowledge of it—included
the power to avoid going against it, there would be no need
for salvation in Christ. But in giving man law, God reveals
to him the abnormality of evil—a sinful violation of His
will concerning the world and mankind—and at the same
time condemns him; for sinful man, lacking the strength
to save himself from sin, lies under judgment. But He who
is without sin has taken upon Himself the whole burden
of our sins and their condemnation under the law; by His
death He has redeemed us. In Christ law died and grace
ascended the throne, and through faith in Christ and union
with Him in the baptismal death man ceases to be a slave
and receives a share in His life.

Nor has this salvation been granted to the Jews alone,
but to all mankind. St. Paul never denied that the Jews
were a superior people, God's elect, but for him they
excelled other nations not because the Word of God had
been committed to them, but because through them the
way had been prepared for the advent of Christ. Any person who believes in Christ and shares in His life and death
must realize that now there is "neither Jew nor Greek"
(Gal. 3:28); if he still thinks to obtain justification through
fulfilling the ritual injunctions of the law, let him know

that "Christ is become of no effect unto you, . . . ye are fallen from grace" (Gal. 5:4). For in love lies the whole meaning of the law, yet the law itself has no power to give love. In Christ love is freely bestowed upon men, and through Him and in Him the law thus becomes unnecessary. In Him "circumcision is nothing, and uncircumcision is nothing, but the keeping of the commandments of God" (I Cor. 7:19).

When Paul and his companion Barnabas returned to Antioch and gave an account of their travels, they met with opposition and censure from the element among Judeo-Christians which continued to regard the observance of Mosaic law as binding upon all members of the Church without exception. One can see from his epistles that Paul had constantly to defend his apostleship and doctrines against the slander of his enemies, who sought to tear from his grasp the churches he had founded.

In Church tradition the so-called apostolic council in Jerusalem has remained the model for all subsequent councils and the standard of catholicity for the Church. In addition to the apostles, the presbyters—the hierarchy of the local community—and through them the whole Church in Jerusalem took part. It was James, the head of that Church, who summed up the deliberations and proposed a solution. By it the non-Jewish Christians were now officially freed of the burden of the law. They were enjoined only from taking part in pagan ritual banquets (Acts 15:20). An epistle to that effect was prepared and sent to the Gentile Christians of Antioch, Syria, and Cilicia. Although this decision was not unanimously or everywhere accepted, a decisive step had been taken: by freeing the converted Gentiles from Judaic law—thereby freeing them from being included in the Jewish nation—the Church demonstrated that she was now fully conscious of her world-wide vocation.

Paul continued his preaching ministry for many more years. Three of his great journeys are described in Acts, but these did not exhaust his apostolic activities. In each city he followed up his preaching by establishing the Church, consecrating bishops and presbyters, and building up a Christian community. Teacher, shepherd, father as well as preacher, he embodied perfectly the pastoral ideal which he himself had formulated. "I am made all things to all men, that I might by all means save some" (I Cor. 9:22). When the dangers of Judaic legalism were paralleled by that of a pagan mystery cult religiosity, in which the moral content of the liberty in Christ conferred upon converts was forgotten, Paul's infinite patience and tireless concern were constantly used in the service of the full doctrine of the Gospel.

In the final analysis everything the apostle said, all the answers he gave, can be summed up in one fundamental, tirelessly repeated affirmation and appeal: "In Christ." These two words give us a pattern for the Christian life. Faith and baptism have united us with Christ; Paul saw Christians as living in such unity with Him, love for Him, and eagerness to serve Him that the whole Church is nothing other than His Body, which He Himself has created through the Holy Spirit. Everything in the Church, therefore—organization, assemblies, variety of gifts, even administrative cares—exists only so that we may grow toward Christ and give back, both to Him and to all around us, that treasure of grace which we have received from Him. If the Church appears in the first chapters of Acts as the advent of the long-promised kingdom of God, Paul's epistles now reveal this kingdom to be the life of Christ Himself, that life which has been bestowed as a gift upon men and which unites them in the Holy Spirit in an indissoluble union with God and with one another.

The great apostle's life ended in martyrdom. In Jerusalem, to which he invariably hastened after every new journey, he was finally seized by the Jews. About to be flogged, he made mention of his Roman citizenship, which entitled him to trial before the emperor. The narrative of Acts records his arrival in Rome under arrest and his two years of preaching activity in the capital, then suddenly breaks off. It is not by chance that the books ends in this manner; its main theme is the journey of the Church from Jerusalem to Rome, from the center of Israel to the center of the empire.

What was left when the ministry of the apostles had been sealed by their blood? There were only insignificant groups of Christians scattered about the world. Nobody knew much about them and at first hardly anyone even noticed their existence. Nevertheless, the first victory had been won: the Good Tidings of Christ had been heard. Throughout the next period of Church history, the time of persecutions, the profound assurance of the apostle will resound: "As unknown, and yet well known; as dying, and behold, we live; as chastened, and not killed; as sorrowful, yet always rejoicing; as poor, yet making many rich; as having nothing, yet possessing all things" (Cor. 6:9 f.).

The Church and the Greco-Roman World

Christ was born when Augustus reigned alone upon the earth, as the Christmas hymn proclaims. The Church has not forgotten that it began when the Roman Empire was at its peak. The Greco-Roman world, which was the Roman state held together by Hellenistic culture, was, after Judaism, the second motherland of Christianity. The myth that this world was unique and universal has been undermined as our historical horizons have broadened and our understanding of other ancient worlds and cultures has extended. Yet it is not merely a myth, and no Christian can be indifferent to the significance of this tradition. For the Christian mind, history cannot be a mechanical chain of cause and effect, nor can the foundation of the Church in precisely that world and at precisely that moment be simply a matter of chance. "But when the fulness of the time was come, God sent forth his Son" (Gal. 4:4). The world that was the "historical flesh" of the Church met Christianity with hostility and persecution, yet it ultimately proved capable of heeding the Christian teaching, and to some extent of responding to it. Nor can it be merely chance that the sacred words of the Gospels were written in Greek, or that the theology of the Church, the human answer to divine revelation, was clothed in Hellenic categories of thought. The Gospel cannot be thoroughly understood if separated from its Jewish, Old Testament sources; it is also inseparable from the world in which the Good News was first destined to be proclaimed.

Although the empire of Alexander the Great fell apart almost within a year of his death, Hellenism conquered with its culture, which gradually became a unifying pattern from Armenia to Spain, from the Sahara to the Danube and the Rhine. The Roman conquests in the second and first centuries B.C. only continued this Hellenization. It was in the world-wide monarchy of Rome that the Hellenistic era reached its apogee. After a century of wars and devastation, there the Pax Romana finally reigned. Roman law everywhere assured a good measure of justice, stability, and well-being. With good roads, economic prosperity, and a widespread exchange of writings and ideas, it is not surprising that the source and symbol of all these benefits, *Roma Augusta* herself, gradually became the object of a cult—the highest value of this newly-unified mass of humanity.

Yet beneath the external glitter and prosperity a deep spiritual crisis was developing. Men were no longer satisfied with the national gods of popular religion who had previously guarded the narrow horizon of their city, tribe, or clan. Many sought new spiritual nourishment in the Eastern mysteries that engulfed the empire. Temples to Isis, Cybele, and Dionysus were erected in the center of Rome, and secret ceremonies, promising immortality and regeneration, were performed. This was an era of premonitions and expectations. "A single Empire, a single world language, a single culture, a single common trend in the direction of monotheism, and single common longing for a Savior"— this is how Harnack has summarized the circumstances in which Christianity began to spread.

People of the Early Church

The Jewish dispersion, which eventually resulted in the establishment of Jewish communities in almost every city of the empire, was, of course, the intended instrument for this expansion. Historians have calculated that there were no less than four million Jews living in the Diaspora, whereas the whole Roman population totalled fifty million. Despite the innumerable religious restrictions that continued to separate the Jews from the "unclean," their constant contact with Hellenistic culture inevitably had some effect on them. In contrast to the Palestinian rabbis, the Jews of the Diaspora felt a need to explain their faith to the outer world. The Septuagint had made the Bible accessible to the Greek-speaking world; later on, the Alexandrian Jew Philo tried to express the faith of his fathers in the categories of Greek thought.

The pagans, meanwhile, were showing a growing interest in the East and its religious core; a number of them became Jews, not by blood, but by the faith which gave central place to the expectation of the Messiah. The network of synagogues that covered the whole empire became the means by which the preaching of the Gospel penetrated the milieu closest to Judaism and accessible to its spiritual influence.

Naturally, we cannot explain early Christian preaching and conversion in terms of any single approach; Paul's epistles make clear how differently he addressed different groups. Yet the center of all preaching was always the *kerygma*, the proclamation of a new event, the news of the Savior who brought salvation and peace. There was no mass preaching to a crowd nor attraction of popular curiosity by outward ceremonies. More than by words, Christianity was served by the actual renewal of life which appeared in the Christian community and was in the final analysis alone capable of proving the life-giving force of the Gospel.

There was a time when it was assumed that the first Christians came from the international "proletariat" which filled the large cities of the empire and which, because of poverty and social inequality, was assumed to be more receptive to the proclamation of love, hope, and new life. Paul's words to the Corinthians seems to confirm such a supposition: ". . . not many wise men after the flesh, not many mighty, not many noble were called" (Cor. 1:26). But one has also to account for James' reproaches of rich Christians, for Pliny's report of the number of Christians "of various classes," and for references in other Pauline epistles to the city treasurer, a member of the Areopagus, and a number of the leading women in Thessalonica.

How many Christians were there at first? Tertullian's claim, "If we alone are your enemies, then you have more enemies than citizens, because all your citizens have become Christians," is obviously rhetorical exaggeration. There was, however, a rapid geographical spread of Christianity, with large churches in Syria, Egypt, Asia Minor, and perhaps in Spain and Gaul. The estimate of historians is that up to the time of Emperor Constantine's conversion at the beginning of the fourth century they were still less than 10 per cent of the whole population of the empire. Thus the Church retained for a long time its character of a small flock, a minority persecuted by the world.

Further Church Development

Since there are few records of the period from the apostolic beginning of the Church to the middle of the second century, a number of historians have been tempted to look for some sort of metamorphosis within it at this period, some break with the original "idea" of Christianity expressed in the Gospels. The organized Church with its hierarchy, doctrine, and discipline, as we see it again in the middle of the second century, they regard as the product of various crises and adaptations to social conditions; the molten, shapeless faith was "Hellenized" by being poured into contemporary molds of thought. Today, however, scholars are giving increasing attention to the voice of Church tradition, which so recently seemed to some of them a tendentious invention. The Gospel, it turns out, must not be separated from the Church; it is the witness to the faith of the Church, to its living experience, and cannot be understood apart from this experience. Fragments of prayers, the signs and symbols on the walls of the catacombs, a few epistles from some churches to others, have acquired new significance and are seen to represent part of a single development, not a series of crises and ruptures. What was not recorded may have lived secretly, retained in the uninterrupted memory of the Church, to be written down only centuries later. It has become increasingly clear that the Church has no need to be restored and justified on the basis of the fragments that have reached us. Rather, only in the light of the Church, in the recognition of its primacy, can the meaning of these fragments be discerned and properly interpreted.

In our limited knowledge of the churches scattered throughout the Roman Empire, the emphasis is on the Christian community gathered for baptism and the Eucharist. This double mystery—rebirth from water and the Spirit and the breaking of bread—was not simply a ceremonial service but the source, the content, the very heart of primitive Christianity.

Tertullian's words, "Christians are not born but they become," explain why the scanty sources of the period speak most about baptism and the Eucharist. Christians became. This meant that each of them could never forget the day when, after the secret growth of the seed cast into his soul by preaching—after doubts, tests, and torments—he finally approached the water of baptism. When he emerged from the holy water, the newly-baptized Christian was brought into a brotherhood, a unity of love. Such is the everlasting significance of the Eucharist, communion always through Christ with one's brothers. One bread, one cup, shared by all and uniting all in one, memory transformed into reality, expectation into the Presence. How the words of thanksgiving preserved from the early youth of the Church must have sounded when pronounced by the celebrant over the offered gifts!

We thank you, our Father, for the life and knowledge which you have revealed through Jesus, your Child. To You be glory forever. As this piece of bread was scattered over the hills and there was brought together and made one, so let your Church be brought together from the ends of the earth into your Kingdom . . . Remember, Lord, Your Church, to save it from all evil and to make it perfect by Your love. Make it holy, and gather it together from the four winds into Your Kingdom which You have made ready for it.[3]

In the light of the Eucharistic meeting, every day and every deed performed were steps on the way to the final victory of the coming Lord; because of the Sacrament, Christians do not look on the Church as a simple human organization, with a leader and subordinates, authority and obedience, but as a living organism imbued with the Holy Spirit.

At the head of the community stood the bishop. His authority was unique. Appointed by the apostles or their successors, the other bishops, he was the head and source of the Church's life. His special gift consisted in transforming the gathering of Christians through the Sacrament into the Body of Christ and in uniting them in an indivisible union of new life. The power to dispense the sacraments

[3] *The Didache*, C. C. Richardson, ed. and trans., *Early Christian Fathers*, "Library of Christian Classics," Vol. I (Philadelphia, 1953) pp. 175-76.

was indissolubly linked with the power to teach; he taught
at the meeting, not by his own initiative but according to
the Spirit; he was the guardian of the apostolic tradition,
the witness to the universal unity of the Church. "One
must look on the bishop as on the Lord himself," writes
St. Ignatius of Antioch in the beginning of the second
century. Therefore "nobody must do anything that has to
do with the Church without the bishop's approval . . .
Where the bishop is present, there let the congregation
gather, just as where Jesus Christ is, there is the Catholic
Church."[4]

The bishop was helped in administering the Church by
the presbyters, or elders. While St. Ignatius compared the
bishops to Christ, he compared the presbyters to the apostles. Installed by the bishop through the laying on of hands,
they helped him in every way and passed on his teachings
and directions to the community. The primitive Church
was a city community, a meeting of Christians in one place
around a bishop, but when the number of Christians grew
and a single meeting of this sort became impossible, the
community split into a network of parishes dependent on it.
Then the presbyters replaced the bishop and became his
fully-empowered deputies, but through the sacrament of the
episcopal laying on of hands all congregations retained their
organic link with the bishop as the beneficent organ of
Church unity.

After the bishop and the presbyters came the deacons,
the "servers." They were the "ears, hands, and eyes" of the
bishop, his living link with his people. In the early Church,
unity in worship was inseparable from actual material aid,
brotherhood, concern for the poor and for widows, for the
burial of their brothers, and for orphans. The bread transformed into the Body of Christ was a part of that daily
bread, the food that Christians brought to their meeting
for the common table and to aid the poor. The deacons

[4] St. Ignatius, *Smyrnaens*, VIII, 1, 2, in *Early Christian Fathers*, page
115.

had the responsibility of distributing the gifts, helping the poor, organizing the *agape* ("love feast," as partaking of the Eucharist was called)—in sum, of carrying out the unity of Christians resulting from their participation in the Sacrament.

St. Ignatius' statement that "without the bishop, presbyters and deacons there is no Church" does not mean that only the hierarchy was active in it. Every member had his function and each supplemented the other in indissoluble union. "Now there are diversities of gifts, but the same Spirit. And there are differences of administrations, but the same Lord. And there are diversities of operations, but it is the same God which worketh all in all. But the manifestation of the Spirit is given to every man to profit withal" (I Cor. 12:4–7). The various organizational forms of the early Church must be understood in the light of an ideal which found expression in service to one's brothers.

In St. Paul's epistles the word "church" is already used to designate both each separate congregation and all Christians, the universal Church. This was so because each congregation, however small, felt itself to be, in the union of bishop, clergy, and people, the incarnation of the whole Church—the appearance and visitation here of the one Christ. Wherever the Christian went he found the same broken bread—"broken to bits but not divided"—heard the same blessing, and was included in the same union. All the churches had one source and one norm: apostolic tradition. Through its bishops each Church could attain the level of the Church as it had first appeared, the miracle of Pentecost and the first community in Jerusalem.

In this network of churches we may distinguish from the very start senior churches in each region which acted as centers of communication. These were the churches most immediately connected with the apostles, the most ancient and largest in membership. Because of the destruction of Jerusalem, the apostolic sees (or "seats") of Rome, Antioch, Ephesus, and Alexandria took on special significance. Rome, in particular, was sanctified by the blood of Peter and Paul and "presided in love," according to St. Ignatius of Antioch. Later Rome was to claim universal authority for its bishop, and the claim was to divide the Church. In the early years we hear nothing of these claims. No one disputed the authority and significance of the Roman Church; she was first and senior, but in union and equality with the others, as the center of the universal consent of all churches. A final formalization of the organization of the Church was still remote, yet behind the inconsistency of differing words and designations appeared the firm contour of the Catholic, or universal and united, Church.

Basis of Persecution by Rome

The persecution of Christians has been variously treated by historians from early times. After the accounts of martyrdom had been embroidered by Christian piety into a shining legend, a later age of enlightenment to which Rome appeared as an ideal of justice and culture attempted to deny or minimize the fact of persecution. Whatever its destructive intention, this attitude has helped to separate genuine documents from the vast hagiographic literature, so that we are now in a better position to explain the persistent struggle against Christianity over three centuries by the Roman Empire, which was in fact basically neither bloodthirsty nor fanatic.

When Christianity appeared, the most varied religions were flourishing in the empire, and Juvenal's satires mock the fascination of these many exotic cults for the Romans. At first the authorities took no notice at all of the Christians and did not perceive the radical distinction between them and the Jews. Judaism, though strange and unusual, was a legitimate religion, and the Church survived its first decades, as Tertullian has said, "under its roof." Even in this period, however, we encounter hostility and frequently even hatred for Christians on the part of the multitude. The lack of temples, the night meetings and secret ceremonies, all

inevitably aroused suspicion, and naturally the most monstrous rumors developed about orgies, magic, and ritual
murders at Christian meetings. Although this created an
atmosphere favorable for persecution, the Roman state was
in general law-abiding and did not permit arbitrary outrages.
The true cause of the conflict must therefore be sought in
the essential nature of the Roman state.

Like all states of antiquity, Rome had its gods, its
national-political religion. This was neither a system of beliefs nor a system of morals (the Roman citizen could and
very often did believe in foreign gods). It was a ritual,
worked out to the last detail, of sacrifices and prayers, a cult
of primarily political and state significance. Rome had no
other symbol to express and maintain its unity and to
symbolize its faith in itself. Although in this troubled
period very few believed in the symbol, to reject it meant
disloyalty, being a rebel. Rome demanded only outward
participation in the state cult as an expression of loyalty;
all that was required of a citizen was to burn a few sticks
of incense before the images of the national gods, call the
emperor "Lord," and celebrate the rites. Once he had
fulfilled this, he was free to seek the eternal meaning of
life wherever he wished.

For a man of the ancient world the validity of such a
demand was self-evident. Religion (the word is of Roman
origin and without synonym in Greek or Hebrew) was not a
problem of personal choice but a family, tribal, and state
matter. One's personal faith or lack of it had nothing to do
with religion, since religion itself had never been a problem
of truth, but only an acknowledgment of the existing system, its legitimacy and justifiability.

The Christians refused to fulfill this self-evident, elementary civic duty. Their act was neither rebellion, condemnation of the state as such, nor even opposition to its
particular defects or vices. Starting with St. Paul, Christians
could boldly declare their loyalty to Rome, referring to their
prayers for the emperor and the authorities. But they could
not fulfill two requirements: they could not recognize the

emperor as "Lord," and they could not bow down to idols, even outwardly, without faith in them. "Lord" in the language of that time meant absolute master and ruler, but for Christians the whole significance of their faith was that the one true Lord, Jesus Christ, had come and ruled in the world: ". . . God hath made that same Jesus . . . both Lord and Christ" (Acts 2:36). This meant that God had given Him all authority over the world, and that henceforth He was the only Master of human life. "One Lord!" We no longer feel the force and paradox of this early Christian exclamation that has come down to us, but it rang out then as a challenge to a world in which lordship had been claimed through the ages by every authority, every state, and every "collective."

The indifference of Christians to the external world, their effort to free themselves from it, has been regarded as a strange way of combating the pagan demands of the empire. In actual fact, by their refusal to fulfill a requirement that was not taken seriously even by those who had imposed it, the whole measure of Christian responsibility in the world was revealed for all ages. By rejecting the formal requirement of the state, they thereby included the state within the perspective of the kingdom of Christ and—however passively—summoned it to submit to the Lord of the world.

Modern observers, even some Christians, regard this conflict as a struggle for freedom of conscience, for the right of a man to make religion his private affair. For the early Church its significance was much more profound. Christianity was not so much a new religion as an upheaval in world history, the appearance of the Lord to do battle with one who had usurped His authority.

Blood of Martyrs

The beginning of the persecutions was illumined by fire in the Eternal City. On the night of July 16 in the year 64 a great part of Rome burned down, and popular rumor accused the emperor himself of arson. In order to distract attention from himself, Nero shifted the blame onto the Christians, showing that the existence of Christianity was known to all. Although Nero's persecution was confined to Rome and its cause was arbitrary, it raised the question about Christians for the first time on the plane of politics and the state, where it was also to be examined in the future. During the rest of the century the frequent rebellions and disorders left Rome no time for the Christians. But the persecutions were gathering head: Church tradition places the martyrdom of Peter and Paul in Rome in this period, perhaps under Nero, and of John the Evangelist in the East under Domitian (81–96).

The beginning of the second century brought the golden age of Roman history under the best emperors that ever ruled her. Their morality was so attractive that the Christians were to create a legend about the posthumous salvation of the first of them, Trajan. The *Meditations* of Marcus Aurelius, the philosopher-emperor, still hold an honorable place in the classical heritage of antiquity. Yet precisely in these days, when all the moral values of the Greco-Roman world seemed to triumph, the tragic conflict with Christianity became fully clear.

Trajan's answer to his friend Pliny the Younger, who, as governor of one of the remote provinces, had asked him about the Christians, has been preserved. How was he to deal with them? The emperor answered clearly and definitely: Christianity was itself a crime and must be punished. Although he forbade seeking out Christians and repudiated anonymous reports, "which are unworthy of our time," from that time anyone accused of being a Christian who did not exculpate himself by offering sacrifices to the gods was sentenced to death. True, the structure of the Roman judiciary enabled Christians to exist even under this condemnation. Rome had no state prosecutor; a private accuser had to bring a case against each Christian, while the state itself at first refused to take the initiative for persecutions. This explains both the relatively long lulls in the persecutions and their individual nature. Still, the situation of all Christians was terrible; they were outside the law, and a single denunciation was enough for the irrevocable process of accusation to result in death.

From this time, for two entire centuries, the line of martyrs was never really interrupted. Sometimes there were outbreaks of mass persecution; for example, in Smyrna in 155, and in Lyons in 167. Sometimes there were individual trials: the martyrdom of Ignatius of Antioch and Simeon of Jerusalem under Trajan, of Telesphorus of Rome under Hadrian, of Polycarp and other Smyrnean Christians under Antoninus Pius, of Justin the Philosopher under Marcus Aurelius, and so on. Whatever the situation, for two hundred years a Christian could not consider himself secure, and of course this awareness of his outcast state, and his condemnation by the world, is a central experience of the early Christian.

The descriptions of the persecutions that have come down to us reveal the whole significance the Church attributed to martyrdom, and explain why the Church seemed to recognize martyrdom as the norm of Christian life as well as the strongest proof of the truth of Christianity. It would be false to reduce the meaning of martyrdom to heroism merely; if the truth of an idea could be established by the number of its victims, every religion could present adequate proofs. The Christian martyr was not a hero, however, but a witness; by accepting suffering and death he affirmed that the rule of death had ended, that life had triumphed. He died not for Christ but with Him, and in Him he also received life. The Church exalted martyrdom because it was proof of the most important Christian affirmation, the resurrection of Christ from the dead. No one has expressed this better than St. Ignatius of Antioch; taken to Rome for execution, he wrote to his Roman friends requesting them not to attempt to save him: "Let me be

fodder for wild beasts. . . . For though alive, it is with a
passion for death that I am writing to you. . . . There is
living water in me, which speaks and says inside me, 'Come
to the Father.' I do not want to live any more on a human
plane."[5]

In the cult of martyrs the Church laid the foundation
for the glorification of saints; each of them is a witness,
and their blood is a seed that promises new shoots. The
Church does not consider its conflict with the Roman Empire a tragic misunderstanding, but the fulfillment of the
promise of the Savior: "In the world ye shall have tribula-
tion: but be of good cheer; I have overcome the world"
(John 16:33). For the Church, persecution was the best
pledge of victory.

Struggle of Christianity To Keep Its Own Meaning

The conflict between Christianity and the world was not
confined to persecution by the state. More dangerous for
the Church than open persecution was its contact with the
ideas and beliefs of surrounding Hellenism. Here it encountered a threat that the faith would be distorted from
within, and the second century was marked by intense
struggle as Christians strove to preserve the purity and
integrity of their doctrine.

St. Paul had already called preaching about Christ "unto
the Greeks foolishness" (I Cor. 1:23). It was extremely
difficult for a man raised in an atmosphere of Hellenism
to understand and really accept Christianity. Inevitably
the philosophers of Athens, meeting on the Areopagus to
listen to St. Paul, interrupted him when he spoke of the
resurrection of the dead. His words about the incarnation
of God, death on the Cross, and resurrection of the body
could not be received without a revolution in their habits
of thought. Greek philosophy taught that in the body we

[5] St. Ignatius, *Romans*, IV, 1; VII, 2, 3, *Early Christian Fathers*, p. 104.

see a prison of the immortal soul, and in the world the Hellene saw only an eternal return, an eternal cycle from which he sought salvation in the motionless world of ideas. Does not the secret of the harmony of Greek art lie in its effort to find and express only the ideal form of the world concealed behind its passing, changeable surface? Not real life, surely, full as it often is of tragic contradictions. The sense of history, its irreversibility, the unrepeating nature of time, and within this time the uniqueness and unrepeated quality of each event and each person, were all profoundly alien to Hellenic psychology. The history of early Christianity, therefore, is a history not of rapprochement between Athens and Jerusalem, but rather of a struggle through which there took place a gradual "churching" of Hellenism which was to fertilize Christian thought forever after.

The Church had first to protect itself from all attempts to reconcile Christianity too easily with the spirit of the times and reinterpret it smoothly in Hellenistic patterns. If the Church had remained only in Jewish molds it would not have conquered the world; but if it had simply adapted these molds to those of Hellenistic thought, the world would have conquered Christianity. Gnosticism, the first enemy with which it came into conflict, was in fact inspired by the idea of reinterpretation and reconciliation.

Gnosticism is the name usually given to a mixture of Greek philosophy and Eastern mysticism, a strange religious and philosophical fusion which emerged from close contacts between the Greco-Roman world and the East. The movement reached its peak just at the time when Christianity was beginning to spread. Typical outgrowths of a transitional, religiously excited age, Gnostic tendencies reflected genuine spiritual needs as well as a superficial attraction to the "wisdom of the East" and a morbid interest in mysterious symbols and ceremonies. As in theosophy, Gnosticism combined a "scientific" approach to religious problems with mystical fantasies and all sorts of secrets.

Men were promised initiation into the ultimate mysteries of existence, but an emphasis on rites and consecrations tended to substitute religious sensuality for genuine religion.

As in our own time, men were groping for a syncretic religion, in which elements of truth from all doctrines, philosophies, and religions might, as it were, be one. It was this effort to combine and reinterpret all religions in its own way that rendered Gnosticism a danger to the Church. It was far from hostile to Christianity—on the contrary, tried to include it within its own fold. Christianity had also come from the East, the homeland of all secret wisdom; it was connected with Judaism, which had a distinctive vogue in the Hellenistic world and also had its mysteries, concealed from the eyes of the crowd. As the Church was taking its very first steps, we see beside it and sometimes even within it seeds of Christian Gnosticism, attempts to interpret the Gospels, avoiding what seemed unacceptable or incomprehensible in them—primarily, of course, the very reality of the Incarnation of God and the humanity of Christ. We sense uneasiness even in St. Paul: "Beware lest any man spoil you through philosophy and vain deceit, after the tradition of men, after the rudiments of the world, and not after Christ" (Col. 2:8).

The danger increased when converted pagans began to outnumber Jews in the Church. Many were attracted to it by the same attitudes that explain the success of Gnosticism. By no means all of them could immediately appreciate the vital distinction between Christianity and the Eastern Hellenistic mystery religions; they saw in the Church what they wanted to see, the crowning of their own religious experience. "These pagans thought that they were under no obligation to abandon their former theories when they became Christian," writes Professor Bolotov. "On the contrary they thought it correct to interpret and understand Christianity with their aid, in a high and perfect sense." This Christian Gnosticism reached full bloom in the middle of the second century, in the teaching of

Basilides, Valentinus, Saturninus, Marcion, and others. Their very number indicates the scale of the movement.

Attraction to Gnosticism cannot be ascribed only to corrupt imagination or interest in exotic mysteries. Its strength —as well as its falseness—was that, although Christ was acknowledged as the *Logos*, Savior, and Redeemer, the essence of Christianity as faith in the Incarnation of God and His coming into the world was corrupted. Christianity was transformed into a special mythological philosophy: instead of the drama of sin, forgiveness, and salvation, a personal encounter between God and man, Gnosticism offered a sort of cosmological scheme according to which the "spiritual elements" in the world were gradually freed from the captivity of matter and evil multiplicity gave way to abstract unity. It was a return in a new Eastern form to ancient Greek idealism.

Some historians have argued that out of the struggle with Gnosticism came a whole metamorphosis of the Church, transforming it into a structured, monolithic organization fortified by the authority of the hierarchy and official doctrine. Berdyaev even regards the condemnation of Gnosticism as a stifling of free thought. In the light of better knowledge of Gnostic documents, such conclusions are hardly still tenable. Nevertheless, the movement did oblige the Church to define more precisely the inner, organic laws of this life and to express in outward forms and formulas what had composed the essence of Christianity from the very beginning. In Gnosticism the Church saw the substitution of an alien and distorted image of Christ for the one by which it lived. The Gnostics referred to secret legends and created a whole apocryphal literature about Christ. Fragments of such Gnostic "gospels" have come down to us, written in the names of Peter, James, Paul, and John. "The image of Christ acquires . . . a character that is not only strange and superhuman but spectral as well. He is present invisibly, sometimes in the flesh, sometimes bodilessly, appearing variously as a child, an adult, or an old man . . . they responded to the curiosity which sought secret knowledge instead of the traditional teachings of the Church, theology and history."[6] The Church faced the necessity of defining on precisely what basis the Gnostic Christ was false and what would enable it to distinguish true tradition about Him from falsehood.

The New Testament

We have seen that acceptance of Christianity had always been regarded as acceptance of the evidence about Christ given by the apostles, the witnesses to His teaching. The apostles interpreted their mission as service or preaching of the Word. Moreover, the Church itself is nothing but the acceptance of this Word, so that the growth of the Church is defined as the growth of the Word. "But the word of God grew and multiplied" (Acts 12:24). "So mightily grew the word of God and prevailed" (Acts 19:20). For the Church, the Word of God meant not only the expression of absolute truth in human language, but primarily the appearance of God Himself and the revelation of His divine life and strength. In the Old Testament God created the world by His Word, maintained life in it by His Word, and began its salvation by His Word. God not only spoke His Word, He acted through it. The prologue to the Gospel of John has been interpreted as an attempt to introduce concrete Judeo-Christian teaching to the abstract philosophical mind. Yet it is wholly rooted in the biblical perception of the Word as divine life, divine action. "And the Word became flesh." This meant not only that in Christ God revealed to man a new doctrine and imparted a new and absolute truth, but that divine life itself had come into the world and had become the life of man. The preaching of the Word of God by the apostles, therefore, was something more than the evidence of eyewitnesses

[6] H. Lietzmann, *Histoire de l'église ancienne*, Vol. 2 (Paris, 1937), p. 83.

about Christ's life. It not only told about Christ, but transmitted Christ Himself; it led men into His life and united them with it. In this understanding of the Word of God there is an organic link between the preaching of the apostles and baptism.

This total dependence of the Church on the Word of God does not mean that it depended solely on its written account in the New Testament text. The image and teachings of Christ as proclaimed by the apostles were not a truth mastered once and for all; "the word of God is quick [i.e., living] and powerful . . ." (Heb. 4:12), and is constantly proclaimed in the preaching of the bishop. Christians commune with it in the sacraments and are inspired by it in prayer; it is the source of the unanimity that links them. In all the sources we find reference to the words and teachings of Christ, which were obviously known to all from the very start.

When records of the apostolic preaching began to appear, since this was evidence of the Word of God, it acquired the same significance as the tradition about Christ in other forms, such as preaching, liturgical prayer, and preparation of new converts for baptism. Since they already possessed the Holy Scriptures of the Old Testament, Christians naturally added these writings to them as their completion, interpretation, and fulfillment.

It is impossible for us to present here even briefly the history of these writings, which has aroused such endless disputes among scholars. One point is obvious: whatever the "sources" of our four Gospels and the relations between them; whatever ingenious hypotheses scholars may have created in their efforts to reconstruct their genesis; they were received by the Church—that is, were recognized— because their content coincided with the image of Christ and the content of His teachings that the Church already knew. The Church did not "sanction" the New Testament writings; it recognized them as the Word of God, the source of its existence from the start.

By the end of the first century, when the apostolic period was drawing to a close, the Church already possessed the four Gospels of Matthew, Mark, Luke, and John. Although they were not perhaps as yet collected into one volume, each had been accepted by the group of churches for which it was written. Very shortly afterward they were combined in one quadripartite Gospel, and in the middle of the second century the Christian apologist Tatian composed the first harmony, or code, of the Gospels. The differences between the four accounts, and even obvious divergences in secondary matters such as chronology and the sequence of events, did not bother early Christians, who were not looking for precise accuracy of detail but for the truth about Christ.

The appearance of the New Testament in the Church as a book, as Scripture, was therefore not a new factor, but a record of the founding tradition. Just because it *was* identical with the original tradition as the Church already knew it, there appeared at first no need of a canon, or precisely fixed list of accepted records or Scriptures. This situation enabled Gnostic teachers to ascribe their own doctrines to the apostles and to present them in the form of "gospels" and "epistles." Hence, the problem of criteria became crucial for the Church in the middle of the second century. Each new doctrine claimed to be a true interpretation of the Gospel—what would enable the "Catholic" Church to judge among them?

These questions were answered by the first generation of Christian theologians, among whom we must especially distinguish St. Irenaeus of Lyons, chief fighter against Gnosticism. First of the great Fathers of the Church, he had known in his childhood Bishop Polycarp of Smyrna and other presbyters who had seen the apostles, and he may have studied in the first Christian school known to us, that of Justin the Philosopher at Rome.

Irenaeus' arguments against the Gnostics may be expressed by the term "apostolic succession," but for him this

meant more than the uninterrupted episcopal laying on of
hands from the time of the apostles; it meant primarily
the unity of the Church and its life in time and space:

Having received this preaching and this faith, . . . the Church,
although scattered in the whole world, carefully preserves it,
as if living in one house. She believes these things [every-
where] alike, as if she had but one heart and one soul, and
preaches them harmoniously, teaches them, and hands them
down, as if she had but one mouth. For the languages of the
world are different, but the meaning of the Tradition is one and
the same . . . Neither will one of those who preside in the
churches who is very powerful in speech say anything different
from these things, for no one is above [his] teacher, nor will one
who is weak in speech diminish the tradition. For since the
faith is one and the same, he who can say much about it does
not add to it, nor does he who can say little diminish it.[7]

For Irenaeus the gospels of the Gnostics are false because they are alien to the witness of the apostles: "Only
that Gospel is true which was handed down from the apostles and is preserved from their time by orthodox bishops
without additions or omissions." We see here the beginning of a New Testament canon and the principle used to
define it: only the four Gospels are genuine, because they
contain the true witness of the apostles; but we know of
their genuineness because they have been preserved and
passed on by the orthodox bishops. In other words, only
the Church can distinguish true Scripture from false, because the Holy Spirit always abides in it.

Thus, ultimately, Irenaeus opposed Gnosticism—the se-
duction of schism and partial interpretation of Christianity
—not by another interpretation but by the very fact of the
Church as a visible, palpable unity which alone preserves
and transmits to its members the whole truth and fullness
of the Gospel. The canon of the Scriptures, the succession

7 Irenaeus, *Against Heresies*, I, 10, 2, *Early Christian Fathers*, pp. 360–61.

of bishops, the interpretation of prophecies, are all only outward forms of this fundamental unity, aside from which they mean nothing. The most significant answer the Church gave to the temptations of the second century was its clear doctrine about itself, its "catholic self-consciousness." Although this self-consciousness had become more precise as a result of conflict, the Church was victorious not by creating something new, nor by metamorphosis, but by realizing and strengthening what it had been from the very beginning.

Sin and Repentance in the Church

By the late second century primitive Christianity may be considered at an end. Although the Christians in the Roman Empire still composed a persecuted minority, this minority had already clearly recognized its universal calling. Educated Christians addressed the emperor and public opinion, pointing out the falseness of the accusations against them and presenting their faith as the true answer to questions of the human mind. After his conversion St. Justin continued his work as a philosopher; in his *Apologies* and other works, he was the first to attempt to explain the truth of Christianity to the Hellenistic intellectuals. Others followed him. The very appearance of these works indicates that an abrupt change was taking place. At first the world as represented by the empire persecuted Christianity and tried to abolish it, but did not argue against it—was indeed quite indifferent to its substance. The Church reacted to this indifference by martyrdom; soon it could be neither abolished nor simply denied, but had to be disputed. Celsus' *True Discourse*, written very early in the third century, was the first scholarly repudiation of Christianity. The writer had studied Christian books and was armed against the new faith by the whole cultural array of Hellenism, but in his arguments we already sense the fear that an alien "barbarism" is undermining the Greco-Roman world.

The Church was now a monolithic and universal organization with a precise "rule of faith," authority, and discipline. At the beginning of the third century it has been estimated that there were up to a hundred presbyters in the area of Rome alone. The Church had its own cemeteries and almshouses, conducting an extensive charitable activity. In Africa almost three hundred bishops gathered for Church synods, and all Asia Minor was covered with Christian communities.

Nevertheless, this period of consolidation was also marked by a decline in the spiritual level of the Christian community, a dimming of the flame rightly associated with the Church's first decades. Of course, there had been grievous failings from the beginning; the change lay in the altered attitude of Christians toward these sins. In the period of primitive Christianity the Church was a community of "saints," that is, baptized, dedicated, and thus newly-purified members of the Body of Christ, and every sin was felt to be a terrible abnormality. St. Paul constantly reminded the new Christian that since he was already consecrated and had received a new life, he should live in accordance with this gift. Although sanctity does not mean sinlessness, since God alone is sinless, it does mean awareness of belonging totally to Christ, body and soul; it means inclusion in His life.

By the middle of the second century we begin to hear, along with hymns to the unity and sanctity of the Church, admissions of sins by Christians. Hermas' *Shepherd*, a second-century Roman document written by a layman, resolutely raises the question of sin in the Church. How is it possible? If baptism gives birth to new life and frees man from the power of sin, what is the meaning of its existence among Christians? It was hard to understand how there could be any repentance "except that which we have made when we entered the water and received in it forgiveness of our former sins . . . For he who has received forgiveness of sins ought not to sin any more, but remain in innocence."

The early Church cut off all who fell away from grace and

rejected the new life. "For it is impossible for those who have once been enlightened . . . if they shall fall away, to renew them again unto repentance; seeing they crucify to themselves the Son of God afresh and put him to an open shame" (Heb. 6:4–6). Unfortunately, however, sin continues to enter men's lives, and they have no recourse but to repent once more. The Church is called upon to save, not to judge, until the Last Judgment. Therefore a "second repentance" was made possible to the excommunicant, permitting him to return to the Church and restoring the forfeited power of his baptism. As gradually developed, this new chance for sinners was guarded by the requirement of confession to the bishop or his representative, sometimes public confession; prolonged evidence of repentance, including various sorts of penance; and reinstatement only by stages in the freedom of Christians to worship together and partake of the sacraments. In very serious cases, restoration of the saving power of baptism was sometimes withheld until the deathbed of the sinner.

Christians did not take the matter lightly. Hermas continues, "If anyone sin, submitting to the temptations of the devil, only repentance lies in store for him, but if he keeps falling in order to keep on repenting, let him not expect good fruits. His salvation is in jeopardy." A little later Tertullian, the African teacher of the late second and early third centuries, warned that "God allows us to knock at the door of this second repentance once, only once." One must "day and night call on God and our Savior, fall at the feet of the priests, kneel before our brothers, begging the prayers of all."

Some historians have regarded this second repentance as a revolution in the mind of the Church, a transformation from a society of the "saved" into a society of "those being saved." This judgment is superficial, however. As awareness of sanctity in the Church presupposes constant repentance and a sense of one's own unworthiness, so now the evidence of decline did not mean that the ideal of a society of saints had been abandoned. Life and history reveal the full force of evil in man, even the "new" man who has been reborn in water and the Spirit. From the beginning the Church had known itself to be a society of saved sinners, and in this apparently contradictory combination of words we may find the explanation for its inconsistency in regard to repentance. Christians were sinners to whom salvation was given. This salvation is not magic; it is given for free acceptance, for struggle, for growth. While in the joy of the first decades the Christians felt more forcibly the wondrous newness of the gift, as time passed they could not help but become aware of the dimensions of the struggle to which it committed them. There is no room in the Church for sin; yet it exists for sinners. Therefore the development of a "discipline of repentance"—an obvious lowering of standards—does not mean a change in the Church's original ideal, but a fulfillment of its eternal task, the salvation and renewal of man.

Many could not accept this realism of the Church, the increasingly obvious way in which it was growing into the very stuff of human history; to them it seemed a betrayal. This attitude at the time led to Montanism, a new heresy that came from Phrygia, long a region of religious fanaticism. About the year 150 Montanus, a newly-converted Christian, with two women, Priscilla and Maximilla, started to proclaim the coming of the Holy Spirit as promised by Christ in the Gospels. They taught that the second Testament, that of the Son, was not yet final. Only in the last divine revelation, in the coming of the Holy Spirit, would salvation occur. This "new prophecy" had been sent by God through Montanus and his two prophetesses. Montanus demanded of his followers absolute moral rigor, celibacy, and voluntary martyrdom, for the end of the world was at hand. Essentially it was an outburst of gloomy eschatology, the last and most extreme expression of the imminent expectation of the end of the world that characterized the first generations of Christians.

But Montanism was in fact a protest against the existing historical Church, and was condemned by the bishops of Asia Minor. It was nevertheless received almost ecstatically in Rome, Gaul, and Africa, and much time was needed before its sectarian nature could be exposed; even Irenaeus of Lyons defended it from condemnation for a long time. The most celebrated conversion to the religion of the new prophecy was that of Tertullian. A fiery African, he has always seemed nearly the quintessence of primitive Christianity; almost no one is so much quoted when there is need to refer to the spirit of the early Church. One of the first Western theologians, teachers, and apologists, he had a great influence on the whole life of the Church. But, like many others, he could not accept its growth and the changes that resulted from it; he was scandalized by the consolidation of Christianity. In his treatise *De Pudicitia* he repudiated what he had written on repentance; he could no longer accept the idea, or the possibility of the forgiveness of capital sins. The Church *could* forgive sins, but it should not do so. Since the Church in which sin still abides is not the true Church, he devoted the last part of his life to struggle against it.

The example of Tertullian best shows us the character of Montanism, with its longing for the original purity and intensity of expectation of the first Christians. There is no denying that the level of Christian life began to decline at this time, yet the Church's victory over Montanism was crucial. It was facing the momentous question of whether it should remain a small band of perfectionists or whether, without altering its final ideal, it was right to accept the masses and start their slow re-education. Should the Church remain outside the world and outside history, or should it accept history as a field for heavy and prolonged labor? It was difficult to fight against Montanism, which was fired with so much sanctity, faith, and self-sacrifice; by condemning it, however, the Church condemned forever all attempts to dethrone the historical, visible Church and to incorporate it into a third Testament.

Beginnings of Theology

The mind of the Church was forged and the Church strengthened by persecution and temptations. The best intimation of coming victory was the first flourishing of Christion thought and the beginning of Christian culture that distinguished the third century. We have barely noted Tertullian in passing. Special mention must be made of the Christian school of Alexandria and its famous teacher, Origen.

Until the third century Christian literature had either been apologetic in character, opposing heresies and paganism, or had consisted of a simple statement of the basic principles of Church dogma. The significance of the Alexandrian school was that it was the first to attempt to reason out these dogmas as an integrated system and to reveal the truths contained in them as sources of thought and knowledge.

We know little of the origins of the Alexandrian school; in all probability it grew out of the teaching of new converts. The city was the intellectual capital of the Hellenistic world, and every sort of preaching there acquired academic overtones. It was natural, therefore, that the foundations for a scientific theology should be laid there, and theology recognized as the highest calling for a Christian.

For the first of the famous Alexandrian theologians, Clement, Christianity was already a higher knowledge—*gnosis* in the full and absolute meaning of the word. "If the Gnostic were offered a choice between the salvation of the soul and knowledge of God, supposing that these two things were distinct (although they are identical), he would choose knowledge of God." Gnosis is the vision of God face to face, the mystical illumination of His truth; the Christian prefers this knowledge of God to all else and sees the purpose of his whole life in it. But a joyous acceptance of the world, a "justification" of it, is also characteristic of

Clement. This was a new transforming experience, for the sake of which Christianity was already firmly rooted in the world and triumphing there. *How Is the Rich Man Saved?* —the title of one of Clement's works—is typical of his general outlook. He did not reject the world, but on the contrary tried to make everything Christian. We find considerations concerning laughter and even domestic arrangements in his writings. Everything is permissible if it is taken in moderation, but particularly if it is subordinated to the knowledge of God and the truth in Him. This was the optimism of the first union, not yet profound and often dubious, between Christianity and Hellenism.

In Origen, the successor of Clement, we see both the features of the heroic period of primitive Christianity and a new spirit which was becoming more and more evident in the Church. A Christian by birth, son of a martyred father, he was inspired by the ideal of martyrdom and his *Exhortation to Martyrdom*, written during the persecutions of Maximinus (235–38), is still one of the best documents of early Christianity. For Origen martyrdom meant more than confession of Christ in the presence of one's persecutors. It was the whole life of a Christian, which in this world can only be the "narrow way" if he is to strive for evangelical perfection. Origen was one of the founders of the theory of asceticism and his influence was immense when, in the next century, monasticism arose within the Church. His desire to follow the teachings of the Gospel to the letter led him, as is known, even to emasculation. He has often been regarded as a pure intellectual, remote from the life of the Church, immersed only in books; but in fact he was first of all a Churchman, deeply rooted in the life and prayer of the Church, and his intellectual contribution can be understood only if we remember that for him everything was subordinated to "the one thing necessary."

When he was very young he assumed the office of instructor, whose duty was to explain the Scriptures to new converts. While devoting himself completely to this work, he soon came to the conclusion that a simple reading of Scripture was not enough. Sitting in his lecture hall were philosophers, scholars, men of great learning. The Word of God must be explained to them as the highest revelation and all its depths uncovered.

The school of Origen soon outgrew its original task; it was open to all who were interested and became a forum for genuine encounter between Christian and pagan wisdom. It was not a matter of Christian wisdom simply overthrowing the pagan, however; here was the first acceptance of Hellenistic values by Christianity in order to convert them to the service of Christ. "I would wish you to use all the strength of your mind for the advantage of Christianity, which should be your highest goal," wrote Origen to his disciple Gregory Thaumaturgus. "To achieve this I desire you to take from Greek philosophy those spheres of knowledge which are potentially an introduction to Christianity, and whatever information from geometry and astronomy may serve to explain the sacred books; that what philosophers say of geometry, music, grammar, rhetoric, astronomy—namely, that they are handmaidens of philosophy —may be said as well of philosophy itself in relation to Christianity."[8] This represented a revolution in relation to profane culture, but in contrast to Gnosticism, Christianity was not subordinated to Hellenism, but Hellenism rather proclaimed as a preparation of the minds of men for the higher revelation and understanding of the Scriptures.

The final meaning of all scholarship, as well as of Christianity itself, was the understanding of the Word of God. Everything was subordinate to this, and there was no limit to the extent to which one could become immersed in its meaning. Yet this understanding required not only a special grace, illumination of the mind by prayer and of the body by ascetic practice, but also scholarly preparation. Origen himself studied Hebrew and in his *Hexapla* copied the whole Old Testament Scriptures six times, in parallel col-

8 Origen, *Epistle to Gregory*, 3.

umns, placing beside the Hebrew original and its transcription in Greek lettering all extant Greek translations of it.
He adopted the methods of the famous Alexandrian literary
school, which had undertaken the study of ancient Greek
literature; and through him these methods became a fundamental part of Christian study of the Bible.

This work was only preparatory, however. There remained the interpretation of the Scriptures, and here Origen struck out on new paths. The basic principle of his
interpretation was the Church tradition about the spiritual
meaning of the Word of God which lay behind the literal
meaning. The Old Testament prefigured the New, while
in the New Testament are revealed the eternal patterns of
Church and Christian life. The Jews did not perceive these
types in their own Scriptures and rejected Christ, whereas
the Gnostics, unable to understand the Old Testament, rejected it on the grounds of being a revelation of a malicious
and vengeful God. According to Origen, all these Old
Testament types became reality in the appearance of
Christ, and therefore He alone is the key to the Scriptures,
just as the Scriptures are for us the only source of revelation about Him. The Old Testament reveals the New, and
the New reveals the coming kingdom of God, "when God
will be all in all" and all these types will be manifested in
an eternal reality.

Origen's contribution to the study and interpretation of
Scripture is very great. Although preaching and theology
had always been based on the Scriptures, he was the first
to formulate a systematically Christocentric conception of
the Old Testament, and in his innumerable interpretations
he was centuries ahead in the development of an ecclesiastical exegesis. We cannot overlook the danger of his approach to the Bible, however. In his extreme allegorism
each word acquired an incalculable number of meanings,
some of them extremely fantastic. Allegory was fashionable
among pagan scholars of literature in Alexandria, and Origen had been influenced by it. Modern scholars are attempt-

ing to differentiate between his typology—that is, the search
for true types and spiritual meanings—and his allegory, in
which he applied arbitrary meanings to certain events and
words. In all likelihood Origen himself was aware of the
distinction. It is difficult, though, to draw a real line between these two approaches, and allegorism was for a long
time a dangerous propensity in Christian theology, often
substituting rhetorical contrivance for the vitality and common sense of the Word of God.

Still more dangerous for the future was Origen's attempt
to construct a Christian theological system. This was contained in his work *Peri Archon* ("On First Principles"),
which has reached us only in a later, somewhat modified
Latin translation, *De Principiis*. Although he maintained
that the only standard for any theology must be the rule of
faith—meaning the tradition of the Church—he did not in
fact discover a way to combine revelation and Hellenistic
philosophy so that the basic idealism of the Greek outlook
might be overcome. On the contrary, his system was an
abrupt Hellenization of Christianity itself; he rejected the
clear doctrine of the creation of the world from nothing-
ness which is the key to any truly Christian cosmology,
and all the unique features of the biblical conception of
the world as history—as reality—and not an illusory tragedy
of free choice. According to Origen, the world evolves from
God and returns to Him, by some incontrovertible law
which makes possible the reality of evil, of freedom, and
of salvation. But since all is eternal in God, this cycle of
creation of the world is eternally repeated, ending unalterably with general restoration and salvation.

Origen ended his long and righteous life as a "confessor"
—one who bore witness to Christ under torture—dying from
injuries suffered during the persecutions of Decius (250).
His longing for martyrdom, which had never slackened
since his childhood, was satisfied. While his figure is unusu-
ally attractive and his example inspiring, his theology was
to play in the end a fateful role in the history of Church

thought, and only with great difficulty was the Church to overcome its temptations and dangers.

Origen started the gradual process of Christianizing Hellenism and the struggle to overcome it within the Church; this struggle was to be the basic theme of the later Byzantine centuries of Church history. Perhaps without his "creative failure" the eventual triumph of Christian Hellenism would have been impossible.

The Last Great Persecutions

The third century was the time of the Church's last, most terrible fight with the empire, but the dawn of coming victory was already approaching. One of the primary reasons for the decline in Christian intensity had undoubtedly been the lull in the persecutions. From the death of Marcus Aurelius (185) until the middle of the third century, the Church lived in relative security. Officially, the prohibition against Christianity had not been lifted, and the long line of martyrs was not actually interrupted, but the over-all situation was greatly improved. People had become used to the Christians, they knew about them. An increasing interest in the East during the Eastern dynasty of the Severi even made Christians—though not Christianity—somewhat popular. Septimus Severus' niece, Julia Mamaea, invited the celebrated Origen to her palace so that she could debate with him in the circle for religion and philosophy which she had founded; later Emperor Alexander Severus placed a statue of Christ in his private chapel; and finally, St. Jerome called Emperor Philip the Arabian the first Christian emperor, which suggests that he had been secretly baptized.

For these reasons the persecution that suddenly burst upon the Church in the year 249 seemed a terrible and unexpected trial and exposed in full clarity how far many, many Christians had departed from the original intensity of faith and way of life.

Emperor Decius (249–51) assumed power at a critical moment. Rome was threatened with ruin by the restored Persian empire and by profound internal disruptions and disorder. Decius believed that salvation lay only in the restoration of the ancient Roman spirit and a return to the neglected and scorned traditions. He gave first priority to the restoration of state worship, and this inevitably led to conflict with Christianity. Except for Nero, Decius was the first representative of Roman power to take the initiative in these persecutions as opposed to the system of private accusation followed by test. In a special edict he ordered all his subjects to prove their loyalty to the national gods by making the sacrifice.

The Church again responded with the blood of martyrs, including not only Origen, as we have seen, but Bishop Flavian of Rome, Babylas of Antioch, and Alexander of Jerusalem. But what startled the Church was the mass apostasy. "Fear struck them," wrote Bishop Dionysius of Alexandria, "and many of the more influential Christians gave in immediately, some giving way to fear, others, as civil servants, to the requirements of their positions, still others drawn along with the crowd. Some were pale and trembling, as if it were not they who were making sacrifices to the idols but they themselves who were being brought to sacrifice; and therefore the crowd mocked them."[9] The same picture appears in the letters of Cyprian of Carthage: "There were some who did not even wait to be summoned to climb onto the Capitol, or to be questioned to renounce their faith. They ran to the Forum themselves, they hastened to their [spiritual] deaths, as if they had wished it for a long time. And—O ultimate crime!—parents brought their children with them, so that they might lose in their childhood what they had received on the threshold of their lives."[10]

[9] Eusebius, *Ecclesiastical History*, VI, 41, 11.
[10] *De Lapsis*, 8, 9.

The persecution passed liked a whirlwind and quickly abated, but it left the Church in ruins. The question arose as to how to deal with those who had lapsed, who now rushed back for forgiveness and reconciliation. While the Church had recognized a "second repentance" at the beginning of the century, now the question was posed anew and more acutely. In the earlier time, lapsed Christians had been the exception, so that a second repentance was also an exception, but now it was a mass occurrence. When we remember what the witness of martyrs meant to the Church —that it was the witness of the Church to itself, the proof of Christ's strength which lived in it—then it becomes clear why the problem of the lapsed caused a lengthy dissension, the last in the series of "temptations of the Church" that marked the late second and early third centuries.

Against this background of dissension the figure of the great African bishop, St. Cyprian of Carthage, stands out clearly. Like Tertullian, he represented the "pure" Christianity that characterized the brief but magnificent history of the African Church. A pagan teacher of rhetoric and professor of literature, Cyprian repudiated everything on his conversion to Christianity. "The spirit descended from Heaven has made me a new man through a second birth. And immediately, in a miraculous way, certainty wiped out doubt." Very soon after his conversion he became bishop of Carthage, the oldest of the African churches. Almost immediately afterward the persecution started. Cyprian hid, not from fear but in order to continue to direct the Church; in his absence the question arose about the lapsed Christians. The latter, knowing the sternness both of Cyprian and of normal Church practice, bypassed the bishop and turned directly to the "confessors"—those who had confessed their faith in Christ and paid for their faithfulness by imprisonment or torture. The Roman state had learned by experience and preferred not to create martyrs; it therefore left the steadfast Christians to rot in jail and subjected them to torture. The confessors were the glory of the Church; their authority was indisputable, and they recommended to the bishop that he accept the lapsed Christians back into Church communion.

This created a difficult situation: there were two authorities in the Church. Cyprian would have liked to defer the question until his return, when there could be a general synod of bishops, but the confessors regarded this as disrespect to their suffering. A paradoxical conflict developed, with the confessors and the lapsed Christians allied against the legitimate bishop and the hierarchy. Alarm spread as well to the Roman Church, crimson with the blood of its own bishop; there the presbyter Novatian opposed Cyprian as a man who had fled and should therefore himself be considered lapsed. In Carthage a whole party was formed against Cyprian, who was obliged to resort to strictness and expel its leaders from the Church. Finally, in the spring of 251 Cyprian returned to Carthage and summoned a synod, which decided the problem by relaxing the discipline of repentance. It divided the lapsed into two categories, depending on the degree of apostasy, and established two forms by which they might again be accepted into the Church. Some could be received only on their deathbeds, while others could rejoin after more or less prolonged periods of repentance.

A rather strange reversal occurred at this point. Those who had demanded that Cyprian accept the lapsed immediately now cried that he was defiling the purity of the Church. They were supported by Novatian in Rome, who had been consecrated bishop under obscure circumstances. With terrible swiftness this new schism of Novatianism spread through all the churches, creating everywhere sects of the "pure" (*cathari*). The name alone indicates the attitude of the schismatics and their enthusiasm for a pure (in contrast to the "fallen") Church. Again, as under Montanism, the Church responded by gathering its forces around its bishops and the undestroyed continuity of catholic life. Africa united around Cyprian, the West around the newly-elected legitimate Pope Cornelius. From Egypt Dionysius of Alexandria, another luminous example of an ecumenical teacher, wrote letters to everyone, begging all to maintain unity. Novatianism, like Montanism, degenerated into a sect, remnants of which still existed as late as the seventh century.

In Montanism and Novatianism we may see what is meant by the evolution of the Church in these transitional decades. Formally, Novatian was right when he invoked tradition in his protest against accepting the lapsed. Cyprian himself had been a typical rigorist before the persecution of Decius. But the teaching of the Church is not a logical system and is not constructed in syllogisms. Novatian, who was true to logic, was torn from the life of the Church, while Cyprian, outwardly self-contradictory, could still boldly state that he had introduced nothing new with the question of the lapsed Christians, for he had taken his doctrine from the life of the Church. In fact, nothing had changed in the nature of the Church or its sanctity, but it had become more deeply conscious of the dichotomy between old and new in its earthly life. Novatian and his followers, for the sake of their principles, were left outside the Church; such is the logic behind every schism. They withdrew in proud scorn for the sullied Church of the lapsed. But in the pastoral heart of Cyprian and his truly catholic way of thinking, this Church of the lapsed remained the same holy bride of Christ which has no room for sin but exists to save sinners.

Cyprian's life ended in the glory of a martyr's death. On September 13, 258, he was summoned to the proconsul. The original documents of his interrogation have been preserved.

Galerius Maximus the proconsul said, "Are you Thascius Cyprian, a priest of the sacrilegious?"

Cyprian answered, "I am."

"The Emperors have ordered you to make sacrifices."

"I will not obey."

"I advise you to think it over."

"Do as you are instructed. There is no need to take counsel in such a righteous deed."

After consulting with the assessors, the proconsul read the sentence: "You have demonstrated that you are an enemy of the Roman gods and the holy laws. The most august Emperors could not convince you to return to performing Roman religious ceremonies. As a warning to those whom you have drawn into your criminal society, you shall pay with your blood for your disobedience to the laws. Thascius Cyprian is to be beheaded by the sword."

"Deo gratia," said Cyprian.

A crowd of Christians accompanied him to the place of execution, with lighted candles and the singing of prayers. His martyrdom was transformed into a triumphant liturgical act. A month before him Pope Sixtus II also bore witness. The police found him surrounded by clergy who were conducting a meeting of the faithful. He died sitting in the episcopal chair, and his deacon Laurentius was killed with him.

With the end of the century came increasing persecutions. The empire was falling, its whole structure rocked under the terrible attacks of Germanic tribes from the north and the Goths and Persians from the east. In these troubled years, when it was natural to seek scapegoats for so many misfortunes, it was not difficult to inflame hatred against the Christians. Edict followed edict, and throughout the empire new names of martyrs were added to the martyrology of the Church. The persecutions probably never reached such intensity as under Diocletian (303), just on the eve of the conversion of Constantine. The largest roster of names of martyrs comes to us from this period. It was as if the Church were revealing, for the last time before its victory, all the strength, beauty, and inspiration of the courageous suffering by which it had survived the first centuries—the strength of its witness to the kingdom of Christ, by which alone it ultimately conquered.

2 THE TRIUMPH OF CHRISTIANITY

Conversion of Constantine

The conversion of the Emperor Constantine resulted in the greatest change that the Church had ever undergone. Its significance was by no means limited to the altered relations between Church and state—the external conditions of Church life. Far more important were the developments in the mind of Christianity itself, the profound internal transformation that took place gradually in the Church community. This process was so complex and many-sided that one must treat with caution the contradictory evaluations of the age of Constantine, indiscriminate condemnation as well as unconditional justification.

In proportion as the struggle between the empire and Christianity was, as we have seen, fated and inevitable, just so, inversely, the peace between them was a matter primarily of a single person, a single will, and a single initiative. No one denies that Constantine played this role, but the evaluations of it have been diametrically opposed. For Eastern Christianity, Constantine still remains the holy initiator of the Christian world, the instrument for the victory of light over darkness that crowned the heroic feats of the martyrs. The West, on the other hand, often regards the era of Constantine as the beginning of an enslavement of the Church by the state, or even as the first falling away on the part of the Church from the height of primitive Christian freedom. It is essential to examine, at least briefly, this long-standing dispute.

In the liturgical texts of the Orthodox Church, the conversion of Constantine is compared to that of Paul—"like Paul, he received a call not from men."[1] But the historian must immediately note the radical distinction between them. What Paul experienced on the road to Damascus was a real and profound crisis, a "transvaluation of all values." Between the old and the new lay an impenetrable line which changed everything in the apostle's life and psychology. This was not true of Constantine. However, it was not by chance that his conversion occurred at the most critical point in his political and imperial career. It was not a matter of political calculation or "Machiavellianism," as some historians have asserted; yet neither was it a transformation of personality, as it had been for Paul. The explanation of Constantine's conversion must be sought in his psychology and religious and political ideology, which alone will furnish clues for an understanding of his place in Christian history.

In Constantine's time the evolution of the Roman Empire, which began with its first contact with the Hellenistic East, reached completion. It had attained its ultimate territorial limits, which had already under Hadrian begun to shrink and were now to waver, shrink further, or divide, according to the pressure of peoples and personalities in the coming centuries—only to recombine or expand once more, and then again divide or contract. Politically, the same final development had been attained. The Roman principality had gradually become a theocratic monarchy, the emperor being the connecting link between God and the world, while the state was the earthly reflection of divine law. The cult of the invincible Sun, which Emperor Aurelian had made the imperial religion in the middle of the third century, was by now closely connected with the

1 From a liturgical hymn on the Feast of St. Constantine.

new religious view of monarchy. The emperor in the world was the same as the sun in heaven; he was a participant in its glorious nature and its representative on earth. The monarch stood apart from simple mortals; he was "consecrated," and therefore all that surrounded him was consecrated. The religious devotion tendered to him, the imperial liturgy, and the sacred ritual that surrounded his whole life symbolized the divine nature of the state and the heavenly system reflected in the world. This evolution of attitude toward the state corresponded to the religious movement of the Greco-Roman world toward belief in a single God; each inspired the other. The Neoplatonism of Plotinus, the swan song of Greek philosophy, the Eastern cults and hermetic scriptures—all the main spiritual and intellectual currents of the period proclaimed one source, one supreme God in heaven.

Constantine was a typical representative of this new religious state of mind. According to his first Christian biographer, Eusebius of Caesarea, his father had already "dedicated to the One God his children, his wife, his servants, and his whole palace." Constantine grew up in the atmosphere of this exalted heavenly religion, purged of coarse paganism. He had always had mystical interests, a faith in dreams, visions, and illuminations. He firmly believed in his election, and his whole political career was marked by his personal contacts with heaven. Such a state of mind does not wholly explain his conversion to Christianity, but it helps us to understand better how Constantine himself received Christianity and how he became the representative of a new approach to the Church and its faith.

Constantine's star began to rise on the political horizon of the empire over the devastation and civil wars of several quarreling emperors who succeeded after Diocletian's abdication. The latter had inaugurated rule by two emperors, both called "Augustus," and two subordinate "Caesars"— each with his own functions—himself as senior emperor keeping supreme authority. This scheme for dealing with the besetting problems of empire did not work well, but

the division of East and West between two rulers within
the Roman framework was the prevailing pattern when
Constantine came to power. Though he had been crowned
at York, Britain, in 306 as the chosen successor of his
father (who briefly followed Diocletian), it was several
years before he could make himself secure. As emperor of
the West, he was obliged to destroy his rival, Maxentius,
who had become established in Rome, in order to unify
the western half of the empire under his rule. Early in 312
he moved out of Gaul and in October approached the
Eternal City with a small army after a bold winter march
across the Alps. The ensuing battle was a matter of life
and death for him, and involved the eventual success or
the failure of his whole "mission," of which he was acutely
aware. He had dared to march against the City. But was it
not defended by all its venerable gods—all the force of tradition, all the glory of the past—as well as by Maxentius?
For a man like Constantine this struggle for the ancient
city may well have meant a sacrilegious break with the past,
and he may have been unconsciously seeking some new
force or sanction which would bolster him in his plan to
revive Rome.

It was at this time of terrible tension and doubt that his
conversion occurred. The descriptions of the event closest
to it in time mention no vision of the Cross nor the traditional words, "In this sign conquer." They say merely that
he was led in a dream to have a new sign inscribed on his
weapons. This done, he conquered Maxentius and entered
Rome. Later the basic narrative began to grow into a
legend, not without the help of Constantine himself. One
point is beyond question: the sign he saw and under which
he won his decisive victory was in his own mind a Christian symbol, and from that time on he counted himself a
Christian.

Did he actually become one? Not until his deathbed,
twenty-five years after the battle of the Milvian Bridge, did
he receive baptism, the only symbol the Church accepts of
becoming a Christian. (It had been his dream to be bap-

tized in the Jordan, perhaps a reason for his long postpone-
ment.) Then what had he been before? The answer to
this question reveals the fundamental paradox in Byzantinism, already fully present in the unique conversion of
the first Christian emperor. In Constantine's mind the
Christian faith, or rather, faith in Christ, had not come to
him through the Church, but had been bestowed personally and directly for his victory over the enemy—in other
words, as he was fulfilling his imperial duty. Consequently
the victory he had won with the help of the Christian God
had placed the emperor—and thereby the empire as well—
under the protection of the Cross and in direct dependence
upon Christ.

This also meant, however, that Constantine was converted, not as a man, but as an emperor. Christ Himself
had sanctioned his power and made him His intended representative, and through Constantine's person He bound
the empire to Himself by special bonds. Here lies the explanation of the striking fact that the conversion of Constantine was not followed by any review or re-evaluation of
the theocratic conception of empire, but on the contrary
convinced Christians and the Church itself of the emperor's
divine election and obliged them to regard the empire itself as a consecrated kingdom, chosen by God. All the difficulties and distinctive qualities of Byzantium, all the
ambiguity of the "age of Constantine" in Church history,
result from the primary, initial paradox that the first Christian emperor was a Christian outside the Church, and the
Church silently but with full sincerity and faith accepted
and recognized him. In the person of the emperor, the empire became Christian without passing through the crisis
of the baptismal trial.

Relations between Church and State

After Constantine's conversion came the so-called Edict
of Milan in 313, defining the principles of his religious

policies. It solemnly proclaimed freedom "for Christians and all others to follow whatever religion they wished," and the properties confiscated from Christian churches during the persecutions were returned to them.

The decision of Milan has been sharply disputed by historians. What did this religious freedom mean? If Constantine, in proclaiming it, had been inspired by the Christian idea that one's religious convictions should be independent of the state, then why was it enforced for so short a time and then replaced by the unlimited and obligatory monopoly of Christianity, which destroyed all religious freedom?

This ambiguity was apparent almost immediately in the schism of the Donatists in Africa. At the time of Constantine's conversion, rebellion had spread in the African Church. After the waves of persecution the atmosphere had become poisoned by suspicion, accusations of deception, and defections. A party of Carthaginian Christians refused to recognize the new bishop, Caecilian, because a certain Bishop Felix, accused of betrayal in surrendering copies of the Scriptures to the police, had taken part in his ordination. This group, supported by many neighboring bishops, had chosen as their bishop first Majorinus and later Donatus, from whom the sect received its name.

Just at this time Constantine was sending generous grants to the Christian communities which had suffered under the persecutions. In Africa his aid naturally went to the "catholics" led by Caecilian. This aroused the Donatists to appeal to the emperor to transfer their case to the judgment of the Gallic bishops, who had not undergone persecution and therefore could not be accused of being compromised. Constantine valued nothing higher than peace, and what attracted him most of all in Christianity was, perhaps, its catholicity, the universal unity of the Church. Wishing to pacify the African Church, he agreed to the request of the Donatists. The chief bishops of Gaul gathered in Rome under the presidency of Pope Miltiades, listened to both sides, and solemnly confirmed the verdict of the synod of Carthage.

The matter had apparently been settled in accordance with all Church rules, as the Donatists themselves had wished. But they appealed again to the emperor, and Constantine then took an irrevocable step, inaugurating the tragic misunderstanding between the theocratic empire and the Church which was to last for many centuries. Instead of simply referring to the decision of the Church, which had been taken independently of him, the unbaptized emperor fulfilled the request of the Donatists and ordered a new investigation.

This was the first blow to the independence of the Church, and the distinction between it and the state became obscured. Later developments in the Donatist rebellion resulted solely from this first fatal mistake. There was a new condemnation of the schism by the Great Synod at Arles, then a new appeal to the emperor. Constantine grew angry —"What madness to plead for judgment from a man who himself awaits the judgment of Christ!"—but again yielded. When he was finally convinced, after so many investigations, that the Donatists were in the wrong, he let loose the full blast of state persecution upon them—the last and most terrible of his errors in the matter. Persecution, which transformed the schismatics into martyrs, only strengthened them. Fire raged throughout Africa and nothing could extinguish it. The Donatist schism, even more than the invasion of the Vandals, was the beginning of the end for the great and glorious African Church.

To the question posed earlier as to the historical meaning of the Edict of Milan, which so briefly suggested a genuine religious freedom, there can be only one answer: Constantine's freedom was not the same as Christian freedom. It would be centuries before the new concept of the individual, stemming from the Gospels, resulted in a new concept of the state, limited by the individual's inviolable rights. We now know how tortuous the development was;

we know too, alas, that Christians themselves have not
always been the bearers of genuinely Christian evangelical
truth. Perhaps the greatest tragedy of our recent history
is the fact that the most Christian of all ideas in our world,
that of the absolute value of human personality, has been
raised and defended historically in opposition to the
Church community and has become a powerful symbol of
the struggle against the Church.

The origin of this tragedy lies in the Church's own
beginnings, when the Christian mind was bewitched by
the conversion of Constantine. Not only did this prevent
the Church from revising the theocratic absolutism of the
ancient state in terms of the Gospel, but on the contrary,
that absolutism itself became an inseparable part of the
Christian world view. Constantine believed in the state as
the "bearer" of religion because it directly reflected and
expressed the divine will for the world in human society;
only in the light of this theocratic conception can the
freedom proclaimed in the Edict of Milan be correctly
evaluated. It was freedom for the cult, for the outward
forms of the worship of God; the state was no longer exclusively affiliated with any particular form. This did not mean
that the state had become religiously neutral, but rather
that the new religious and philosophical monotheism which
Constantine had represented before his conversion regarded
all exterior forms of religion—the cults of all gods—as more
or less closely approaching the single highest deity, and in
the long run saw everything as relative.

From this point of view the Edict of Milan was not a
beginning but an end. It was the last expression of the religious syncretism in which ancient paganism was to dissolve
and die. Yet the theocratic nature of the state remained
untouched; religion was primarily a state matter, because
the state itself was a divine establishment, a divine form
of human society. Freedom was granted so that, in the
words of the edict, "the divinity abiding in the heavens

might be mercifully and favorably inclined toward us, and
to all who are under our authority."

Although this freedom must be regarded as the last
manifestation of imperial syncretism, the Edict of Milan
reveals something new that was to follow. The emperor did
not conceal his special sympathy for Christianity, and declared openly that he was granting freedom to non-Chris-
tians "for the peace of our time," although his heart belonged wholly to the new faith. This was freedom for the
transitional period, in expectation of the painless triumph
of Christianity. Paganism was already doomed to ruin and
persecution by the theocratic nature of the empire and by
the persisting pagan concept of the state. Constantine considered himself the religious lawgiver of the empire, and as
a Christian he could not combine Christianity with pagan
falsehood. The more he became aware of his Christianity,
the more obvious became his hostility to paganism. Two
logics, two faiths, the theocratic and the Christian, were
interwoven in this ambiguous union which was to define
the fate of the Church in newborn Byzantium.

Donatism was only an introductory chapter in the history
of the new relations between Church and state, whose
significance was to be revealed far more fully and tragically
in the Arian controversy that took up the whole first century of the age of Constantine.

The Arian Disturbance

In the Arian quarrel, a large number of threads were
gathered in a single knot, with many problems drawn into
it. This marked the start of the great theological disputes
which were to persist through almost five centuries of
Church history, leaving as a heritage the inspired writings
of the Fathers and teachers and the crystallized formulas
of the ecumenical councils. This struggle to attain the truth,
however, was immediately complicated by the involvement
of state power. It ceased to be a purely ecclesiastical matter

and acquired a new, political dimension. In the course of
the controversy the faith of the Church was crystallized,
and the gradual and painful birth of Christian Byzantium
took place as well. Although the fourth century was outwardly one of the most tragic in the history of the Church,
it was at this time that the vision of a Christian world was
born which, despite all the problems it posed, was never
to be erased from the mind of the Church.

The dispute began in Alexandria, the capital of Christian
thought. Arius, a scholarly Alexandrian presbyter and
preacher, began to teach that Christ, as the Son of God
and one of God's creations, must necessarily be recognized
as created in time, since His birth could take place only in
time. He had been born of God as an instrument for the
creation of the world, and therefore "there was a time when
He was not." Consequently the Son of God was wholly
distinct from the Father and not equal to Him.

For the rank and file of modern Church members it is
difficult to understand, first, how such a doctrine, which
obviously contradicted the most basic principles of Christianity, could arise; and second, how the dispute could have
had so many after-effects, rending the Church asunder for
a space of fifty years. To understand it, we must realize that
for Christians of that time theology was indeed "a matter
of life and death, a heroic spiritual feat, a confession of
faith and a positive solution to the problems of life."[2] In
disputes centered apparently upon words and definitions,
the participants were in fact defending and protecting the
vital significance of Christianity—what today we might call
the existential aspect implied in the term "salvation." Salvation is not a magical act taking place outwardly; it depends
on how wholeheartedly man accepts and absorbs the divine
gift. Theology, then, which signifies comprehension, expression, and confession of the truth in words, becomes the
highest calling of man. It restores man's participation in
the divine meaning; it is his rightful heritage as a rational

[2] G. Florovsky, *The Ways of Russian Theology* (in Russian, Paris, 1937),
page 11.

being. Theology is the expression of faith in rational terms;
not its subordination to reason, but the extension, rather,
of reason itself to the dimensions of revelation.

The Church had lived from the beginning by faith in the
Father, Son, and Holy Spirit—in the experience of the
Triune God. The meaning of the Gospels lies in the revelation of the Trinity as perfect unity, love, and life. "The
grace of the Lord, Jesus Christ, the love of God, the Father,
the communion of the Holy Spirit" is the liturgical blessing we encounter in St. Paul's letter. But if the source of
salvation and the strength of Christian life lies in this
revelation of the Triune God, then the revelation should
also enlighten human reason and enable it to penetrate the
mystery revealed by Christ. The acceptance of truth has
always meant effort, crisis, and growth. "Natural" reason
conflicts with revelation as in a contradiction or paradox.
How can the primitive faith of the Church in a Triune God
be reconciled with the equally unquestionable affirmation
of His unity, the monotheism that led Christians to follow
the Jews in repudiating all paganism? This faith must be
revealed and the experience explained. So the theological
question of the Trinity, fundamental in its nature and
chronologically the first to arise, troubled the mind of the
Church.

Even in the second century the Apologists, defenders of
the Christian faith to the empire and the public, had tried
to explain faith in the Trinity by basing it on the concept
of the Logos familiar to Greek philosophers. The Son of
God, Christ, is the Word of the Father, by which He
creates and saves the world and by which He is linked to
the world. In the "Word" we in turn recognize God and
join ourselves to Him. But the danger of such an explanation is that the concept of the Logos in Greek philosophy
has what might be called an instrumental nature. The
Logos was always the bond, the intermediary link, the
unifying principle; it was not an independent source existing by itself. Although in the Fourth Gospel the Word is

understood in the spirit and light of the Old Testament
as the living and acting God, it might in the Greek conception easily be taken to be some divine quality or force
given to the man Jesus which distinguished Him from the
rest of mankind. In other words, the concept of the *Logos*,
which was common to Christianity and Hellenism, still
had to be purified of its exclusively cosmological significance
in Greek philosophy. The Apologists of the second century,
however, lacked the words and the philosophical gift to do
this. Their writings are ambiguous and inconsistent. While
they were wholly orthodox for the Church, which read them
in terms of its own faith, they could be understood by outsiders as identifying the Father with the Word in the way
that a man might be identified with his reason or his
thought.

At the beginning of the third century a movement called
Monarchianism had arisen, again in the West. This was a
doctrine of the Trinity which defended the "monarchy" of
the Father. It reflected the fear of retreating from the position of radical monotheism and a confused conception of
the faith of the Church as being faith in three gods. The
Monarchians taught that only the Father was God; in their
teachings about Jesus Christ and the Holy Spirit they split
into two groups—one which taught that Christ was a man
on whom the divine force had descended, making Him the
Son of God and uniting Him with the Father in a unique
way; while the second taught that Father, Son, and Holy
Spirit were three different modes of the appearance of the
One God in the world. First He revealed Himself as the
Father, then as the Son, and finally as the Holy Spirit. The
latter doctrine was called Modalism, and its chief representative, the scholarly Roman presbyter Sabellius, was expelled from the Church under Pope Callistus (217–22).

Out of the struggle against these heresies come the first
attempts to give an orthodox description of the mystery
of the Trinity and to express it in human terms. In the
West there was the theology of Tertullian before he re-

treated into Montanism, and in the East that of Origen. Despite the great difference between them, both had a common inadequacy: they identified God only with the Father, the view that had led to Monarchianism. The Trinity "arises," "becomes," if not in time, in any case hierarchically; it is a "disclosure" of God the Father—although according to the experience of the Church it is precisely the triune quality of God that is His complete form—the mystery of the Three who have one life in perfect love.

Thought had not yet caught up with faith, and words were helpless to express experience. Faith comes before theology, and only for that reason may we speak of theological development as the gradual acceptance, discovery, and refinement of faith, which has been complete from the start. From the examples of Origen and Tertullian we may see that the first attempts at this discovery were incomplete, even heretical. It was difficult to find words to express the faith, and centuries would be required to remake thought itself in the spirit of Christianity.

Such was the situation at the beginning of the fourth century, when Arianism first appeared. For lack of words, thought broke away, drawing faith after it and distorting the most basic and vital truths of the New Testament revelation. In this sense Arianism, as it slowly and painfully worked itself out, marked the end of all these confusions, for it was to enable the Church at last to express its faith in the Trinity in words "proper to God."

Arius was mistaken in his view, for he approached the solution to the theological problem of the Trinity solely as a philosopher and weighed the whole problem by logic. He interpreted two basic and particularly vital truths of Christianity, that of the One God and that of the salvation of the world by the Son of God, as abstract principles. He was a convinced monotheist, not in the Old Testament sense, but in the spirit of the philosophical monotheism which predominated at that period in the Hellenistic world.

This meant recognition of some abstract One or Entity which lay at the base of all that existed, as its source and as the unifying principle of all multiplicity. God was One, and there could not be any multiplicity in him; if He had a Son, then the Son was already distinct from Him. The Son was not He and not God. The Son was born, and birth is the appearance of something which has not been before. The Son was born for creation, for salvation, but He was not God in that unique and absolute sense which we use when we call the Father God.

Arianism was a rationalization of Christianity. Here living religious experience was no longer fertilizing thought, forcing it to see and understand what it had not previously understood. On the contrary, here faith was dried out by logical analysis and distorted into an abstract construction. Arianism was in tune with the times in its strict monotheism and desire to prune out everything irrational and incomprehensible. It was more accessible to the average mind seeking a "rational" faith than were the biblical images and expressions of Church tradition. As one historian has noted, it deprived Christianity of its living religious content and distorted it into an abstract theism of cosmology and morality.

The first reaction to Arianism was that of active believers who were horrified by this distortion of the sacred principles of the Church. Arius was censured by his own bishop, Alexander of Alexandria; but this was only a censure, not an answer. In his rebuke Alexander himself went astray, unable to find adequate words. Arius appealed for support to his former friends from the school of the famous Antiochene theologian, Lucian. As educated theologians, many of them occupied episcopal chairs. Especially noteworthy were Eusebius of Caesarea, whose *Ecclesiastical History* is a chief source of our knowledge of the early Church, and Eusebius of Nicomedia, who was to baptize the Emperor Constantine at the time of his death.

These friends supported Arius, and not only for personal

reasons. In these years there arose within the Church an intellectual class eager for rational explanations of the faith, which was beginning to be somewhat embarrassed by the insufficiently philosophical nature of Church doctrine. The Arian heresy seemed to them completely suitable as a "modern" interpretation of it, one which would be acceptable to broad circles of educated people. In this way the local Alexandrian dispute gradually spread throughout the East.

At this point the Emperor Constantine intervened. We must imagine what the conversion of the emperor himself meant for the Church after three centuries of persecution, if we are to understand why his court had immediately become a center of attraction, not only for opportunists and careerists, but for those genuinely inspired by the victory of Christ who dreamed of extending it throughout the world. Emperor and empire were becoming providential instruments for the kingdom of Christ. Around Constantine there sprang up a group of Christian counselors, a sort of unofficial staff. A prominent place among them was taken very early, as soon as Constantine came to the East, by Eusebius of Nicomedia, first of an unfortunate series of court bishops. Constantine himself could not, of course, understand the essence of the theological dispute, but he was disturbed by this new dissension within the Church.

Council of Nicaea—First Ecumenical Council

These were the years of Constantine's triumph. His victory over Licinius in 323 had finally confirmed his supreme power, and he pictured a united empire, spiritually renewed by a united Church. Suddenly, instead of his dream there was sad reality: new disputes and divisions. In all likelihood his Christian counselors gave him the idea of summoning a council of bishops, the customary means used by the Church to settle controversy. Constantine wanted to make of this council the symbol and crown of his own victory

and of the new position of the Church in the empire. And
so the first ecumenical council was summoned at Nicaea
in the spring of the year 325. It was universal, not in the
number of bishops attending (tradition defines it as the
council of the 318 Fathers), but in its conception and
significance. For the first time, after centuries of semi-
subterranean existence, prelates gathered from all parts of
the Church, many still with the marks of wounds and
mutilations received under Diocletian. The unprecedented
magnificence of their reception and the hospitality and
kindness of the emperor confirmed their joyous assurance
that a new era had begun and that Christ was indeed
victorious over the world. Constantine himself was the first
to interpret the council in this way. He had designated it
for the twentieth anniversary of his reign and wanted a gala
occasion and rejoicing; as he said in his speech to the
assembled bishops on the opening day, disputes were "more
dangerous than war and other conflicts; they bring me more
grief than anything else."

The importance of the Council of Nicaea lies, of course,
first of all in the great victory the truth sustained there.
It left no records or "Acts," as the other ecumenical councils have done; we know only that it condemned Arianism
and inserted in the traditional baptismal symbol of the
faith a new precise definition of the relationship of the
Son to the Father, by calling the Son "consubstantial"
(homoousion) with the Father, and consequently equal to
Him in divinity. This term was so precise as to exclude any
possibility of reinterpretation. Arianism was unconditionally condemned.

But the new definition, too, was to be for many long
years a stumbling block and a temptation, and it plunged
the Church into yet another lengthy dispute, which took up
the next half-century. Hardly any other fifty-year period
in the history of the Church has had such significance in
defining its future. The immediate reason for the controversy was that the condemned Arians not only did not sur-

render, but by means of very complex intrigues were able to bring the government authorities over to their side. The participation of the emperor in the life of the Church was a chief element in this new struggle, and one must say from the start that the events of the fourth century from this point of view were more than destructive—they were truly tragic.

The temporary triumph of the Arians would have been impossible even with the help of the emperor if the Church, which had condemned Arius almost unanimously, had remained united both in its condemnation and in accepting the constructive doctrine of Nicaea. But Nicaea had introduced confusion and doubt into men's minds. Most of its participants easily accepted the condemnation of Arianism, which too obviously distorted the original tradition; but the constructive doctrine about the Trinity contained in the term *homoousion* ("of one substance") was a different matter. This term had been proposed and in fact thrust upon Constantine, and through him upon the Council, by a small group of bold and far-sighted theologians who understood the inadequacy of merely condemning Arius and the need to crystallize Church tradition in a clear concept. For most of the bishops, however, the word was incomprehensible. For the first time a creedal definition had been made to contain a term alien to the Scripture. Even the meaning was dubious; would not this "one in substance" bring back into the Church the temptation of Sabellianism, so recently overcome? Did it not merge Father and Son again in "one essence"? Still, the council at Constantine's request had dignified it as a symbol of faith without probing much into its ramifications of meaning. The bishops considered it their main work to condemn heresy; as for the symbol of faith, in practice every Church had its own, which was in essential—but not necessarily literal—agreement with all the others.

The council had seemed to end successfully, except for the mistake of Constantine, who repeated his action against the Donatists by exiling Arius and his followers, thus again confusing the judgment of the Church with that of Caesar. At this point the group of court bishops began to exert its influence. It consisted almost wholly of friends of Arius, led by Eusebius of Nicomedia. They had accepted the condemnation, since nearly all the bishops had shown themselves against him at the council; but with reluctance and with hope of revenge. Since they could not openly oppose the council, they resorted to intrigue, and taking advantage of the general indifference of the bishops to the constructive Nicene definition, began to minimize it and to direct their forces against the group of theologians who alone understood its full significance.

Rumors and accusations were set in motion having nothing to do with theology. The first victim was Eustathius of Antioch, whose reputation with the emperor they succeeded in blackening and who was sent into exile. They then turned their intrigues against young Athanasius, recently elected bishop of Alexandria and probably the moving spirit in the creation of the new term. Again without engaging in theological dispute, his enemies first succeeded in having him condemned for alleged canonical wrongdoing by the episcopal council at Tyre in 331, and later in having him exiled by the emperor to Trier on the Rhine. Constantine could not bear rebels, and they contrived to present him to the emperor as such. After this there was no difficulty in bringing back Arius himself; he signed a questionable repentance and was received into communion. Constantine, who had never understood what the dispute was about, thought all was well—that the Church had restored peace within itself and that only enemies of peace could now rake up the past. Opportunists triumphed everywhere, while the Church as a whole was obviously uncomprehending and silent.

But Constantine's days were drawing to an end. In 336, the same year that Athanasius was sent into exile, he celebrated the thirtieth and last jubilee of his reign. He was already a different man. His mystical tendency had grown with the years; toward the end even matters of state withdrew into the background of his interest. The speeches and celebrations of the jubilee were illuminated by the light burning ever more strongly in his soul. Shortly before his death, through the laying on of hands, he became a communicant. He no longer put on imperial robes. His dream of baptism in the Jordan was not to be, but he was baptized by Eusebius of Nicomedia, and the joyous certainty of the nearness of Christ and His eternal light never again left him.

The Emperor Constantine died on a sunny noon of Pentecost in the year 337. However many mistakes and perhaps even crimes there may have been in his life—such as the murder of his son Crispus, a dark family drama never finally solved—it is hard to doubt that this man had striven unwaveringly toward God, had lived with a thirst for the absolute, and had wished to establish a semblance of heavenly truth and beauty on earth. The greatest earthly hope of the Church, the dream of the triumph of Christ in the world, became associated with his name. The love and gratitude of the Church is stronger than the pitiless but fickle and frequently superficial judgment of historians.

After Constantine

Only after the emperor's death did the Arian dispute begin to reveal its full significance. Constantine was succeeded by three sons, Constantine II, Constans, and Constantius, among whom the empire was divided. The usual strife of succession destroyed the first two in 340 and 350, respectively, leaving Constantius sole ruler. He was to play a fateful role in the life of the Church. While his father had connected his position as an "outside bishop of the Church" with his conversion and immediate election by Christ, Constantius interpreted his power *over* the Church as self-evident. The ambiguity of the age of Constantine was beginning to bring forth its first poisoned fruit. Although the late emperor could make mistakes and frequently did, he was a great man with a genuine desire for justice. Constantius, on the other hand, though partial to Christianity, was a small man and immediately sought the support of a group of shameless flatterers and opportunists who clung to him.

At first, it is true, the Eusebians had to give way. Constantine II demanded that all the exiled bishops be returned to their thrones. Athanasius, who had never recognized his dethronement and had been supported by the Western churches, was met with love by the people of Alexandria. But the Eusebians had a strong weapon against him: he had been deposed by a council of bishops, and only a council could restore him. The overwhelming majority of bishops had absolutely no notion of the ideological dimension underlying the whole struggle against the Alexandrian "pope." He seemed to them a restless person and had, moreover, been canonically dethroned. In the winter of 337-38 in Antioch, the center of Eusebian intrigues, an epistle was composed to the emperors and to all the bishops of the Catholic Church, accusing him of returning illegally to his throne.

Athanasius replied through a council of sixty-two Egyptian bishops, and appealed as well to the judgment of the whole Church. The epistle of the Egyptian council demonstrated that he was innocent of the absurd accusations raised against him and pointed out the real significance of the whole affair, the desire of his enemies "to abolish the orthodox and do away with the condemnation of the Arians at the true and great council." Here for the first time we note alarm at the intervention of the emperor in Church affairs. "By what right were the bishops who condemned Athanasius summoned by an order of the Emperor?"

But the Egyptian bishops were late in remembering that external authority had no rights within the Church. What about Nicaea itself? In any case the question was now transferred to its true theological battleground, and the West, hitherto silent through ignorance of Eastern matters, became involved. The Eusebians had to get rid of Athanasius immediately and used all their influence on Constantius. They chose their own bishop of Alexandria, a certain Gregory of Cappadocia, and demanded that the emperor help him take the Church of Alexandria away from the deposed and condemned Athanasius. From this moment there was open alliance between Constantius and the Eusebians. The prefect of Egypt, a friend of Arius, was ordered to give Gregory all possible help. On hearing that Gregory was approaching the city, the people rushed into the churches to defend them from the heretic. Police intervened and outrages developed, with churches being emptied by armed force. The police sought Athanasius, but he succeeded in hiding. In March 339 Gregory solemnly entered Alexandria, where a persecution of the supporters of Athanasius began. The Eusebians had triumphed once more.

Athanasius, however, was not a man to give in to force. He possessed great energy and absolute faith in the righteousness of his cause, and the ordeals which the great Alexandrian Father and teacher underwent all his life long apparently added to his strength. A truly epic struggle began between this giant and all the forces combined against him. From a hiding place somewhere near Alexandria, he sent his famous and explosive *Encyclical Letter*, which was a cry for help. "What has passed among us exceeds all the persecutions in bitterness. . . . The whole church has been raped, the priesthood profaned, and still worse, piety is persecuted by impiety. . . . Let every man help us, as if each were affected out of fear of seeing the Church canons and the faith of the Church held in scorn."

Shortly after this we find Athanasius in Rome, where other victims of the Eusebian terror were gradually gathering. Until this time the West had taken no part in the post-Nicene dispute; the term *homoousion* had been accepted without argument or doubt, and only now, belatedly, did

they learn from Athanasius and his friends of the difficulties
in the East. The situation became as complex as it was
tragic when Pope Julius gave his defense of Nicaea and
Athanasius such a Roman tinge that the East inevitably
united to oppose it.

The Roman Position

Already by the end of the second century we have seen
the gradual development in the West of a Roman self-
consciousness. The Roman Church was the most ancient
Western Church and the only Western apostolic see, consecrated by the names and blood of the apostles Peter and
Paul. Christianity in the West developed from Rome, so
that most of the Western churches regarded the Roman
Church as the Mother Church, from which they had received the tradition of the faith and apostolic succession.
While Rome's position in the West was exceptional, the
Church of St. Peter was the object of special respect in the
East as well, so that Ignatius of Antioch referred to it as
"presiding in love." After the fall of the apostolic commu-
nity in Jerusalem, Rome undoubtedly became the first
Church, the center of that universal unity and consent
which Irenaeus of Lyons contrasted with the splintered
Gnostic sects.

But alarming signs appeared very early: the Roman
bishops were more and more inclined to regard their primacy, which no one disputed, as a special power, and their
"presiding in love" as presiding in power and authority.
Thus in 190–192, Pope Victor demanded in an ultimatum
that the Eastern churches accept the Roman practice of
celebrating Easter. Rome held this celebration on the first
Sunday after the Jewish Passover, while in the East it coincided with the Jewish holiday. Victor based his demand
on the authority of the apostles Peter and Paul. He was
answered by one of the senior bishops of the East, Poly-

crates of Ephesus, who referred in turn to a tradition that had reached him directly from the apostles. That is, he simply repudiated the Roman claim to force its practice on other churches. "I have lived in the Lord sixty-five years, I have read all the Holy Scriptures, and I fear nothing, whatever might threaten me. Greater men than Victor have said: It is better to listen to God than men." In reply Victor in an encyclical letter simply excluded the churches of Asia Minor from communion with Rome, and this decisive measure evoked protests even in places where the Roman practice, not the Eastern, prevailed.

Later, in the middle of the third century, a dispute arose between Rome and Africa over the question of the baptism of heretics. Pope Stephen also required unconditional submission to the Roman decision. The African bishops through Cyprian of Carthage answered: "None of us claims to be a bishop of bishops or resorts to tyranny to obtain the consent of his brethren. Each bishop in the fullness of his freedom and his authority retains the right to think for himself, he is not subject to any other and he does not judge others." Stephen was answered still more sharply by Firmilian of Caesarea in Cappadocia, one of the pillars of the Eastern Church: "There are many distinctions within the Church, but what is important is spiritual unity, unity of faith and tradition. What boldness to claim to be the judge of all! Stephen by this claim excludes himself from the universal unity of the episcopate."

Thus very early we see both acknowledgment of the universal significance of Rome as the first Church to express the common consent and the common unity, but also a reaction against a specifically Roman interpretation of this significance. In each case, however, the reaction was merely to a concrete situation and never to the matter of the Roman claims in their essence. Thus a Roman tradition was gradually allowed to develop. When East and West later came to face it, it was too late; for Rome the tradition was already sanctified by antiquity and interpreted as true.

The Arian dispute was an important step in the history
of this gradual divergence. Athanasius appealed to Rome
because he had no one left to appeal to in the East. The
Eusebians wrote to Rome to make their condemnation
of Athanasius universal. Both appeals were in accordance
with the concept of the universal unity of the Church as a
universal communion, a unity of life such as we have already observed in the second and third centuries. But Pope
Julius interpreted them in his own way, in the light of the
gradually developing, specifically Roman tradition. He conceived his role as that of an arbitrator of Eastern matters,
and wrote the East demanding that the whole problem be
decided at a council in Rome—even appointing the date
of the council. It was almost an ultimatum.

In Antioch the pope's letter caused dismay. One must
not forget that, at this time, for the overwhelming majority
of Eastern bishops the problem was Athanasius, not the
Nicene faith. Athanasius, to their minds, had been deposed
by a legitimate council and a review of this decision, not
in the East but in Rome, seemed an unprecedented defiance
of all the canonical norms accepted by the Church from
ancient times. The Eusebian leaders began to play on this
dismay. Only a year after receiving the papal epistle, in
January 341 an answer came to Rome signed by Eusebius
of Nicomedia (who by this time had managed to transfer
across the Propontis to the new Eastern capital, Constantinople) and by two other senior Eastern bishops. In it the
pope was respectfully but somewhat ironically put in his
place. It should be noted that Julius had put himself in a
difficult position by accepting into communion, along with
Athanasius, Marcellus of Ancyra. The latter really did interpret the Nicene definition incorrectly, with clearly Sabellian overtones. He had undoubtedly been rightly condemned in the East. But theological refinements were
poorly understood in the West, and Nicaea had been accepted in a purely formal way. They saw in Marcellus only
a martyr to the truth. Meanwhile, from the East Julius was

offered a choice between two condemned fugitives and the whole Eastern Church, which was united in condemning them.

On receiving this answer, Julius immediately summoned a council of Italian bishops in Rome, where he solemnly proclaimed his agreement with Athanasius and Marcellus. In a new epistle to the Eastern bishops, he expressed the Roman point of view in plain terms: "Do you not know that the custom is that we should be written to first, and that judgment is rendered here? What I write you and what I say we received from the blessed Apostle Peter." Julius was completely sincere, as well as morally superior to the Eusebians. The Catholic West rightly took pride in his dignified epistle. But there is irony in the fact that, in defending the truth, he really did break with the tradition of the Eastern Church and in effect forced it to unite against him; while in its opposition it was at the same time repudiating Athanasius and the Nicene faith and defending the original concept of the Church, which it was not to reject even when it finally returned both to Nicaea and to Athanasius.

Countermeasures in the East

The East responded by holding a great council, which met in Antioch in the summer of 341 to dedicate the "Great Golden Church" that Constantine had not been able to finish before his death. About a hundred bishops attended. Nothing shows better that Church history cannot be reduced to black and white formulas than the fact that this council, which again condemned Athanasius, has still remained in the tradition of the Eastern Church one of the authoritative "local councils," and the canons it adopted are still included in the canonical collections.

The Council of Antioch of 341 was the breaking point in the Arian rebellion. The Eusebians wanted no theological

disputes but simply the destruction of the defenders of
homoousion. But now it was necessary to answer the Western accusation of heresy in specifically theological fashion.
By returning to theology for the first time since Nicaea, the
Eastern bishops started down the road which would bring
them after decades of tormenting distortions to a deliberate
acceptance of that council's decisions.

In answer to the accusation of the pope, the Fathers at
the council solemnly affirmed an old pre-Nicene creed,
which has been ascribed to Lucian of Antioch, in which
faith in Jesus Christ is expressed in the following terms:
"God of God, the Whole of the Whole, the One of the One,
the Perfect of the Perfect, the King of the King . . . Non-
distinct image of the Divinity of the Father, both of His
Being and of His strength, will, and glory." This was an
antiquated form of the pre-Nicene doctrine about the same
homoousion ("consubstantiality") in older verbal garments.
Their agreement with *homoousion* was not apparent to the
Antiochene Fathers, nor did they perceive that only the
Nicene definition expressed finally and with utmost preci-
sion what they were describing in so many images: the
perfect divinity of the Son and His perfect unity with the
Father. On the contrary, *homoousion* seemed to them an
alien and dangerous term, and they found confirmation of
their fears in the heresy of Marcellus of Ancyra, who had
returned to the Sabellian confusion of the Son with the
Father. Yet Rome had accepted Marcellus. Thus we cannot
speak of a struggle between the orthodox West and the
heretical East. There were too many factors on both sides
of misunderstanding and incomprehension. Much had to
be burned away in the purifying fire of suffering and division.

The Council of Antioch seemed to make possible a theological agreement with the West. But there remained the
problem of individuals—of Athanasius first of all. Under
the pressure of the Emperor Constans, still in power in the
West, it was decided to review his case at an ecumenical

council in Sardica (Sofia). This council, in turn, had hardly convened in 343 when it immediately split—again because the Westerners did not comprehend the complexities of the situation. The Easterners agreed to a general review of Athanasius' case, but before the review they regarded him as deposed and insisted that he be absent during the discussion. The Westerners refused to fulfill this condition, referring to Rome's justification of him. The Council split, and the peace overtures that had been made were nullified.

Political pressure by Constans on his brother continued, and the military situation in the East made Constantius particularly sensitive to it. Matters went so far that when Gregory of Alexandria died in 345, Constantius, without ecclesiastical consultation, simply summoned Athanasius to occupy his former post. Knowing to what he owed this summons, Athanasius demanded a written rescript, and since he had never recognized his deposition, returned. His return was a triumph. Even his most violent enemies were reconciled by the *fait accompli.*

But the political wind very soon shifted again. In 353, after several civil wars, Constantius emerged as sole ruler of the whole empire and immediately showed that his conciliatory attitude had been due only to expediency. The Arians and semi-Arians were far more obedient to state authority than the Nicaeans, and they became the support of Constantius. Nicaeans were persecuted everywhere. Athanasius was not touched at first, for Constantius had appointed him in a personal rescript. Both the emperor and his counselors understood that, while Athanasius was defended in the West, his condemnation could not be universal. Therefore it was necessary first to crush the West and bring it into submission to state authority. In 352 the deceased Pope Julius was succeeded in Rome by Pope Liberius. The emperor demanded that he summon a council and condemn Athanasius. The pope tried to defend himself, but without success. In 355 three hundred Western bishops in Milan, where Constantius' court was at the time,

yielded to brute force. "My will is the canon for you," said
the emperor when the bishops asked to investigate the question canonically, and all except a few very steadfast ones
signed the condemnation. Those who resisted were immediately exiled. Liberius, who had refused to accept the decision of the council, was also exiled. Imperial officials
passed all through the West, collecting signatures from
bishops to make sure of their stand.

Thus forty years after the conversion of Constantine the
Church lay prostrate at the feet of his son. Only Athanasius
remained, a living challenge to force and a witness to the
independence of the Church. On the night of February 8,
356, when he was presiding at a vigil, the church was surrounded by soldiers. On the order of the bishop the people
began to sing "Praise the name of the Lord!" and started
to disperse. Along with them, unnoticed in the darkness,
Athanasius also left, disappearing for six years. In vain
the angry Constantius ordered all the monasteries of Egypt
searched; the desert and the monks hid their bishop. And
immediately his fulminating and accusing voice rang out.
During his years in hiding he wrote his *Apology to Constantius*, which was devastating for the emperor, and his
History of the Arians, in which he laid bare the whole theological dialectic of the post-Nicene dispute. In the face of
triumphant force, he alone remained undaunted.

Until this time no one had as yet openly opposed Nicaea,
and the Arian minority had been able to create the impression of unity among the Eastern bishops only on the
question of individuals and by their general opposition to
the West. But now their hands were loosed and all opposition destroyed. In every important see were obedient executors of the instructions from the court oligarchy. Then in
the autumn of 357, in Sirmium on the Danube, the Arians
cast aside their masks. They had composed a creedal statement (the so-called second formula of Sirmium) which was
already almost openly Arian, and the bishops were required
to accept it under threat of state sanctions. The manifesto

of Sirmium, confirmed by imperial authority, rang out like
a trumpet from one end of the empire to the other.

End of Arianism

This apparent final victory of Arianism turned out to be
fatal to it. The Sirmium statement was so obviously Arian
that it inevitably produced a reaction among all the sane
elements in the Church. The coalition they had been able
to knit together against Athanasius, Marcellus, and Rome
now fell apart, and the Eastern Church, which had not
hitherto been aware of the full extent of the danger, began
to come to its senses.

The healing process was gradual, and the whole weight
of the state, a load on Church life which was never again
lifted, was even more apparent. Bishops began to split into
theological parties; new creedal statements were composed.
There were struggles, mutual excommunications, councils,
and congresses. The Church historian Socrates later compared this period to a night skirmish in which no one
knows who is his enemy or his friend.

Arianism led to the denial in fact of the very essence
of Christianity. This was demonstrated with particular force
by the extreme Arians, the so-called Anomoeans, who affirmed that Christ was absolutely distinct from God. The
Church had never recognized so clearly the need for a
precise theological answer, a firm confession of faith. Everyone understood the inadequacy of mere reference to previous creeds; the figurative expressions used in them were
interpreted by the Arians in their own way. Yet the Nicene
term *homoousion* still seemed suspicious. The first theological reaction to Arianism therefore united the majority
of the Eastern bishops around the term *homoiousion*. The
Son was "of like substance" with the Father, of the same
nature as the Father; this was the first step. By taking it, the
Easterners acknowledged the need for philosophical terms
to express their faith; they themselves took the road for

which they had previously condemned the defenders of Nicaea.

The Arians once again kept the upper hand, however. On the commission ordered by Constantius to prepare for the new ecumenical council, they managed to convince the confused bishops that all harm came from the use of the term "substance," which it would be best simply to forbid, calling the Son "like the Father in all." With this came new divisions, new disputes. The weary Constantius decided to unite them all in a compromise with a theological minimum, since a precise creed seemed a constant source of difficulty. At the council convened in Constantinople in 360 to dedicate the Church of St. Sophia, it was proclaimed that "the Son is like the Father"—the qualification "in all" was discarded. Such a definition might be acceptable to anyone except, of course, extreme Arians, but it deprived the faith of the Church of its vital content, its joyous certainty in the Incarnation "for our salvation" of God Himself. At the same time, for various imaginary crimes, all the bishops who disagreed were deposed and exiled. The Church was ruled by a new state religion.

Constantius might think he had completed his father's work and achieved the longed-for peace in the Church, but since it was based on a meaningless compromise, the peace was bound sooner or later to end. A year and a half after the triumph of the Homoian party (as the new Church-state coalition was called), Constantius died. A reaction now took place, not against any particular theology this time, but against Christianity itself: for two and a half years (361–63) the mysterious and tragic shadow of the Emperor Julian the Apostate lay across the empire. His first act was to establish complete religious freedom. He is reported to have hoped that the Christians would dispute so bitterly among themselves that they would discredit their faith in all eyes. Actually the brief reign of Julian demonstrated that the Church when left to itself might solve its difficulties independently.

Once more the great Alexandrian exile Athanasius returned in triumph to his city. He was not there long, for when Julian learned that he had baptized several pagan women, he issued an edict for his expulsion, and the much-traveled bishop again went into hiding. His brief stay in Alexandria, however, was marked by one of the great, historically decisive acts of his life: the calling of the Alexandrian Council of 362. Rigor and intractability might have been expected of him, persecuted for so many years by the whole anti-Nicene East. Yet Athanasius, who had identified his entire life with the Nicene definition and had never once wavered, even when the whole Church seemed united in rejecting him, was the first to understand that the errors of the East were not pure heresy and was able to discern allies and brothers among them. He understood that real incomprehension lay back of their rejection, and he perceived in their inadequate words their complete return to the truth. For this alone he deserves his title "Great." The work of the Council of 362 was a gesture of reconciliation. It solemnly affirmed the Nicene Creed, but with sufficiently lucid explanation to bring back, as to the only salvation, all who had sought the truth in shadows and rebellion and had not despaired of finding it.

The first to be restored was the West, which had been made to abandon the *homoousion* definition only by imperial force. In 363 the legions put on the throne the elderly general Valentinian, who, when the bishops asked to be permitted to summon a council, answered: "I am a layman and consider that it would be improper for me to intervene in this; let the hierarchs meet and decide as they wish." In this atmosphere of freedom the Western Church simply and completely returned to its original acceptance of the Nicene Creed.

The situation in the East was more complex; Valentinian had appointed as emperor there his brother Valens (364–78), who continued officially to protect the Homoian party. Outwardly the life of the Church continued disturbed, the years of divisions, mutual accusations, and excommunica-

tions taking their toll; yet beneath this sorry surface the
mighty neo-Nicene flood was growing ever greater. A
uniquely important role in this restoration was played by
three bishops customarily called the Great Cappadocians.
They are Basil the Great, Gregory the Theologian, and
Gregory of Nyssa, who with Athanasius are the greatest
Fathers and teachers in the tradition of the Eastern Church.
As the Council of Nicaea and the struggle to support it is
forever connected with the name of Athanasius, so to these
three, and especially to Basil the Great, the Church owes
its final triumph.

Their main contribution was theological; they were rich
in the experience of the post-Nicene disputes, which had
revealed the difficulty of expressing the faith of the Church
in words, and they were thinkers and philosophers of genius.
They perfected the creation of a theological language,
crystallized its concepts, and expressed all the profound
significance of the orthodox doctrine of the Holy Trinity
contained in Athanasius' *homoousion* and in the Nicene
Creed. They forced the whole Church to perceive its own
truth.

The bright image of Basil the Great particularly illumines the epilogue of this long, troubled, often apparently hopeless struggle. A sick man who dreamed constantly
of monastic solitude, of reflection and creative work, still
he devoted his whole life to the reconciliation of Christians,
and his tact, patience, and persistence knew no limits. How
often there appeared to be no way out of the blind alley
of division that now seemed part of the very flesh of the
Church! Despite insults, misunderstandings, and slander,
the great Cappadocian archbishop never slackened his
efforts. His service was blessed and recognized before his
death by the elderly Athanasius, who was able to spend the
last years of his life peacefully among his people. Basil
completed this work. He died in 379, just before the last
triumph of Nicaea, the Second Ecumenical Council—like

Moses, leading his people to the Promised Land but not entering it himself.

New Relation of Christianity to the World

All the complexity and ambiguity of the Church's new position in the world was revealed in the Arian rebellion. Victory frequently alternated with defeat, and freedom from persecution with dependence on authority. It must be acknowledged that the modern Christian tends to judge the age of Constantine unfavorably. We have recently become sensitive again to the eschatology of the early Church, and the question arises whether these centuries of union and peace with state, culture, and society were not a fatal mistake—whether the Church did not become worldly during this time and reject "the one thing necessary." As always in tragic periods of decline, the Christian mind is subtly tempted to refuse the highway of responsibility and withdraw into pure "spirituality."

Yet only the pain of historical defeat hinders us from perceiving that during these fateful decades a Christian world began to evolve which was far more significant than its actual historical framework. By this I do not mean any particular form of relation between Church and state, nor the formal adoption by the public of Christian ceremonies, symbols, or customs, but rather that profound transformation of the human mind which lay behind all these developments—almost imperceptible at first, but crucially important in its consequences. This was the inoculation of the human mind and conscience with the image of Christ. After Constantine, Christianity became indeed the fate of the world, so that fundamentally whatever occurred in the world became somehow connected with Christianity and was resolved in relation to it. This is the vital significance of the period.

The first impression of the fourth century is usually that

of a nominal conversion. Outwardly it was indeed filled
with disputes about Christianity; splendid churches arose
in the cities; the services were more majestically performed,
and gold and precious stones appeared on the vestments.
But do we see any moral transformation of society? Did
Christianity influence the laws, customs, or principles of
the state that had adopted it?

It is true that Constantine declared Sunday a day of rest,
freed the churches and the clergy from taxes, granted
bishops the judiciary right, and protected the family. But
a part of his "Christian" legislation was directed toward the
privileges of the Church, and the rest—the legislation that
really strove to humanize life—continued the trend of Roman law toward philanthropy, which had begun in the third
century. In any case, we do not note any sharp break or
crisis of conscience, and in many ways the fourth century
was marked, on the contrary, by a greater enslavement of
man than before. Indeed, the iron Middle Ages are fore-
shadowed in the greater pressure on him from the state.

When we judge this period, however, we must not forget
that the problem of the Church's influence on the world
was posed for it in a different way than it is now posed
for us. We judge and measure the past by standards of
Christian achievement and quality of life, because behind
us lie centuries of gradual development of this urge toward
the ideal in the human mind, progressively infecting all
aspects of life with a thirst for absolute perfection. We
speak of problems of the state, culture, and society; but
they became "problems" only in the light of the image
of the perfect Man and the perfect life that illuminated
the world, and in the light of our new knowledge of good
and evil. We often forget with what difficulty and what
struggles this growth of a perspective took place.

The first obstacle the Church encountered was not any
particular imperfection or defect of the state or society, but
paganism itself. It is impossible to evaluate truly the
achievements of the period without understanding the na-

ture of this struggle. We think of paganism as primitive idol worship and consider the victory of the Church something simple and self-evident. But behind the worship of idols, actually making it far less primitive, lay a very particular and integrated perception of the world, a complex of ideas and beliefs deeply rooted in man, which it was no easy matter to eliminate. Even today, two thousand years after the appearance of Christianity, it has not completely disappeared. In its most general and simplified form it can be defined as the subjection of man to irrational forces which he senses in nature—a concept of the world and of life in it as a fate dependent on these forces. Man can somehow propitiate them or redeem himself by sacrifice and worship. To some extent he can even control such forces with magic; but he can never comprehend them, still less liberate himself from them. His whole attitude toward the world is determined by fear and the sense of dependency on mysterious powers; he can invoke or "charm" them, but cannot make them intelligible or beneficent.

Christianity regarded paganism as a terrible lie about the world, which enslaved man and was consequently a lie about God; and it used all its forces in the struggle for the human soul. Only in the light of this conflict can we completely understand what now seems to us the increasing worldliness of the Church. During the period of the persecutions, Christians were the little flock which, being legally condemned, was outside the state and public life. It could not undertake any role in the world except to bear witness by word and blood. But now the situation was radically changed. After Constantine the masses began to pour into the Church. In addition, through the conversion of the emperor, even before the official condemnation of paganism, the Church was placed in a central position in the life of the empire, the place occupied by the official religion in previous times.

We have seen that the function of this official sort of

religion in state and society was to protect the public well-being by worship and sacrifice, to place the lives of all under the protection of the gods, and to ensure their obedience to divine laws and their loyalty to the state. If Christianity had been only eschatology, a call to reject the world and turn wholly to the coming kingdom "not of this world" (as many think today), the acceptance of this function would indeed have meant that the Church had become worldly. But the witness of the martyrs had demonstrated that Christians do not separate religion from life, but affirm that the whole man and all his life belong wholly to the kingdom of Christ. The entire meaning of the Christian message was that the kingdom of God had drawn near with the coming of Christ and had become the seed of a new life here and now in this world. In the light of the reign of the Lord, nothing in the world could any longer claim to be an absolute value: neither the state, nor culture, nor the family—nothing. Everything was subordinate to the One Lord; such was the significance of the Christian refusal to give this title to the emperor.

But now the world itself had accepted and recognized the Lord. The emperor had placed his kingdom and the whole empire under His protection, and he wished to receive from the Church the sanction he had previously expected from the gods. Could the Church refuse this? Of course not, if it had affirmed, in the words of Athanasius, that "in the Cross there is no harm, but healing for creation."

To abolish paganism meant, therefore, not simply to abolish idols and idol worship, but also to appease the eternal need which had nourished them, the need for divine aid, for a divine sanction for human life and everything great and little in it. More than that, it meant revealing the true meaning of life and illumining it with a new light. Historians sometimes assert that, in struggling against paganism, Christianity itself adopted pagan elements and ceased to reflect the evangelical reverence of God "in spirit and in truth." Churchly piety, the development and increasing complexity of worship, and the reverence for saints and their relics which grew so swiftly in the fourth century—the increasing interest in the material aspect of religion, the holy places, objects, and reliquaries—all have been attributed directly to pagan influence in the Church and regarded as a compromise with the world for the sake of a mass victory.

The Christian historian is not required in his defense of Christianity simply to reject this accusation or to deny that there are any analogies between Christianity and pagan forms of religion. On the contrary, he may boldly accept the charge, for he can see no harm in such analogies. Christianity adopted and assimilated many forms of pagan religion, not only because they were the eternal forms of religion in general, but also because the intention of Christianity itself was not to replace all forms in this world by new ones, but to fill them with new and true meaning. Baptism by water, the religious meal, the anointing with oil, these basic religious symbols and rituals were not invented or created by the Church but were already present in the religious usage of mankind. The Church has never denied this link with natural religion, but from the first it has attributed to the connection a meaning which is the reverse of what modern historians of religion see in it. The latter explain everything by "borrowings" and "influences," while the Church, in the words of Tertullian, has always asserted that the human soul is "by nature a Christian," and therefore even natural religion—even paganism itself—is only a distortion of something by nature true and good. In accepting any particular form, the Church in its own mind has returned to God what rightly belongs to Him, always and in every way restoring the fallen image.

In other words, we must ask not only whence the Church took a particular form and why, but also what meaning it has given it. Particularly interesting from this point of view was Church building, which flourished so luxuriantly during and after the reign of Constantine. In the early era of persecutions the Church of course had no public buildings, but the first Christians sharply contrasted their concept of religion with the Judaic attitude toward the Temple at Jerusalem, on the one hand, and the pagan attitude toward a temple, on the other. For paganism the temple was the sacred dwelling of a god, but "sacred" meant distinct from "profane"—wholly contradictory to it. The temple united men with the divinity as much as it divided it from them. In the temple one could make sacrifices for people, propitiate the god, and render him what was due, but outside it everything remained profane and divided from the deity.

But the basic Gospel of Christianity was that from now on God had chosen man himself as His temple, and He no longer dwells in man-made temples. "Know ye not that your body is the temple of the Holy Ghost which is in you?" In this way the contradiction between sacred and profane was overcome, because Christ had come to sanctify man and his entire life, to make it sacred again and to unite it with God. In calling themselves the Body of Christ, Christians of course could not help connecting these words with the words of Christ himself about the destruction of the Temple in Jerusalem and its restoration in three days. The place where Christians gathered was sacred, and the sanctity of the gathering made any place and the whole world a Temple.

The Visible Church

Yet now the Christians themselves were beginning to build churches, and after the time of Constantine, Church building became one of the main features of Christian life. Did this mean a break in the mind of the Church, a return to the well-trodden road of a temple concept of religion? The answer is contained in facts which might at first appear to have only archaeological interest. The basic model of the Christian temple in the fourth century was the basilica. This was not in origin a religious building but specifically profane, designated for large gatherings—for the court, for trade, or for politics. This meant that in building their own churches Christians deliberately rejected as prototypes both the pagan temple and the Temple of Jerusalem, described in detail in the Bible. In the light of Christianity a temple acquired a completely new meaning, incompatible with the old. The pagan temple was subordinated architecturally to its religious function as the house of a god; in its center, therefore, stood an idol or a depiction of the god. The Christian church, on the other hand, was wholly subordinate to the concept of the Christian gathering, and so was its architecture. In the center of the building stood that which transformed this gathering into a Church, uniting Christians into a living temple of the Body of Christ: the table for the celebration of the Eucharist. The appearance of Church buildings, therefore, changed nothing essential in the Church, but on the contrary, the building itself acquired a new significance.

With Constantine, the Christian church emerged into full view and ceased to be a place of semisecret meetings, so that gradually it became the center of religious life in the city. In Constantinople, his new capital, which was ceremoniously opened in 330, he had originated the plan for a Christian city which was to be the standard for all city construction in the Christian Middle Ages. The Church building was its mystical center or heart. A church crowned the city with its cupola or protected it with its sacred shadow. The idea itself was admittedly borrowed from paganism, and historians are still arguing as to what inspired Constantine in his rebuilding of ancient Byzantium—whether it was the vision of a sacred center for the Christian empire or echoes of ancient dreams of a philosophical city. For later generations, in any case, Constantinople remained the specifically Christian center of the empire. In the Church building, from then on, man's whole

life received a religious sanction. The Church gatherings
in it gradually came to coincide with gatherings of citizens.

A new "physical" link was established between the
Church and the world. The martyr who had suffered in
this city was naturally distinguished from the throng of
martyrs as its own saint, the spiritual patron of the city;
and the prayer offered in the Church "for all and in behalf
of all" was now perceived to be primarily a prayer for that
particular place and for these people. It naturally came to
include their daily needs and embraced man's whole life
in a new way, from birth to death, in all its forms: governmental, social, or economic. Frequently, it is true, the
Christian saint assumed in the popular mind the significance formerly held by the local god or "genius," and the
Church service was interpreted as a ritual religious sanction
for all aspects of life. Yet at the same time the Church
building and the cult were now becoming the main channels or forms for preaching Christianity to a still semipagan
world—the school for a new Christian society. By responding to all the needs of this world and assuming the function
previously performed by paganism, the Church united
everything from within with the Good News, and placed
the image of Christ in the center of life.

Whatever may be said about the swift development of
the cult of saints, even of its monstrous distortions, the
fact remains that the image of the saint himself and his
life as it was read in the Church spoke of a new meaning
in life and summoned the people to Him by whom this
saint had lived and to whom he had completely given himself. However much men may have brought into the
Church what they had seen and sought in pagan temples,
when they entered it they now heard those eternal and
immutable words about the Savior crucified for our sins—
about the perfect love that God has shown us—and about
His kingdom as the final goal of all living beings.

One historian has called the essential nature of this
evolution in Church life the "consecration of time." While

its highest point and final meaning remained the Sacrament—that is, the anticipation of all the fullness and joy of the kingdom of God and of the timeless and eternal presence of Christ among those who have loved Him; and while the narrow way of baptismal renunciation of the sufficiency of this world was still the only road leading to the Sacrament; yet the rays of the Sacrament now illumined this world as well. The consecration of time, the consecration of nature, the consecration of life, a firm faith that "in the Cross is no harm but healing for creation," the gradual illumination of all things by the image of Christ—this was the affirmative significance of what has so often been regarded as the growing worldliness of the Church. This "worldliness" should not be measured by its inadequacies or distortions, which were all too frequent, but by its positive inspiration; it revealed in a new way the same old catholicity, the Church's integrated and all-embracing awareness of itself as a seed cast into the world for man's salvation.

There was pressure from the state and enslavement of bishops. Yet in the final analysis it was Athanasius and Basil who were glorified by the Church as the "rule of faith"—not Eusebius of Nicomedia—and it was their truth that the state itself accepted and to which it submitted. This was not an accident. For the first time the principle of objective truth, independent of everything else in the world, was proclaimed superior to all powers and authorities. Today we hardly remember that the idea of objective truth, proclaimed by the whole modern world, entered the mind of man at this time, in the midst of disputes over words which may seem to us trifling; and that in them the mind of modern man was in the making: his faith in reason and freedom, his fearlessness in encountering reality whatever it might be, since there is something stronger than the external buffetings of reality: the truth.

Yes, there was a reconciliation with the world, an acceptance of its culture, the forms of its life, its language and thought. Basil the Great and his friend Gregory the Theologian would recall with gratitude all their lives the golden years spent at the pagan university of Athens (along with Julian the Apostate). Basil would even write a little treatise for young men on the value of studying secular—that is, pagan—literature. Gregory hymned the joyous mystery of the Trinity in classical stanzas. Yet this reconciliation took place under the sign of the Cross. It introduced into the world itself the image of absolute perfection, and therefore a judgment and a conflict. Everything was consecrated, but the coming Kingdom cast its shadow over all; the world had become finite and was recognized to be a pathway, struggle, and growth.

Rise of Monasticism

There is no better illustration of the unique quality of this reconciliation of the Church with the empire than the rise, in the same fourth century, of monasticism. Its importance in the history of the Church is not inferior to that of the conversion of Constantine.

The origin of monasticism is usually associated with the name of St. Anthony. His life had been described by Athanasius, and this document has always remained the standard of the monastic ideal, and defined the whole later development of monasticism in the Church. Outwardly Anthony's life followed a very simple pattern. He was born in Egypt around 250 in a Coptic Christian family. When he was still very young, he heard in church the words of the Gospel: "If thou wilt be perfect, go and sell that thou hast, and give to the poor, . . . and come and follow me," and he was shaken by them. He gave away all his property and devoted himself entirely to ascetic feats, starting in his own village but very soon withdrawing into the desert, where he spent twenty years in complete solitude. Athanasius has described this period of his life, often very realistically, as a ceaseless struggle with the devil. Later the second period began: followers thronged to him from all sides, and he emerged from his seclusion to become their teacher and leader. The principles of his ascetic doctrine were set forth by Athanasius in the form of speeches which Anthony addressed to the monks. "Then monasteries arose on the mountains," wrote Athanasius, "and the desert was inhabited by monks, men who had rejected all earthly goods and had inscribed their names in the heavenly city."

Monasticism acquired its present form somewhat later, from St. Pachomius the Great. Also a native of Egypt, he was the first to create a life in common and the regulations for it; the rule of Pachomius has formed the basis for later monastic rules. Under his guidance, in the Thebaid on the upper Nile, was created a unique monastic state numbering thousands of persons. It was visited in 357–58 by St. Basil, who on his return from Asia Minor created a monastic community there, with his brother, Gregory of Nyssa, and his friend Gregory the Theologian. Even before this, Anthony's disciple Hilarion had brought the monastic life to Syria and Palestine, and in the same period it began to flourish in the West as well.

Monasticism attracted more and more people into the desert, to the monasteries, and it soon acquired a particular significance even for those who did not become monks. Descriptions of the lives and feats of the hermits—*The Life of Anthony, The Life of Paul of Thebes* (written by St. Jerome), *Historia Lausiaca, The History of the Monks,* and so on—were to become for centuries the favorite reading matter of all Byzantine society. Characteristics of monastic worship penetrated to the city churches, where the services came to be decked in the same colors. Our liturgical regulations even today are those of the Monastery of St. Sabas in Jerusalem. Monasteries arose within the cities themselves; by the middle of the sixth century in Constantinople alone there were seventy-six. Monks assumed a more active role in Church life. They had begun as a movement of laymen; neither Anthony nor Pachomius had had any hierarchical rank; they apparently considered the monastic life incom-

patible with the priesthood, and even more with the episcopate. But gradually monasticism was transformed into an
official and even a higher Church calling, so that in later
Byzantium only monks could become bishops. Beginning as
a physical withdrawal into the desert, the monastery was
established in the very heart of the city. It became one of
the most integral signs of that Christian world whose history had begun with the conversion of Constantine.

What was the meaning of this swift growth and development? Many historians, again deceived by external analogies, insist on deriving it from some non-Christian source,
seeing in it the usual "metamorphosis" or transformation
of the "white" Christianity of the early Church into the
"black" Christianity of the Middle Ages. There is an
analogy here in the ascetic practices worked out in such detail by the monks, the basic forms of which we do indeed
encounter outside Christianity as well. Solitude, struggle
against one's thoughts, "concentration of attention," im-
passivity, and so forth—all allegedly entered Christianity
through the ascetic stream which in that period was growing in strength; and this stream was in turn connected with
dualism, with the recognition that matter was evil and the
source of evil. Monasticism, by this evaluation, is thus
presented as a Christian form of Manichaeism, a dualistic
sect which had great success in the fourth century.

On the other hand, while renunciation of the world is
fundamental as its original inspiration, it must be recognized that this renunciation cannot be considered something so absolutely new for the Christian mind as to need
derivation from Manichaeism or Neoplatonism, as Harnack
and other historians have held. While in the course of its
development monasticism borrowed much from other ascetic traditions, and while there were even extreme tendencies and distortions within it, neither these borrowings
nor the distortions were the reasons for its rise, just as Greek
philosophy did not give rise to Christian theology, although
its language was used in theological development.

In fact, painstaking studies of the early records carried on in the last few decades have indicated that monasticism is only the expression under new conditions of the original evangelical concept of Christianity which had ruled the life of the early Church. Renunciation of the world is a condition for Christianity: ". . . Who does not leave his father and his mother . . ." Renunciation is neither condemnation nor denial of the world, but in Christ the glory of the coming Kingdom was revealed to man, and in its light "the image of this world passes." All is now driven toward that final point, and everything is measured by it. In this world, however, evil continues to reign; it hinders us from reaching the Kingdom, tearing us away from it by thousands of temptations and illusions. The road of the Christian is to be the narrow road of struggle; does not the Gospel speak of the strength of evil, of the struggle against it, or of renunciation for the sake of the Kingdom?

In the era of persecutions, the simple fact that a man belonged to the Christian religion already separated him from the world and its life. As Karl Heussi, the historian of monasticism, has written, "It is enough to imagine the situation of the first Christian communities within the pagan world, their complete separation from public life, from the theater and the circus, from all celebrations, the limited space in which their outward lives proceeded, to be convinced of the 'monastic' nature of early Christianity, which lived within the world but separated from it." Yet the closer the world came to the Church and the more it penetrated into its inner life, as we see in the moral decline of many Christians at the end of the second century, the stronger grew the monastic tendency within the Church itself among those who strove by a standard of high evangelical idealism to hold themselves apart. We find many examples of this isolation of ascetics even in the third century, and it may be said that by the beginning of the fourth all the component parts of monasticism were present. Athanasius has stated that "before Anthony no single monk had yet known the great desert," yet the decisive influence for Anthony himself was that of a hermit from a neighboring village already "trained in a life of solitude." One of the most recent investigators of early monasticism has written:

The supernatural essence of Christian life has always required some absolute expression which would reveal the complete freedom of the Christian in relation to all the realities of this world. Martyrdom was the first response to this demand, born from outward conditions; when these conditions changed and the world ceased to struggle against Christianity, but, on the contrary, proposed an alliance which could and very often did become more dangerous for spiritual values, which were not susceptible to "naturalization," monasticism became a sort of affirmation of their independence . . . It brought nothing essentially new into the Church of the first centuries; it was an expression in a new form, created by new circumstances, of what is customarily called the "eschatological" nature of Christianity, of which the first Christians had been acutely aware and which they had expressed in martyrdom. From the very beginning the ideal of chastity and of voluntary rejection in general of certain comforts, which were not evil in themselves, also developed alongside martyrdom. When the latter disappeared, monasticism inevitably became all that martyrdom had embodied and expressed.[3]

One might ask whether the essence of the early Church, the source and expression of its entire life, had not been the unity and the assembly of all together, crowned and expressed in the sacrament of communion by all with one bread and one cup. Does not the monastic ideal of solitude as a condition for salvation contradict the original experience of the Church? Yet here again, it was a reaction to the danger of easy sacramentalism, which had gained strength in the fourth century. The assembly of the Church became more and more obviously an assembly of citizens and its separation from the world as a "sacrament of the coming

[3] L. Bouyer, *L'Incarnation et l'Église-Corps du Christ dans la théologie de St. Athanase* (Paris, 1943), p. 24.

age," increasingly nominal. Monasticism was a reminder that while the pledge and source of new life was the Eucharist and the grace it bestowed, still acceptance of it was a free act by man, so that Christ's deed in no way diminishes human freedom or effort. While practicing asceticism in solitude, the monks convened on the Lord's Day for the Eucharist, the assembly. Yet in their solitary asceticism they reveal the whole range of responsibility imposed on the Christian by his participation in the Sacrament, and demonstrate what absolute demands it makes upon the conscience of those whom it sanctifies.

Struggle against the devil, whom the Gospels call the "Prince of this world," construction within oneself of a new man after the image of Christ, and as a final goal, "deification"—that is, communion with God and acquisition of "peace and joy in the Holy Spirit," as St. Paul had previously described the kingdom of God—these were the monastic ideals, and this was the experience that became imprinted upon the immense monastic literature. In the course of centuries the experience would be more and more precisely described, and the "art of spiritual life" analyzed to the last detail. By comparison with this experience, with its depth of perception of man and its knowledge of him, scientific psychology frequently appears petty and trivial.

It must be flatly stated that until now monasticism has shown us the only practical "success" of Christianity, unique in nature, tested by experience, and confirmed by thousands of examples. (This does not, of course, exclude the possibility of other approaches to the spiritual life.) In the course of centuries, the visage of the sainted monk has towered over the whole Christian world and illuminated it. In this visage, emaciated by fasting, vigil, and asceticism, washed by tears of repentance and illumined by spiritual vision, the body itself transformed into a spirit, innumerable generations of Christians have perceived undoubted proof of the reality of a new heaven and a new earth.

How can we reconcile the almost complete dominance

of this monastic image with the development of the Christian world? Would not the triumph of monasticism deprive it of all meaning? If monasticism and the desert were recognized as the highest norm even by those who were building that Christian world or dealing with it, would not this "building" itself become an illusory and sinfully vain matter? Here we touch on the last and most important apparent contradiction of the age of Constantine in Church history.

Outwardly, it was true, the Christian way seemed to split into irreconcilable contradictions. The Church building protected and sanctified the whole world and all its life; but tens and thousands of Christians escaped from that world and sought salvation outside it. If each approach had constituted a condemnation of the other, there would be only absurdity. But the uniqueness of the age of Constantine was that both monasticism and the building of a Christian world were regarded—not in terms of theory but in living experience—as equally essential and complementary. Harnessed together, they preserved the integrity of the evangelical outlook, though perhaps only the vision of it.

The world receives a Christian sanction and is blessed by the Church, but monasticism became the "salt" which does not allow the world to absorb Christianity and subject it to itself. In the light of this eternal reminder, the world already regarded itself as an image that passes—as a way to another, final reality which completes and judges all. The monks withdraw, but from the desert they bless the Christian empire and the Christian city, and they never weary of praying for them; they interpret this very abnegation as a service to the world for its salvation. It is a concept perhaps only embodied as a miracle or an exception; the world, even in its new Christian aspect, continued to be the same unadmitted idol, requiring services to itself, while monasticism frequently turned into spiritual individualism and disdain for the rest of life. Nevertheless, an inner standard for Christian action in history had been found.

State Religion—Second Ecumenical Council

With the reign of the Emperor Theodosius the Great (379–95), the first cycle in the development of new relations between Church and state came to an end. An edict of 380 declared Christianity the required faith and made it finally the state religion. The freedom announced in the Edict of Milan was ended, but it had been doomed from the start. It was precluded by the very nature of the ancient state, whose basic feature, a theocratic conception of itself, was actually reinforced by the conversion of Constantine. In Constantine's reign the persecution of paganism began. It grew in strength under his sons; in 341 the "madness of sacrifices" was forbidden by law, and in 353 all cults of idols were condemned and their temples closed. True, these laws were hardly enforced in practice; paganism still represented a considerable force, which explains the attempt to revive it under Julian. Culture, the school, and learning would long remain almost a monopoly of pagans. Still, the conversion of the emperor doomed it to disappearance, and this process was accelerated by the extent to which the emperors drew closer to the Church.

It must be frankly admitted that the Church demanded of the state that it combat paganism and itself denied the principle of toleration. It had forgotten the words of Tertullian, addressed to the persecutors of Christianity: "Both common right and natural law require that each man bow down to the god in which he believes. It is not right for one religion to violate another." In his work *On the Confusions of Pagan Religions* written for the sons of Constantine, the Christian writer Firmicus Maternus exhorted them: "Come to the aid of these unfortunates; it is better to save them *in spite of themselves* than to allow them to perish [emphasis supplied]." But the minds of Christians, in which the evangelical ideal of religious freedom had flared up briefly during the experience of martyrdom, were blinded for a long time by the vision of a Christian theocracy that would bring men to Christ not only by grace but by law as well. Much time passed before the pagan nature of this theocracy was recognized. State sanctions gave the Church unprecedented strength, and perhaps brought many to faith and new life, but after Theodosius the Great it was no longer only a community of believers; it was also a community of those obliged to believe.

Later, at the Second Ecumenical Council in Constantinople (381), the first chapter of the great theological disputes was completed, and Nicene orthodoxy triumphed. The council itself was far in spirit from the victorious radiance shown by the bishops when they met at Nicaea. Now wounds from many years of division had to be healed and the whole weight of the Arian rebellion was felt. Many personal questions were decided, with inevitable sacrifices and compromises. Gregory the Theologian, inexperienced and naïve in higher church politics, had stubbornly defended the truth of Nicaea in the Arian capital, but was now apparently unneeded and withdrew from the council. The bitterness of this remained with him to the end of his life. The Church was "reconstructed" for its new official existence with no little difficulty, and not all had enough wisdom, patience, and flexibility for it. Behind the dogmatic unity we begin to sense a jealousy on the part of the ancient seats of Antioch and Alexandria of the growing significance of the Church of Constantinople. Afar off, the see of St. Peter was also alarmed at this rise of a second Rome. The spring of orthodox Byzantinism was over, and the heat and burdens of the long journey were beginning.

St. John Chrysostom

One name must still be mentioned, that of St. John Chrysostom. The real situation of Church life in those decades is best sensed in his life and writings, and one may also discern in them all the depth and difficulty of the process that had begun. A presbyter of Antioch famed for his eloquence, John was made bishop of Constantinople in 398 and devoted himself zealously to his pastoral duties, the first of which was preaching. His central concern was the Christian life of his flock in its variety and everyday reality. Before him was a world that had accepted Christianity but was still so close to paganism, so deeply poisoned by sin and ignorance, that it did not take the faith itself too seriously. People crowded into the churches, but outside church walls—and indeed, sometimes within them—were moral irresponsibility, hatred, and injustice.

Chrysostom was more than a great preacher; he built houses and shelters for the poor, exposed the rich, and attacked luxury. His social indignation was derived directly from the Gospel—all evil, he claimed, proceeds from "these cold words: mine and thine." All men are equal, all have the same needs and the same rights. "Put God in the place of your slaves; you grant them freedom in your wills. But free Christ from hunger, from the want of prison, from nakedness." Everything was to be renewed by Christianity: the family, society, and the concept of religion. Chrysostom was not afraid to expose moral corruption even in the palace, and this was the beginning of his way of the cross.

Condemned by false brothers and sent away by the emperor, he died on his way to a remote place of exile. Byzantium seems never to have rendered to any other of its saints such love, such honor, and such faithfulness. Modern concepts of social justice, political equality, and the general duty of organized help to the poor came much later. Chrysostom's life, however, was a constant reminder to Byzantium of the ultimate source of all social inspiration, because of the now almost forgotten reverence he paid to poverty as the image of Christ Himself.

3 THE AGE OF THE ECUMENICAL COUNCILS

Development of Church Regional Structure

In 395 Emperor Theodosius the Great on his deathbed divided the empire between his two sons. Honorius received the West and Arcadius, the East. Theoretically the empire continued to be one state with two emperors, but in practice, from that point on, the Eastern and Western roads inevitably diverged.

In the fourth century there had begun an evolution in ecclesiastical structure which was inevitable in view of the new position of the Church in the empire. Its general significance may be defined as the co-ordination of external Church structure with the imperial administrative structure. This development was not a revolutionary one, since it continued trends begun long before the conversion of Constantine—the gradual development of several large ecclesiastical regions, each united around a senior Church. The Council of Nicaea, in its sixth canon, sanctioned this situation. It recognized the *de facto* primacy of Rome in the West, of Alexandria in Egypt, and of Antioch in Syria. Since these primacies arose spontaneously, each expressed all the particularities of local conditions, the growth of the Church in given parts of the Roman Empire. Thus Rome was the only apostolic see in the West and had exclusive importance there. There was a difference, however, between the canonical or jurisdictional primacy of Rome over neighboring Italian churches and its moral authority, which was recognized, as we have seen, beyond the borders of Italy in Africa, Spain, and Gaul. The African Church from the beginning had had a special structure and canonical practice; the highest authority there was the regular synod of bishops, who met twice a year. In the East the canonical forms of ecclestiastical union differed again, depending on various historical conditions. In Egypt there was almost complete centralization: all authority was concentrated in the hands of the Alexandrian bishop or "pope," in relation to whom the bishops held a position which by modern analogy one may define as that of a vicar bishop. In Syria, on the other hand, the local bishop was much more independent, although here, too, the center of agreement had from the first been the Church of the second city of the empire, Antioch. Though less important than these three apostolic seats, Ephesus was still a center for Asia Minor. In other areas there were no such large centers and the churches were usually grouped around a *metropolis* or capital of a province. It is characteristic, for example, that the Church of Jerusalem, once the mother of all Christians, represented itself at the end of the third century as a simple bishopric in the orbit of the metropolis of Caesarea, the civic center of Palestine. Only after the fourth century, because of Constantine's special interest in the holy places and the flood of pilgrims, did its ecclesiastical significance also begin to grow.

While from the beginning the indivisible nucleus of Church structure had been the local Church or community or meeting headed by one bishop, presbyters, and deacons (for this nucleus flows from the very nature of the Church as the visible incarnation everywhere of the "new people of God"), it is quite clear that the relations or canonical links between the churches differed and were determined by local peculiarities of their growth and the development of Christianity itself. One thing is undeniable: the links were conceived and felt to be just as essential and elemental as the structure of each community; no single Church was self-sufficient, if only because its bishop received consecration from other bishops and in this way expressed and manifested the oneness of the gifts and life of the Spirit throughout the universal Church. The forms of this bond still differed, however. In some regions the highest canonical authority was the union of a group of churches around the Church of the main city in a province, whose bishop was recognized as *metropolitan*; in other areas such provinces in turn were united around some still more ancient, great, or apostolic Church, thus composing an ecclesiastical "region." In Egypt, on the other hand, there were no metropolia, but all the bishops had the archbishop of Alexandria as their immediate primate.

Metropolitan councils decided general matters; they were the court of appeals for complaints against the local bishop and regulated relations between bishops, changed boundaries of bishoprics if necessary, and so forth. All the bishops of a province under the chairmanship of the metropolitan participated in the consecration of new bishops. Decrees of the councils concerning Church structure, discipline, and such matters received the name of canon (rule); and starting with the fourth century, collections of canons began to appear. For example, in that century eighty-five so-called apostolic canons were widely distributed, and they form the foundation of the Orthodox canonical tradition to the present day. The canons of the ecumenical councils were gradually added to them, as were those of the local councils having general ecclesiastical significance, such as the Antiochene council of 341, mentioned in the preceding chapter. The canonical collections received their final form much later, but study of the canons even at this early stage demonstrates the gradual development of Church structure. We may note here that the Second Ecumenical Council concentrated attention solely on the Eastern half of the empire, and from this time the difference in canonical evolution between East and West becomes fully discernible.

Nicaea had taken note and sanctioned the form of the universal unity of the Church, its catholicity, as it had evolved toward the end of the third century. This did not hold back the development of form, however; in the course of the fourth century we see an increasingly definite co-ordination of Church structure with that of the state. The empire was divided into "dioceses," and the second rule of the Ecumenical Council of 381 notes a corresponding division of the Church, too, into dioceses: the ecclesiastical region of Egypt, with its center in Alexandria; the East, centered at Antioch; Pontus, centered at Caesarea of Cappadocia; Asia, centered at Ephesus; and Thrace, at Heraclea. In this way the previous structure was combined, as it were, with the new, in which the decisive factor became the civic importance of the city. Dioceses were in turn divided into "provinces," and the latter into "eparchies"; we must remember that all these terms are taken from Roman administrative terminology. Later the principle according to which "the administration of Church affairs must follow civil and rural administration" was officially sanctioned by Church rule.[1]

The Byzantine Idea of Church and State

Alongside this natural process of co-ordination, perceptible even before Constantine's conversion, we now observe the creation of a sort of imperial center of the Church, wholly linked in its rise and development with the changing relationship of Church and empire and with the ambiguous but fully obvious weight of imperial authority itself in Church affairs. We have seen that a kind of ecclesiastical general staff grew up around Constantine almost immediately after his conversion and strove to influence the Church

[1] Canon 17, Chalcedon.

through the emperor, thus counterbalancing, as it were, the previous centers of catholicity. Its members included Constantine's old friend Osius of Cordova and the two Eusebiuses and their group. The Christian emperor inevitably created around himself a new center of attraction for the Church, but this must not be regarded—as it is by some historians—as the enslavement of the Eastern episcopate in rudiments of that "caesaropapism" with which they constantly charge the Eastern Church.

We must from the start perceive the unique profundity of the Byzantine concept of relations between Church and state, which are linked not by any concordat or juridical limitation of power, but by the truth; which is to say, by the faith of the Church, which the emperor first, and through him the empire itself, recognized as its truth, and as a truth superior to themselves. The religious attitude of the empire was not at all a matter of indifference to the Church. A heretical or apostate emperor would mean the downfall of the Christian world, a new defeat of truth by a lie, over which it had only just triumphed—a new defection of the world from Christ. We must not forget that the modern lay state, which arose out of the failure and decay of this Christian experience, was born at a time when Christianity itself had lost its universal appeal, and religion became for a long period the private affair of each individual, particularly a matter of his fate after death. But the success or failure, the errors and achievements, of Byzantium can be evaluated only if we assess the completely different experience of Christianity itself, in that period, as primarily a sense of the cosmic victory of Christ over the "Prince of this world." In this victory the conversion of Constantine acquires a special significance, as already noted: here the state, hitherto the main instrument of diabolical malice against the Church, bowed down before Christ. But in doing so it immediately reacquired all the positive significance that Christians, beginning with St. Paul, had never denied it. To orthodox and heretics alike, the concept of a religiously neutral state was equally alien, as was the concept of "clericalism"—the hierarchical subordination of state to Church—which arose later in the West. In the Eastern concept the Church embraced the whole world and was its inner essence, standard, and the source of gifts of the Spirit within it; but it was not the *authority* in worldly political matters, nor even the source of authority. The latter was granted to emperors and rulers; they should be guided by the truth of the Church, but they did not receive authority *from* the Church.

Only in this light can we understand why orthodox and heretics alike exercised influence over the emperor, and not merely from opportunism and ambition. Each sincerely believed in his own truth and wished to make it the norm for the Christian empire. The drama of the East lay in the fact that this vision turned out impossible to fulfill, and in actual life frequently alternated with evil. The state itself was still too set in its pagan categories, continuing to believe itself the final goal and value, and religion only its instrument. While for the state, too, the fate of the Church and its dogmatic disputes were not matters of indifference, this was for other reasons. Any division within the Church immediately reflected on the tranquility of the state.

Constantinople vs. Alexandria

In the fourth century there arose really two new centers of attraction for the Church: Constantinople and Jerusalem. Constantine's interest in the Holy Land, his mother Helen's search for the wood of the Cross, the adornment of Jerusalem with magnificent churches, all have a special significance if we take into account the fact that the second holy city for Constantine was Constantinople, which he founded. There was perhaps even a subconscious sense of a special mission in the history of salvation: the city of the Cross and the city arising out of the victory of the Cross;

the reign of Constantine crowning the victory of Christ; the world with two centers—the King of the Jews and the king of the Romans—reconciled in His sight. Through the centuries this mystical vision of Constantinople as a holy city would broaden and deepen, but it undoubtedly originated with its first emperor. Eusebius of Nicomedia made no mistake when he exchanged his ancient and celebrated see for the still obscure city of Constantinople, for here lay the highway of historical Christianity.

When the new capital was founded in 330, this imperial center was allotted a suitable position in the Church. It was at first the modest seat of one of the suffragans of the metropolitan of Heraclea; but it was doomed to elevation, if the expression may be allowed. Constantinople was created to be a second Rome, and the Christian center of the empire as well. In the Church of the Twelve Apostles, which he had built, Constantine prepared in the midst of the twelve symbolic tombs of the apostles a thirteenth, for himself. Did not this conversion of the empire fulfill the prophecy of the apostles? It is from this thirteenth tomb that his title as "equal to the apostles" came.

True enough, the omens of Constantinople were sometimes doubtful; for many years it was a center of Arianism, and Athanasius had elevated Alexandria in the eyes of the Church by his struggle for truth and freedom. Even when Constantinople became orthodox, the hostility of Alexandria did not slacken; it reappeared in a ridiculous attempt to support a certain Maxim the Cynic against St. Gregory the Theologian; in a passionate and hasty "Council at the Oak" in 402, which condemned Chrysostom; and also during the struggle of Cyril against Nestorius, despite the justice of that cause in the main.

Yet fifty years after the founding of the city, the Fathers of the Second Ecumenical Council were already proclaiming that the bishop of Constantinople held primacy of honor after the bishop of Rome, because Constantinople was the "New Rome, the city of the Emperor and the

Senate."[2] For a time this changed nothing in the basic structure of the Eastern Church, which was defined at the same council. Constantinople was not allotted any region, and formally its bishop continued to be one of the bishops of the diocese of Thrace, headed by the metropolitan of Heraclea. In fact, however, the canon that confirmed his "primacy of honor" made him a unique center of the whole Eastern Church and defined the entire empire as his region. The two forms of ecclesiastical structure—that which had developed organically and that which Constantinople now symbolized—obviously did not coincide, and one of them would sooner or later have to submit to the other. Here lay the explanation of the prolonged conflict between Alexandria and Constantinople, which kept smoldering and flaring up intermittently into bright flame throughout these centuries.

The Christological Controversy—Nestorius and Cyril

The period between the fourth and eighth centuries is usually called in textbooks of Church history the era of the ecumenical councils. Its predominant significance, of course, was the entry of the human mind into the "mind of truth"; its highest point was the Fourth Ecumenical Council at Chalcedon (451), at which the doctrine of the God-Manhood of Christ was proclaimed. Not only theology but external political events closely connected with this Christological controversy were decided at Chalcedon, but the most profound contribution of the period was its searching inquiry into the meaning of the God-Manhood of Jesus Christ for the world and for mankind. For a question as to the nature of Christ is always a question as to the nature of man and his task. The passion engendered in this discussion may be explained by its vital significance.

The first theological theme to be taken up by the councils,

[2] Canon 3, Second Ecumenical Council.

that of the Trinity, had already been discussed in Christological terms in the disputes of the fourth century. The
whole concept of Christ's Incarnation and earthly achievement depended on whether He was recognized as God or
as a "creature." Was He really both God and man, or was
the same gulf still between mankind and its Maker, with
man still doomed to enslavement and sin, death, and separation? The triumph of the Nicene term *homoousion* was
the first clear answer. Christ was God; the Incarnation of
God was real. Yet the Nicene recognition, with such difficulty put into words, led inevitably to a further question
in the mind of the Church. If God were united with man
in Christ, how was such a union possible, and what could
be discerned as man in it? Would he not "burn up" in this
contact with God? Would not the whole concept lead
again to some illusion? If Christ is God, what is the value
and significance of His human achievement?

This was not a search for an abstract formula which
would satisfy the Greek philosophizing mind, nor yet a
prying into divine secrets, but a reflection on man's freedom, on the meaning of his achievement and personal
effort. Directly connected with the Arian disputes, this
question had been posed and unsuccessfully answered by
one of the leading supporters of the Nicene Creed, Bishop
Apollinarius of Laodicea, who interpreted the union of God
and man in Christ as requiring the elimination of some
element of human nature. The divine Mind, the *Logos*,
replaced the human and created *logos* in Jesus; since the
mind is the highest and dominant part of man, and since
the Man Jesus had the divine Mind itself, He was God.
Apollinarianism was immediately condemned as a heresy;
there could be no genuine salvation if the fully human
were replaced in Christ by a cut-down and diminished
version of man. Yet again, as with Arius, mere condemnation was not a positive answer. The dispute and the search
for a theologically adequate solution began in earnest at the
beginning of the fifth century, in the conflict between
Nestorius of Constantinople and Cyril of Alexandria.

Nestorius and Cyril belonged to two different trends or schools of Christian thought, two distinct psychological attitudes toward Christianity itself, which had gradually formed long before the start of the Christological dispute. These were the schools of Antioch and Alexandria. The differences between them had many causes: different philosophical influences, that of Aristotle on the Antiochenes and of Plato on the Alexandrians; the opposition between Semitic realism and Hellenistic idealism; differences in religious practices and traditions. In interpreting Holy Scripture, the Antiochenes feared allegories, symbols, multiplications of "spiritual meanings," everything that flourished so richly in Origen's theology. They particularly sought literal meaning and historical accuracy in the understanding of the text and only later drew their theological conclusions. These conclusions have been called "anthropological maximalism" by a modern investigator. In this country of voluntary and heroic asceticism it was the human effort of Christ that first attracted attention; this was the justification for the efforts of His followers, and a witness to human freedom. Although this approach was basically correct and evangelical, one might very easily overstep a fine line and divide Christ Himself, distinguishing His human effort in such a way as to give it an independent significance. The Good News of the Son of God become man might pale before the image of the Man of Righteousness.

Thus in Syria, which was called the diocese of the East, a definite theological tradition gradually emerged. Its spirit was already apparent in Diodorus of Tarsus, one of the main participants in the Second Ecumenical Council; it was systematically expressed by his disciple, Theodore of Mopsuestia, in whose doctrine the dangers of the Antiochene—what was then called the "Eastern"—way were clearly revealed. Theodore distinguished two "subjects" in Christ, and for him the union between them was not a union of personality (though he does employ this expression in another meaning) but a union of will, of consent; not so much union, indeed, as co-ordination of the two.

This union was developing and growing . . . Christ as "Perfect Man" grew like all men in body and soul. He also grew in knowledge and in righteousness. And as He grew He received new gifts of the Spirit. He struggled, overcame His passions and even His lusts. This was inevitable, so Theodore thought, if Christ were really man . . . Theodore concentrated his whole emphasis on the human achievement; God only anoints and crowns human freedom.[3]

This "ascetic humanism" achieved its final and by now obviously heretical form in Theodore's disciple, Nestorius. A brilliant preacher, scholar, and ascetic, he was invited in 428 by Emperor Theodosius II to be bishop of Constantinople. With a zeal that sometimes went to extremes, he began a struggle against pagans and heretics and also a moral reform of the clergy of the capital. His passionate nature immediately made him enemies, among whom was the emperor's sister Pulcheria. Hostility to the bishop increased and spread far beyond Constantinople; naturally, everything that happened in the capital had empire-wide echoes.

Nestorius wanted to purify the great city of heresies. He took up arms in particular against calling the Virgin Mary *Theotokos*, or "Birth-Giver of God," a term which had long since come into liturgical use. Theodore of Mopsuestia had also rejected it: "It is madness to say that God was born of a virgin," he said. "He who had the nature of the virgin was born of the Virgin, not God the Word . . . He who was of the seed of David was born of a Virgin." By this term, however, even before any more precise theological definition, the Church had expressed its faith in the absolute union of God and man in Christ. All that was said of the Man was said of God, too, and vice versa; this was the meaning of the evangelical assertion: "And the Word was made flesh."

Nestorius was opposed by Cyril, archbishop of Alexandria. Representing the Alexandrian theological tendency in

[3] G. Florovsky, *The Byzantine Fathers of the Fifth to the Eighth Centuries* (in Russian, Paris, 1933), p. 10.

his habits and methods, Cyril also inherited the theological clear-sightedness so forcefully revealed in Athanasius. He continued the tradition stemming from Ignatius of Antioch and Irenaeus of Lyons, according to which the inner standard and criterion of theology was recognized to be the Church's experience of salvation by Christ and in Christ. In the same way every theological construction, inevitably abstract to the extent that it used words and concepts, should be checked by its "existential" importance as by a tuning fork in order to discover whether it revealed or in any way diminished the salvation (not the knowledge) the Gospel proclaimed.

Cyril was a passionate man, a fighter. He did not always discriminate in his means of combat, and frequently did not find the right words, but he always had a true sense of the danger in the issue and gave himself wholly to defense of the truth. In the preaching of Nestorius he immediately discerned a basic distortion of the meaning of Christianity. Cyril felt that the whole essence of salvation lay in the unity of God and man in Christ, that unique Personality in whom all men come in touch with the Father, and He perceived a diminution and denial of this in the Nestorian rejection of *Theotokos*. He immediately took up a defense of the term in his *Epistle to the Monks* and later in a direct appeal to Nestorius, begging him to put a stop to the "universal scandal" he had caused.

Constantinople greeted this protest with displeasure. There the sad case of Chrysostom was still well remembered; the bishop of Constantinople had been condemned unjustly and without a hearing by a council under the chairmanship of Theophilus of Alexandria, Cyril's uncle, and Cyril himself had taken part in the condemnation. Those were the years when the bishops of Alexandria had tried to put a limit to the uninterrupted growth of Constantinople's ecclesiastical influence. The capital had reason to fear the powerful, abrupt, and influential Cyril. Theological dispute was again complicated by Church politics.

Third Ecumenical Council

While Cyril continued to expose Nestorius, at first in letters to him, such as his celebrated *Dogmatic Epistle*, and later in special theological works, Nestorius took advantage of the complaints of certain Alexandrian clerics against their bishop and planned to have him condemned at an ecclesiastical court. Cyril's personality and his unlimited authority throughout all Egypt had won him many enemies. Instead of giving a theological answer to a theological accusation, Nestorius simply attempted to crush him with the support of the emperor, the weak-willed and indecisive Theodosius II. Perceiving the danger, Cyril turned to Rome. There Nestorius was already disliked for his one-sided support, given without consultation with Rome, of the Pelagians, heretics who were disturbing the Christian West at the time. Cyril sent examples of Nestorius' teachings to Pope Celestine; they were sharply condemned by the local expert on Eastern matters, John Cassian, an abbot of Marseilles. In August 430 a council of bishops under the leadership of the pope condemned the doctrine of Nestorius. The bishop of Constantinople was given ten days from the time he received the Roman decision to recant from his errors.

This decision was transmitted to Constantinople through Cyril, whom the Pope empowered to be his representative. When he had learned the decision of the Roman council, Cyril convened his own bishops in Alexandria, who of course confirmed the condemnation of Nestorian doctrine. The council also approved a formula of recantation in the form of twelve "anathemas" which Cyril had composed for Nestorius. All this material was sent to Nestorius and to the bishops of the main Eastern churches—John of Antioch, Juvenal of Jerusalem, Acacius of Berea, and other friends of Nestorius and followers of Theodore of Mopsuestia. Meanwhile, Nestorius, in order to parry what seemed to him

a new attack by the ambitious Alexandrian, who had converted even Rome to his side, persuaded the emperor to
summon an ecumenical council. The *sacra*, or summons,
of the emperor, sent out to the bishops in November 430,
called them to Ephesus on Pentecost of the following year.

Outwardly the history of the Third Ecumenical Council
was tragic. It met in an atmosphere of mutual suspicions,
offenses, and misunderstanding. Again, as in the Arian dispute, it was not a simple conflict of black and white, of
heresy against orthodoxy; there was also a real misunderstanding due to different shades of thought and use of
words. Again the synthesis had to be arrived at by lengthy
and tormenting analysis, the gradual process of finding a
meeting ground between words and traditions.

The Eastern bishops, under the leadership of John of
Antioch, attacked Cyril although they, too, were disturbed
and frightened by the extreme and provocative conclusions
drawn by Nestorius from the premises with which they were
familiar. They did not take their position simply out of
friendship for Nestorius; Cyril's language and theology
seemed to them plainly unacceptable. His twelve anathemas
then led to a storm of protests and condemnations in
Syria. Theodoret of Cyrrhus, leading light of Antiochene
theology, was especially outspoken against them.

The criticism of Nestorianism which was developed by St.
Cyril of Alexandria did not convince the "Easterners," but
alarmed them. This did not mean that they were all extreme
Nestorians, but that they feared the opposite extreme. It must
be recognized that St. Cyril could not find words which were
above dispute and did not give precise definitions. His theological experience was not confused or ambiguous, but for all his
theological perspicacity he did not have the great gift of words
which had so distinguished the great Cappadocians.[4]

One theological formula he used was especially dangerous and later condemned: "One nature of God the Word

4 *Ibid.*

Incarnate." Cyril thought this was a quotation from Athanasius the Great, but the phrase had actually been composed by Apollinarius of Laodicea, already condemned by
the Church, whose followers, in order to disseminate his
views, had signed his works with the names of undisputed
Church authorities. The formula could be interpreted as a
denial of the human nature in Christ, being wholly swal-
lowed up by the divine. According to this doctrine (the
Easterners thought) man was not saved but consumed in
the flaming contact with Deity. It is understandable, therefore, that the Easterners should gather at Ephesus in alarm;
while not wholly in agreement with Nestorius, they came
primarily to expose and condemn the heresy of Cyril. The
imperial letter summoning them had been couched in language sharply hostile to Cyril. "Essentially the council was
summoned against Cyril," writes Mgr. Duchesne.[5] This
must be kept in mind for a fair judgment of his conduct
there. It has been subject to criticism even by Orthodox
historians, for whom St. Cyril is one of the greatest Fathers
and teachers of the Church. Some historians have tried
to rehabilitate Nestorius,[6] and in modern literature about
Ephesus he is frequently depicted as a martyr, with Cyril
as his persecutor, who condemned his enemy in his absence.
But we must remember that when Cyril arrived in Ephesus
with his bishops, he encountered obvious support for Nestorius among the imperial officials who had been entrusted
with organizing the council. Cyril wanted a theological solution. They were preparing to condemn and depose him,
not on theological grounds, but simply for "disciplinary"
reasons and with the open encouragement of state authorities.

Two weeks passed in waiting for the Easterners; the
Roman legates were also late. The mood became more intense and uneasiness spread in the city. Cyril decided to

[5] L. Duchesne, *Histoire Ancienne de l'Église* (Paris, 1928), Vol. 3, p. 343.
[6] See, for example, J. F. Bethune-Baker, *Nestorius and His Teaching*
(Cambridge, England, 1908).

wait no longer and on June 22 opened the council, despite
the disapproval of the imperial officials and a protest signed
by sixty-eight bishops supporting Nestorius. Thus it was a
council of Cyril's supporters alone. But the population of
the city, led by Memnon, bishop of Ephesus, supported
him. Nestorius, also in Ephesus, was sent three summonses
to appear. He rejected them; from an accuser he had suddenly become the accused. Then Cyril proceeded to a trial *in
absentia*; the bishops approved his writings against Nestorius and the bishop of Constantinople was unanimously
condemned. The emperor's representative, Candidian, protested, but feared to act openly since the whole city was for
Cyril. When the bishops emerged from the church where
they had been in session until late at night condemning
Nestorius, they were met by an immense crowd with flaring
torches and escorted home in triumph.

Four days later the caravan of Easterners finally arrived.
Indignant at what had happened, they immediately formed
their own council and condemned and deposed Cyril and
his supporters for heresy and disturbing the peace of the
Church. Although they did not even enter into communion
with Nestorius, the rebellion became an open one. When it
was all over the Roman legate, who arrived last, joined
Cyril, and reaffirmed the condemnation of Nestorius.

Cyril's council held several more sessions. It affirmed the
Nicene Creed, forbidding anything to be added to it. This
was to be the argument used by the Orthodox against the
addition in the West of *Filioque* ("and from the Son") to
the description of the Holy Spirit, "which proceedeth from
the Father." It forbade the creation of new creeds and
solved several canonical problems; among others it recognized the ecclesiastical independence of the Church of
Cyprus from Antioch, to which it had been previously
subordinated.

Both sides, and Candidian as well, sent reports of all the
proceedings to the emperor. Each tried to represent the
matter in the most advantageously partisan light. We have
seen that the sympathies of Theodosius had been with

Nestorius and the Easterners, but now the mood in Constantinople began to shift. Church members expressed themselves more clearly as opposed to him and processions of monks in the capital demanded his condemnation. Even his friends, who were indignant at Cyril's procedure, silently accepted his condemnation. It can be truly said that the condemnation of Nestorius was accepted by the whole Church.

But for the Easterners the main problem was not that of Nestorius but of what seemed to them an even more vicious heresy, the doctrine of Cyril himself. The emperor wavered. His first reaction was typical. He wished to restore peace by removing the controversial individual from each camp: Nestorius and Cyril. The state would never understand that such methods were inevitably doomed to failure. He then summoned representatives of both parties to Constantinople, but no agreement could be reached between them. Then Nestorius himself resigned from his see, thus permitting the election as his successor of someone acceptable to all. Cyril, ignoring the emperor, simply returned to Alexandria, where he was under the protection of a devoted following and any attempt to touch him would result in popular rebellion. The powerless Theodosius had no recourse but to recognize the facts and be reconciled to the division.

The freedom thus granted to the Church proved beneficial. Although at first there were insults and mutual excommunications, men were found who were able to rise above personalities and party solidarity. The century-old bishop Acacius of Berea wrote to Cyril, proposing that he forget the polemical aspects of the case so that the problem could be solved in its essence. Could an interpretation of Cyril's theology be found that would be acceptable for Easterners? Again there were lengthy statements of faith; both sides were sincere, but behind each stood the phantom of heresy. Cyril's explanations satisfied many, and late in the year 432 Paul of Emesa was sent to Alexandria from Antioch with an expression of the faith of the East which Cyril in turn accepted. Now peace could be restored. Cyril entered into communion with Paul, and the latter returned home with the signed formula of union.

Gradually most of the Easterners also signed it, and in 433 communion between Egypt and Syria was re-established. The formula of union "was, strictly speaking, the dogmatic result and epilogue of the Council of Ephesus. This formula was composed in the theological language of Antioch . . . but the borderline between orthodoxy and Nestorianism is therefore all the more clearly expressed."[7] It was the victory of orthodoxy over both extremes: Christ was "complete God and complete man . . . He is of one nature with the Father in divinity and of one nature with us in humanity, for a union of the two natures has been made; therefore we confess one Christ, one Son, one Lord . . . we confess that the Holy Virgin is *Theotokos* because God the Word was made flesh and became man, and from her conception united with Himself the temple received from Her."

This was the language of Antioch, but in accepting it Cyril conceded nothing for which he had fought. The confession of one Person in Christ was positively expressed, and the saving faith in the real union of God and man in one Person was protected.

Such was the orthodox epilogue of Ephesus. The storm died down, although slowly and painfully. Nestorius languished in a remote Libyan oasis, the insults he had suffered unforgotten. Nevertheless, despite Cyril's intensity and sometimes unhappy choice of words, truth had triumphed. The Church had little time, however, to enjoy its victory.

The Monophysite Heresy

Nestorianism had been overcome rather easily. It had been defended only by the leaders of the school of Antioch,

[7] Florovsky, *op. cit.*, p. 15.

who feared the extremes of Alexandrianism more than they sympathized with Nestorius. As for the mass of Christians, they had long been more aware of the divinity of Christ than of His humanity, and they experienced the mystery of the Incarnation more as a manifestation of God than as a free and complete union of man with Him—a union in which God and man remained distinct. The condemnation of Nestorius, therefore, only accelerated the process which had been perceptible from the very start of the Christological dispute, and led to the formulation of the most significant and—in its consequences for the Church—tragic heresy of the time: Monophysitism.

We already know that in his dispute with Nestorius Cyril had used a doubtful definition of Christ as "One nature of God the Word Incarnate." To Cyril this did not mean a merging of God and man, but only the real fact of their union in one Person or personality. He was thus able to recognize and accept the truth of the Antiochenes and their defense of the complete man in Christ. For many of his followers, however, this seemed a dethronement of Christ, a humiliation of God. They interpreted any distinction of two natures in Christ (so essential for a correct understanding of the Gospel) as a subversion of all Christianity and a denial of that "deification" of man or ultimate oneness with God which was the final goal of salvation. "God became man so that man could become deified," says St. Athanasius. Particularly in monastic experience of the struggle against "nature," against human weakness and sinfulness, it was psychologically very simple to overstep the line dividing struggle *for* the true nature of man from struggle *against* man, and end with a denial of the essential goodness of human nature. "Deification," or becoming one with God, began to be seen as the destruction within oneself of everything that is human, which was regarded as low and unworthy, "a bad smell that soon would pass away." In such a context, a theological emphasis on the manhood of Christ became incomprehensible. Did not the whole joy of

Christianity and the whole justification of intense ascetic feats lie in the fact that Christ was not man, and that each of us has the possibility of overcoming our humanity? Such were the psychological presuppositions of Monophysitism.

As soon as Cyril died, in 444, an open rebellion broke out against the agreement of 433, under the slogan of return to an emphasis on Christ's "one nature" (*mia physis*). The signal was raised in Constantinople by one of the generally recognized authorities of Eastern monasticism, the archimandrite Eutyches. He affirmed that the humanity assumed by Christ differed from ours. It was, therefore, irreverent to compare Christ with men, even in respect to his humanity. Everything "Eastern"* seemed detestable to Eutyches; he conducted an immense correspondence, had influence at court, and tried in every way to expose the Antiochene heresy, especially that of its main representative, Theodoret of Cyrrhus. Alarm naturally spread throughout the East. Theodoret presented accusations against Eutyches, but the court was now openly opposed to the Antiochenes. New persecutions of the Easterners began. By imperial decree, the twelve anathemas of Cyril, which he himself had silently bypassed in the agreement of 433, were proclaimed a rule of faith. Cyril's successor, Dioscurus, systematically prepared for the triumph of Alexandria and "Alexandrianism" in its extreme form.

Even in Church circles in Constantinople, however, the extreme position of Eutyches frightened many. At the insistence of Eusebius of Doryleum, who had once been the first to attack Nestorius, the bishops then in the city about their own affairs, under the chairmanship of Flavian of

* Here the term "Eastern" refers, of course, to Syria and Antioch, as often during the disputes of these centuries, according to the regional divisions noted on p. 116. The broader perspectives of East and West—Byzantium and Rome, or Asia and Europe—are also intended where appropriate, it is hoped without confusion to the reader. Thus Eastern monasticism, mentioned just above, refers to the Orthodox Byzantine tradition as contrasted with Rome and the West.

Constantinople, reviewed the doctrine of Eutyches and were obliged to condemn it as unorthodox. Eutyches absolutely refused to confess two natures in Christ. According to ancient custom, he complained to Rome, but Pope Leo the Great, when he learned of the proceedings of the court, which Flavian had sent him, wholly approved the decision of Constantinople.

The storm began again. Especially indignant were the monks, blind supporters of Cyril, followers less in spirit than in letter of some of his expressions, which he himself had rejected. The emperor, still the same weak-willed Theodosius, who inclined toward Eutyches and had not obtained a reversal of his condemnation from Flavian, decided once more to summon an ecumenical council—again in Ephesus. This time there could be no doubt of what he wanted from the council. Theodoret of Cyrrhus, the generally recognized leader of the Antiochene school, was forbidden to participate and the chairman, appointed ahead of time, was Dioscurus of Alexandria, whose Monophysite sympathies were no secret to anyone. Pope Leo refused to come to the council, since Attila's hordes were then approaching Rome, but he sent two legates and a dogmatic epistle addressed to Flavian of Constantinople.

What took place in Ephesus on August 8, 449, has been known throughout history as the "Synod of Robbers." Everything transpired under conditions of sheer terror. Dioscurus reigned, relying on the band of fanatic monks who flooded the city. He had what amounted almost to a formal order from the emperor to acquit Eutyches and destroy all opposition to the doctrine of the one nature. Under threat of beatings and pressure from the police, all the necessary decisions were made. Almost no one heard the indignant exclamation of the young Roman deacon: "I protest!" Half dead from beatings, Flavian still managed to write a letter to the Pope; he was deposed and exiled. The rest, giving way to force, signed. The Church had never before experienced such shame. The emperor ratified

this disgrace with state sanctions, and all the enemies of
Eutyches started on the bitter road of exile. Again force
and heresy triumphed over the Eastern Church.

Evil can only act by force, however, and sooner or later
it is itself exposed. Regardless of all obstacles, the Roman
legate Hilarion succeeded in returning to Rome, telling the
pope what had occurred and transmitting Flavian's appeal.
Shortly afterward came Eusebius of Doryleum and mes-
sengers from Theodoret of Cyrrhus. Leo immediately sent
ambassadors to Constantinople demanding from Theodosius a review of the whole matter. By now Theodosius
was dead and had been replaced by his sister, Pulcheria,
who in theological matters supported the moderate policy
of the deposed Flavian. In Constantinople the atmosphere
immediately changed; there was an end to the violence
of the fanatics. Pulcheria and her husband, the Emperor
Marcian, understood that the time had come once and
for all to settle the theological question that had plunged
the Church into such rebellion, and so establish a lasting
peace. Another ecumenical council, first assigned to Nicaea
but later transferred to Chalcedon, a suburb of Constantinople, opened there in the Basilica of St. Euphemia on
October 8, 451.

Council of Chalcedon (Fourth Ecumenical Council)

Outwardly the leading role of the Fourth Ecumenical
Council at Chalcedon fell to the share of the Roman
legates. The East, again divided and weakened by disputes,
accepted the mediation of Pope Leo. His *Dogmatic Tome*,
written for the council of 449, was accepted as the norm
of orthodox doctrine. This was a moderate policy, com-
bining Cyril's thought with the language of the Antiochenes. It clearly and precisely confessed two natures in
Christ. The same policy was supported by the imperial
couple's representatives, who conducted the debates, but

this time without imposing their theology. After accepting Leo's epistle as the rule of faith, the council in several stormy sessions condemned the action in Ephesus in 449 and those chiefly responsible for it, especially Dioscurus. Most of the bishops considered their task finished, but the emperor and the legates demanded a *Horos*—a general obligatory and clearly ecumenical creed. Almost against the will of the council, a commission was appointed on which both theological schools were represented, as well as the Roman legates. It was this commission that presented to the council the famous text of the dogma of Chalcedon:

We, then, following the holy Fathers, all with one consent, teach men to confess one and the same Son, our Lord Jesus Christ, the same perfect in Godhead and also perfect in manhood; truly God and truly man, of a reasonable soul and body; consubstantial [*homoousion*] with the Father according to the Godhead, and consubstantial with us according to the manhood; in all things like unto us, without sin; begotten before all ages of the Father according to the Godhead, and in these latter days, for us and for our salvation, born of the Virgin Mary, the Mother of God [*Theotokos*], according to the manhood; one and the same Christ, Son, Lord, Only-begotten, in two natures, unconfusedly, unchangeably, indivisibly, inseparably, the distinction of natures being by no means taken away by the union, but rather the property of each nature being preserved, and concurring in one person [*prosopon*] and one substance [*hypostasis*], not parted or divided into two persons, but one and the same Son and Only-begotten, God the Word, the Lord Jesus Christ; as the prophets from the beginning have declared concerning Him, and the Lord Jesus Christ Himself has taught us, and the creed of the Holy Fathers has handed down to us.

Two natures in union "unconfusedly, unchangeably, indivisibly, inseparably." Even one untried in theology and philosophy inevitably senses that in these words was found at last the golden rule for which the Church had so earnestly longed. The words are all negative—what can human lan-

guage say of the mystery of Christ's Being? But this negative definition has an inexhaustible religious meaning: it
guards, describes, and expresses forever what composes the
very essence of Christianity, the joyous mystery of the Gospel. God is united with man, but in that union man is
preserved in all his fullness; he is in no way diminished.
And now God is wholly in him: one Person, one Mind, one
striving. This is the meaning of God-Manhood; the Chalcedonian dogma gave mankind a new measure. What might
seem outwardly a mere rhetorical balance of words expressed in fact the faith, hope, and love of the Church,
the moving force of all our Christian life. God comes to
man, not to diminish him, but to make the divine Person
human.

The *Horos* of Chalcedon ended the dialectical opposition of Antioch and Alexandria. After the "thesis" and
"antithesis" came this synthesis, from which a new chapter
emerged in the history of Orthodox theology, that of Byzantium. Chalcedon is the theological formula of historical
Orthodoxy. Expressed once more in Antiochene language,
in a paradoxical way it reveals the faith of Cyril of Alexandria, who remains the forerunner of Chalcedon and the
great teacher of the meaning of divine Incarnation. The
historical limitations of each school were burned away and
the ambiguity and inadequacy of words overcome. All
Orthodox theology flows from the "miracle" of Chalcedon,
and unendingly reveals and interprets that source.

Incidentally, the Council of Chalcedon was a triumph
for Constantinople, whose primacy as a center of the Christian Church was finally confirmed in the famous twenty-
eighth canon. After confirming the third rule of the Second
Ecumenical Council, "in view of the fact that the city is
honored by the presence of the Emperor and the Senate,"
the canon also introduced a new element: from now on the
bishop of Constantinople was allotted the dioceses of Pontus, Asia, and Thrace, and the bishops of barbarian peoples
subject to these dioceses. In this way the two systems out-

lined earlier found a formal co-ordination: Constantinople
became the center of a definite region, or patriarchate as
it was later called, like Antioch, Alexandria, and Jerusalem,
which was also elevated at Chalcedon. It likewise retained
its primacy of honor over the more ancient sees, in recognition of its civic significance. Nothing shows better the
spirit of this evolution than the episcopal synod, which developed literally by itself in these years around the archbishop of Constantinople. Bishops from the provinces
would come to the capital on business, and the practice
arose of convening them to review various ecclesiastical
matters. This was the seed of future patriarchal synods, the
first budding of a completely new, centralized concept of
the authority of the first bishop of a region, which became
dominant later on. It represented a victory of the imperial
structure of the Church over the last remnants of its pre-
Nicene form.

All attempts to halt the growth of the influence and importance of Constantinople proved useless. Roman historians frequently represent this growth as a deliberate
policy on the part of its bishops, allegedly ambitious and
power-seeking, who intentionally subjected the East to
themselves. This is a very superficial judgment, however.
The fact is, among the bishops of Constantinople at that
time we see no special ambition; Gregory the Theologian,
St. Nectarius, St. John Chrysostom, even Nestorius and
finally Flavian—none could be compared in ambition with
the "popes" of Alexandria: Theophilus, Cyril, and Dioscurus. If there was such a policy of expanding domination,
it was of course at Alexandria, not in Constantinople. Some
historians do not see that this growth of Constantinople
was inevitable and would have taken place even if all its
bishops had been like Gregory the Theologian, whose mod-
esty and kindness hindered him from discerning that Maxim
the Cynic was a sinister adventurer. The roots of the development lay deep in the very foundations of the new
vision of a Christian *oekumene.*

Alexandria's last and hopeless attempt to retain its hegemony had been the Synod of Robbers at Ephesus in 449, two years before Chalcedon, of which the disgrace inevitably made reaction against it all the stronger. Antioch had been weakened and deposed by Nestorianism; now it was Alexandria's turn.

Reaction to Chalcedon—the Road to Division

The proclamation of Chalcedonian dogma, like that of Nicaea before it, long preceded its actual acceptance by the mind of the Church. While Nicaea triumphed in the end over the whole Church, Chalcedon unfortunately led to a separation of the churches on the historical plane that continues to the present day.

We have seen earlier the psychological and religious roots of Monophysitism. For the overwhelming majority of Christians today the doctrines of the Trinity and of two natures in Christ remain abstract formulas which do not play a significant role in personal belief; at the time, however, the Chalcedonian definition seemed to many a real apostasy from earlier religious experience. When one adds that it was composed in the sober language of the Antiochenes, that the council acquitted and received into communion the chief enemy of Eutyches and the former friend of Nestorius, Theodoret of Cyrrhus, and that it solemnly condemned the Alexandrian archbishop Dioscurus, one can understand why it inevitably provoked historic reactions. Actually the decisions of the council rejoiced only a small handful of Antiochenes and the Roman legates. It was accepted by the moderates in Constantinople. In Egypt, however, it seemed a betrayal of the precepts of the great Cyril. Now the Syrian monks joined the Egyptians. Chalcedon was a rehabilitation of Nestorius! Under this slogan the monastic movement against the council, pulling with it the mass of believers, immediately assumed threatening proportions.

The echoes and tragic consequences of this reaction cannot be explained by theological and psychological causes alone. Behind the Monophysite crisis lay something more than a mere relapse into the more extreme delusions of the Alexandrians. Its importance in the history of Orthodoxy was great because it revealed all the contradictions and—to speak frankly—the temptations inherent in the union of the Church with the Roman Empire under Constantine. While Chalcedon was spiritually and theologically indeed a miracle, an inexhaustible source of theological inspiration, it marked a sharp break in the relations between Church and state and in the history of the Christian world.

All this must be kept in mind in order to understand the significance of the reaction against it in the East. The council represented a triumph, not only of absolute, objective, timeless truth, but also of the faith of the empire, the faith of Constantinople. If the empire had really been what it proclaimed itself to be—what the best men of the time envisioned it to be, a universal, supranational Christian state—this triumph of imperial orthodoxy and of Constantinople would have been thoroughly justified, both historically and ecclesiastically. But unfortunately here, too, the discrepancy between theory and practice was fairly acute. The unity of the empire, culturally and psychologically, must not be exaggerated. Official documents have preserved for us its concept of itself, but if we depart from them the picture is completely different and, to be candid, a sad one. Beneath a thin layer of Hellenism and Hellenistic culture, established in the cities and among intellectuals, the old national passions continued to seethe and ancient traditions lived on. In the outskirts of Antioch, John Chrysostom was obliged to preach in Syrian; Greek was no longer understood there. Modern research demonstrates with increasing clarity that the Syrian and Coptic masses felt the power of the empire to be a hated yoke. Moreover, in the eastern part of it an output of Syrian Christian writings appeared, stemming of course from the Greek but showing the possibility of independent development. One need mention

only the name of St. Ephraim the Syrian in the fourth
century to feel the depth and potential of this "Eastern"
version of Christianity.

The main source of nourishment for the reaction against
Chalcedon and for Monophysitism was monasticism. In its
origins least of all connected with Hellenism, this movement was nourished in the fourth and fifth centuries primarily by local national elements—Syrian and Coptic—in
Syria and Egypt. In the support the monks gave Athanasius
when in hiding from the police, we may perhaps discern a
tinge of the defense of one's own man against outsiders.
When they backed Cyril and rioted at the Synod of Robbers, the monks were openly defending their own Church
from the alien imperial center that was creeping in on them.
The struggle against Chalcedon, aside from its theological
significance, now acquired new importance, both religious
and political. The ethnic passions that had seethed beneath
the surface found an outlet in Monophysitism, and the
struggle against "two natures" threatened to turn into a
rebellion against the empire itself.

When the bishops returned from Chalcedon, they were
met in many places by popular opposition. In order to bring
the Patriarch Juvenal to his city of Jerusalem, troops had
to intervene. In Alexandria the soldiers who were guarding
Patriarch Proterius, appointed by Constantinople to replace the deposed Dioscurus, were locked in the Caesareum
by an inflamed mob and burned alive. At first the government resorted to force and tried to impose the terms of
Chalcedon, but when Marcian, last representative of the
dynasty of Theodosius the Great, died in 457, there began
a period of compromises with the Monophysites.

For two centuries this problem was dominant in imperial
politics. In Alexandria in March 457 the people elected
their own Monophysite patriarch, Timothy Aelurus, and
Proterius was killed. In 475 the Monophysites controlled
the seat of Antioch as well, and elected a certain Peter
the Fuller to occupy it. The authorities understood that be-

hind Monophysitism stood immense popular forces which threatened the political unity of the empire. Also in 475 the usurper Basiliscus, who had driven out Emperor Zeno for a short time, published his *Encyclion,* which in fact condemned Chalcedon, and required the bishops to sign it. From five to seven hundred of them did so! Zeno, after returning to power in 476, at first supported Chalcedonian orthodoxy, but under the influence of the patriarch of Constantinople, Acacius, and in view of the undiminishing growth of Monophysitism in Egypt, Syria, and Palestine, in 482 he published his *Henoticon,* a dogmatic decree in which he rejected both the *Tome* of Leo and the creedal definition of Chalcedon without naming them. The Monophysite patriarch of Alexandria and Antioch signed it, but the people refused to follow them; in Alexandria alone a crowd of thirty thousand monks demanded that the patriarch repudiate the *Henoticon.* More important, the emperor, by accepting the signatures of the hierarchs of these cities, recognized their legitimacy.

There was a Chalcedonian patriarch in Alexandria as well, however (appointed to succeed Proterius), and he then appealed to Rome. Pope Felix III demanded that Acacius of Constantinople, leader of the policy of compromise, should accept outright the dogma of Chalcedon and Leo's epistle. This failing, he solemnly deposed and excommunicated Acacius in July 484, and so began the first schism with Rome, which lasted for about thirty years until 518. Thus, by trying to preserve the Monophysite East, Constantinople lost the orthodox West; the "schism of Acacius" was one link in the long chain of disagreements that led to final separation. Emperor Anastasius I (491–518) openly supported the Monophysites; in 496 he deposed the patriarch of Constantinople, Euphemius, for refusing to compromise with the Monophysite patriarch of Alexandria. In 511 Macedonius of Constantinople shared a like fate for faithfulness to Chalcedon and was replaced by the declared Monophysite Timothy. In 512 Anastasius appointed to the seat of Antioch the leading Monophysite theologian, Severus of Antioch, who solemnly condemned Chalcedon at the Council of Tyre in 518. Every year the division between orthodox and Monophysites became more profound and impossible to retrieve. In Palestine and Syria, it is true, some of the monks under the leadership of St. Sabas, founder of the famous Palestinian monastery, remained faithful to orthodoxy and did not recognize the Monophysite hierarchy, but the main mass of Syrians and practically all Egypt were ready prey to heresy. It was not by chance that the orthodox there received the name of Melkites or emperor's men.

Chalcedon represented a theological synthesis, but not an imperial one. The Monophysite schism demonstrated with increasing clarity that the price paid for the union of Church and empire—or rather, the price paid by the Church for the sins of the empire—was the first great tragedy of the young Christian world.

Last Dream of Rome

The forty-year reign of Justinian (527–65) represented the last attempt of an emperor to preserve the unity of the Roman "universe," the climax and apogee of that world in which dying antiquity had entered into union with Christianity. From the beginning Justinian was fascinated by Rome's great past, and behind all his policies lay a dream of the former glory of the empire, of the majesty of imperial power and the mission of Rome, rather than sober recognition of reality. "We hope that God will return to us the lands which the ancient Romans ruled as far as the two oceans," he wrote. But this was a dream. In reality Roman unity no longer existed.

Byzantium, for its part, was increasingly turning its back on the West and shifting its center of interest eastward. From the fifth century on, we clearly perceive the progressive orientalization of the empire in its culture, psychology, art, and court ritual. New Christian churches were arising beyond its borders in Georgia, Armenia, and Persia; the Byzantine mission developed eastward, and it was characteristic that the break with Rome in 484 did not particularly disturb anyone in Byzantium. The Church unfortunately submitted to history, and history widened still further the gulf between the two halves of what had once been a united *oekumene*. The fact is, although the East was connected by organic succession with Rome, a new Byzantine world had developed, while the Roman West under barbarian attack plunged deeper and deeper into the chaos of those Dark Ages from which Roman-Germanic Europe would later emerge.

The beginning of the barbarian invasions, the great migration of peoples, was marked in 355 by the appearance of the Huns in eastern Europe. Under their onslaught the Germanic tribes which had settled there began to break through the borders of the empire. The eastern region was saved by Theodosius the Great. Repelled from the south, the German tribes moved west. The first wave at the beginning of the fifth century rolled as far as Rome, but was beaten off. Nevertheless, the barbarians gained a foothold within the empire. The Visigoths in Italy, the Vandals in Africa, and the Franks in Gaul as "allies" recognized Roman rule, and the victory over the Huns on the Catalonian plain in 451 may still be regarded as a Roman victory. But Rome itself was falling apart; betrayals, conspiracies, and murders, one after the other, pursued the helpless Western emperors, and in 476 the last of them ignominiously disappeared. In 493 Theodoric's Ostrogoths founded their kingdom in central Italy. Even then, all these peoples continued nominally to recognize the supreme and sacred authority of the Byzantine emperor, and their princelings willingly accepted empty court titles from Constantinople; nevertheless, the West was plunging into barbarism and darkness.

This history of decay was just what Justinian did not recognize. His whole mind, life, and actions were controlled by the Roman idea in all its universalism. He assumed power at a crucial period; from the beginning of the sixth century the pressure of the restored Persian empire on Byzantium had increased, and his vital interest demanded that he concentrate all his forces on the East, as the events of the next century showed so clearly. Justinian bought off the Persians, however, and threw his armies westward under the command of Belisarius. In 534 Africa was taken from the Vandals; the next year the Byzantines occupied Sicily, and on December 10, 536, Belisarius entered Rome, which had been abandoned by the Ostrogoth king. The dream had become reality, and in 559 it was crowned by the restoration of Roman dominion in Spain. When he died, Justinian believed that the ancient unity of the empire had been restored.

He wanted not only external but internal restoration as well. The very first years of his reign were marked by a colossal systematization of Roman law, known as the "Code of Justinian." Its reputation has not been exaggerated; Justinian's Code preserved the heritage of Roman law and made it the foundation of the new world born out of the decay of the empire, thus establishing our historical origins. Finally, alongside this juridical work went a profound administrative and financial reform. The empire again found its strong state structure. Justinian was the last great Roman emperor.

Justinian and the Church

One cannot understand Justinian's significance in history, especially in the history of the Church, without understanding that he was also the first ideologist of the Christian empire, who brought the union of Constantine to its logical conclusion. In his reign occurred the first synthesis of

Christian Byzantinism, and this in turn was to define the whole future course of Eastern Orthodoxy.

Justinian never distinguished Roman state tradition from Christianity. He considered himself to be completely and fully the Roman emperor and just as organically a Christian emperor. Here lay the source of his whole theory, in the unity of the empire and the Christian religion, which to him was self-evident and completely indivisible. But here, too, may be found the ambiguity and, one must frankly admit, the inner fallacy of his theory. On the one hand it demonstrated that the mind of the empire had undoubtedly changed under the influence of Christianity; Justinian always felt himself to be the servant of God and the executor of His will, and the empire to be the instrument of God's plan in the world. The empire had placed itself irrevocably under the symbol of the Cross, and its purpose was to guard and spread Christianity among men. Justinian's interest in missionary work, his contributions to Church charity, and his generous material support of the Church must never be forgotten or minimized, nor can his sincere faith and genuine interest in theology (which was not merely political) be denied. His Code deliberately opens with a confession of the "Catholic faith" in Christ and the Holy Trinity, and on the precious throne of St. Sophia, the symbol, heart, and protection of the empire, are engraved the words: "Thine own of Thine own are offered Thee by Justinian and Theodora." In a certain sense they actually express the mind and inspiration of the emperor. The empire now belonged wholly to the Christian God.

Most Orthodox historians, however, do not perceive the tragic flaw in Justinian's theory. Some of them—those who are hostile to Byzantium on the whole—consider him a theoretician of caesaropapism, the subordination of the Church to the state, and regard this as the source of all evils in the history of the Orthodox East. Others, on the contrary, see him as the creator of a "symphony," a truly Orthodox theory of relations between Church and state, and interpret the errors and violence of his reign as inevitable earthly shortcomings. But the fatal element of Justinian's theory lies in the fact that there is simply *no place for the Church* in it. By planting Christianity sincerely and deeply at the heart of all his official acts, the great emperor actually managed not to *see* the Church, and therefore based his whole concept of the Christian world on false presuppositions.

One must hasten to admit that the word "Church" is encountered innumerable times in his writings, and that he defined the mission of the pious emperor to be "the maintenance of the Christian faith in its purity and the protection of the Holy Catholic and Apostolic Church from any disturbance." But what was the real situation behind these words?

Two Communities

We know that in the minds of Christians from the beginning the Church had been a new community, a new people of God, created through the sacramental new birth by water and the Spirit. This birth had given Christian life a new dimension. It had introduced it into a Kingdom that was not of this world, and had brought it into communion with the life of the world to come, still concealed from sight, so that while remaining on this present earth the Christian became a citizen of another world as well, through the Church. "You have died and your life is hidden with Christ in God." The Church, in other words, had been divided from the world not by persecution or rejection alone, but by the incompatibility of its most sacred essence with anything earthly.

As late as the fourth century the borderline between the Church and the world had been clear; by no means all believers accepted baptism, so strong was the awareness of the break connected with this sacrament. St. Basil the

Great, for example, was baptized as an adult, and St. John Chrysostom denounced those who put off baptism, thus postponing the time when they would part with their "pleasant" lives. By the fifth century, however, this external borderline gradually began to be effaced; the Christian community increasingly coincided with Byzantine society as a whole. Yet still in the doctrine and mind of the Church the principle remained inviolate that the Church is a community "not of this world," as distinct from a "natural" community, and if we explore the text of the liturgy we see that it still remains a closed assembly of the faithful and not a public service which anyone who enters may attend.

The fact that the bounds of the sacramental community of believers coincided with the bounds of the natural community—an inevitable result of the acceptance of Christianity by the whole empire—does not in itself represent a departure from the original teaching of the Church about itself. Had it not been sent to all men? Its methods of preaching and action among men changed somewhat; its services developed and became more solemn; the Church embraced human life more widely; but essentially it remained what it had been and should be, an assembly of the people of God, summoned primarily to bear witness to the kingdom of God. The Eucharistic prayer still preserves this eschatological aspiration, and each liturgy proclaims the ultimate otherworldliness of the Church and its adherence to the age to come.

The coincidence between these two communities meant, however, that from the time of the Christianization of the empire the boundary between the Church and the world had gradually shifted from an external one dividing Christian from pagan to an inner one within the Christian mind itself. The Christian belongs both to the Church and to the world, but he must recognize the ontological distinction between them. Striving as a Christian to illuminate his whole life with the light of Christ's teachings, he still knows

that his final value and final treasure, "the one thing necessary," is not of this world; it is the kingdom of God, the
final union wich God, the perfect joy of eternal life with
Christ. He anticipates this joy in the Church, in its assembly, when in the breaking of bread it "heralds the death of
the Lord and confesses His resurrection." While joined to
the world through each of its members and being itself a
part of it, the Church as a whole is the mystery of the
kingdom of God, the anticipation of its coming triumph,
and therefore also, in the final analysis, free and distinct
from the world.

All the urging of the preachers and theologians of the
fourth and fifth centuries was mainly directed toward maintaining in the Church community an awareness of just
these two planes in Christian life. Their efforts explain
much about the growing complexity of liturgical ritual and
the growing emphasis on the "awesome" nature of the Sacrament as the appearance in this world of a Reality that
is absolutely other, heavenly, and incommensurable with
it. Finally, monasticism by its withdrawal also bore witness
to this. By preaching, services of worship, and asceticism,
the Church struggled against the temptation to transform
Christianity into a "natural" religion and merge it completely with the world.

Here lay the deepest of all the misunderstandings between the Church and the empire. The Roman state could
accept the ecclesiastical doctrine of God and Christ comparatively easily as its official religious doctrine; it could
render the Church great help in rooting out paganism and
implanting Christianity; and finally, it could Christianize
its own laws to a certain extent. But it could not really
recognize that the Church was a community distinct from
itself; it did not understand the Church's ontological independence of the world. The religious absolutism of the
Roman state and the emperor's belief that he was the representative of God on earth prevented it. The trouble was
that the conversion to Christianity not only did not weaken

but actually strengthened this belief and brought it to its
logical conclusion. We have seen that the unique feature
of the conversion of Constantine, and its significance for the
future, lay in the "directness" of his election by Christ—in
the fact that he "accepted the call like Paul, not from men."
In the mind of Constantine himself, this had placed the
empire in a special position in the sacred history of salvation
and made it the completion and crown of the events that
had led through the Old and New Testaments to the final
victory of Christ over the world.

The more the Church coincided in scale with the empire
—the more imperceptible became the outward difference
in their boundaries—the stronger was the identity between
them in the thinking of the state, under the authority of
the autocrat installed by the power of God. Outwardly the
structure of the Church remained untouched. With the
destruction of paganism, the emperors unconditionally rejected the sacred or priestly functions they had performed
in ancient Rome in consequence of the state's theocratic
nature. The sacramental, educational, and pastoral authority of the hierarchy was in no way limited, but on the contrary surrounded by unprecedented honor and privileges.
Only the hierarchy, in theory at least, continued to be the
all-powerful expression of Church faith, and the state recognized that it was obliged to protect, spread, and confirm
the teaching of the Church as established by its councils.

But it is characteristic, and has been overlooked by many
historians, that the problem of relations between Church
and state in Byzantium was almost imperceptibly and unconsciously replaced by the problem of relations between
the secular authority and the hierarchy. In the imperial conception, the Church had merged with the world, but because this was a Christian world it had two complementary sources for its existence, structure, and well-being: the
emperor and the priest. In Byzantine literature the comparison of the relations of Church and state to those between body and soul gradually became classic. The state

was conceived to be the body, which lived because of the presence within it of its soul, the Church. There is a radical distinction, however, between this pattern and the doctrine of the early Church, which it actually never rejected, since this would have meant rejecting its own life.

The early Church felt it was itself a body, a living organism, a new people, completely incompatible with any other people or any natural community. Only within this organism and only in relation to it is there meaning for the work of the hierarchy, whose purpose is to manifest this unity and transform the Church into the image of Christ Himself. Theoretically all men in the empire were called and could become members of this body, but even then the world would not become the Church, because in it and through it men commune with another world, another life, that which will come in glory only after the end of this one.

In official Byzantine doctrine, however, the state was compared to a body, not in this early Christian sense, nor because all subjects of the empire had become Church members. Actually the figure was derived wholly from pagan premises which had not been replaced, according to which the state itself was conceived to be the only community established by God, and embraced the whole life of man. The visible representative of God within it, who performed His will and dispensed His blessings, was the emperor. He was obliged to be concerned with both the religious and the material well-being of his subjects, and his power was not only from God but was divine in its own nature. The only distinction between this pattern and pagan theocracy was that the empire, by the choice of its emperor, had found its true God and true religion in Christianity. Christ had left his authority to forgive, heal, sanctify, and teach to the priests. Therefore they must be surrounded in the state with special honor, for on them, on their prayers and sacraments, would depend the prosperity of the empire.

In the early Byzantine way of thinking, what the Church consisted of was the hierarchy, the dogmas, the services, the

Church buildings; all this was indeed the soul of the world, the soul of the empire. But the idea of the Church as a body or community had dropped out of sight and was replaced by or exchanged for that of the state. There is no longer a problem of Church and state, but only one of the relationship between two authorities, the secular and the spiritual, within the state itself. This latter problem is what Justinian deals with in his legislation and religious policy, and this is the significance of his reign in the history of the Church.

"Symphony"

Justinian's solution is known in history as the idea of "symphony," best expressed in his famous *Sixth Novella*. "There are two great blessings," he writes, "gifts of the mercy of the Almighty to men, the priesthood and the empire (*sacerdotium et imperium*). Each of these blessings granted to men was established by God and has its own appointed task. But as they proceed from the same source they also are revealed in unity and co-operative action." The priesthood controls divine and heavenly matters, while the empire directs what is human and earthly. But at the same time the empire takes full care of preserving Church dogmas and the honor of the priesthood. And the priesthood with the empire directs all public life along ways pleasing to God.

This doctrine might indeed have been "theoretically the best of all that exists," as one Russian historian asserts, if the state, proclaimed to be as essential and as great a blessing as the Church, had really re-evaluated itself in the light of Christian teachings about the world. Christianity had never denied either the benefit of the state or the possibility that it could be enlightened by the Light of Christ. Yet the meaning of the Church's appearance in the world as a community and a visible organism was that it revealed the limitations of the state, destroying its claim to absolutism forever, however "sacral" its nature might be; and it was just this sacral quality that had been the essence of the ancient pagan state. The Church revealed to the world that there are only two absolute, eternal, and sacred values: God and man, and that everything else, including the state, is first limited by its very nature—by belonging wholly only to this world; and secondly, is a blessing only to the extent that it serves God's plan for man. Therefore the "enlightenment" of the state means primarily its recognition of its own limitations, its refusal to regard itself as an absolute value. It was for this enlightenment that Christians had suffered and died in the era of persecutions, when they rejected the right of the state to subject the whole of man to itself. Hence the true postulate for a Christian world was not a merging of the Church with the state but, on the contrary, a distinction between them. For the state *is only Christian to the extent that it does not claim to be everything for man*—to define his whole life—but enables him to be a member as well of another community, another reality, which is alien to the state although not hostile to it.

The whole drama of Byzantinism lay in the fact that historically this re-evaluation never took place, either under Constantine or after him. Justinian's theory was rooted in the theocratic mind of pagan empires, for which the state was a sacred and absolute form for the world—its meaning and justification. One cannot speak of the subordination of the Church to the state, because for subordination there must be two distinct subjects. But in the theocratic conception there is not and cannot be anything that is not related to the state, and religion is essentially a state function. It is even a higher function, which in a certain way subordinates everything else in state life to itself; but only because the state itself is religious by nature and is the recognized divine form for the human community. The state is subject to religion; but religion itself has the state as the goal of its functions, and in this sense is subject to it as the final value, for the sake of which it exists.

"The well-being of the Church is the defense of the empire"—in these words of Justinian lies the key to his whole
theory. He accepts wholly the distinction between imperial
and spiritual authority, and regards the latter as the bearer
of the truth, with which it is the first duty of the state to
be in harmony. He understands that "empire" and "priesthood" have distinct tasks. But all this—the distinction between them, the truth, and their distinct assignments—all
exist essentially for the well-being and strengthening and
blessing of the empire, the ultimate and absolute value.

It is characteristic that even Justinian's love for monasticism, which he proved by founding dozens of monasteries
throughout the empire—a monasticism which apparently
repudiated the religious absolutism of the empire by the
very fact of its existence—had for him precisely the same
source of inspiration. "If these pure hands and these consecrated souls will pray for the Empire, its armies will be
stronger, the well-being of the state will be greater, fertility
and trade will flourish, due to God's undoubted favor."
Even those whose only purpose was to bear witness that
"the image of this world passes," and that we may use it
only "as if not using it," were included in this ancient utilitarian conception of religion and became, in the emperor's
regard, a source of material (not even spiritual!) well-being
for the empire.

In Justinian's synthesis the Church appears to dissolve,
and the awareness that it is radically alien to the world
and the empire disappears once and for all from state thinking. The first chapter in the history of the Christian world
ends with the victorious return of pagan absolutism.

Reconciliation with Rome—Break with the East

The fate of the Church itself under Justinian best illus-
trates the situation just described. From the very first years
of his reign, the emperor demonstrated that he regarded

the religious unity of the empire as just as self-evident and natural as state unity. Stern measures were taken against all possible heretical sects, the remnants of ancient schisms and disputes. Justinian resolved to settle still more firmly with paganism and with its citadel, the university at Athens, which had recently been basking in the glory of the last of its great pagan philosophers, Proclus. In 529 the university was closed and replaced by the first Christian university, in Constantinople. Campaigns of mass conversion began in the capital and Asia Minor. The few remaining pagans were obliged to go permanently underground.

When he was still only heir to the throne under Emperor Justin I, Justinian began his religious policy by a solemn reconciliation with Rome. Even then the plan of restoring the ancient empire in the West was maturing in his mind. In the chaos that reigned there the only link left with Byzantium and Roman tradition was the papacy. Its authority was unshakable, even among the German barbarians, although they belonged officially to Arianism, the heritage of Ulfila the Goth, who had baptized them in the fourth century at a time when Arianism was triumphant. In these years of decay and destruction the papacy remained true to the empire, regardless of strained relations between them. The price of reconciliation between the churches, however, was the signing by the patriarch and the bishops of a document composed by Pope Hormisdas which was more violently papistic in content than anything the Eastern Church had ever seen before. The late Orthodox patriarchs Euphemius and Macedonius, themselves victims of Monophysitism and already revered as saints in Constantinople, had to be condemned by their own Church, merely because they had ruled it in 484 when communion between Rome and Constantinople was sundered. Justinian needed peace with Rome at any price.

He had relied on the papacy to restore his power in the West, and the papacy was unwavering in its loyalty to Pope Leo and the Council of Chalcedon. But the situation in the

East when he ascended the throne in 427 was diametrically opposite. In Egypt the Church belonged wholly to the Monophysites; in other provinces supporters of the *Henoticon*—semi-Monophysites—ruled. The Antiochene Church was headed by the intellectual leader of all Monophysite theology, Severus. Justin and Justinian first began by attempting to restore the imperial episcopate to the faith of Chalcedon by force, but the new bishops, appointed and consecrated in Constantinople, had to occupy their seats with the help of the police. The masses rioted, whole monasteries had to be dispersed, and curses against the "synodites" resounded everywhere. Only Palestine was wholly orthodox, except for an insignificant minority. In Syria, in Edessa (an ancient town near the Persian border), in the outlying regions of Asia Minor, the Chalcedonian hierarchy was seated by force. Egypt they did not dare to touch at all, and Severus of Antioch and the other Monophysite leaders went into hiding there.

Shortly afterward, in 531, Justinian sharply changed course and abandoned the use of force, replacing it by a policy of compromise. Usually this reversal is ascribed to the influence of his wife Theodora, a secret Monophysite, who constantly helped the persecuted leaders of the heresy. Other historians mention a unique division of spheres between husband and wife; Justinian's support of orthodoxy and Theodora's of Monophysitism they claim were a political maneuver to preserve the unity of the empire, by allowing both sides access to imperial power. Whatever the case, Justinian could not help but comprehend the threatening significance of this religious division, behind which the separatism of ancient nationalisms was ever more clearly visible.

The expelled monks were allowed to return to their monasteries. A huge number of them settled right next door to the emperor himself, where for decades they were a center of secret Monophysite intrigues around Theodora. The emperor was still counting on a theological agreement. In 533 he arranged a three-day discussion in which twelve theologians participated, six on each side. Despite the peaceful tone and high theological level of the debate, it had no result. Soon afterward Theodora succeeded in making a certain Anthimus, almost openly a Monophysite, patriarch of Constantinople. An encounter with Severus of Antioch, whom the emperor had managed to entice out of Egypt for theological discussions, completed Justinian's apparent conversion to the Monophysite camp.

Just then, however, the Roman Pope Agapetus himself appeared in Constantinople. The patriarch's heresy was exposed, he disappeared, and the orthodox Menas was elevated to his seat by the pope's own hand. Justinian again changed course. In an edict of 536 Monophysitism was once more solemnly condemned, the books of Severus of Antioch were removed from circulation, and entry to the capital was forbidden to heretics. He resolved on an even more drastic step: after so many years of almost official recognition of the Monophysite hierarchy in Egypt, he now sent an orthodox bishop there with unlimited powers, and a wave of terror once more rolled through the country.

Now a decisive development took place: the rise of an independent, parallel Monophysite hierarchy, which changed to a final and irreversible schism what might hitherto have been considered a theological divergence. There had been parallel patriarchs at times before this. But now with the help of Theodora a certain Bishop John, exiled for heresy, succeeded in being transferred to the capital on the pretext of needing medical attention, and here, concealed from the police by the empress, he began to consecrate priests in his own house. Later he managed to pass secretly throughout almost all Asia Minor for the same purpose. A little later another secret bishop, Jacob Baradai "the Ragged," traveled through Syria in the guise of a beggar. On this journey, with the help of two exiled Egyptian bishops, he consecrated bishops as well. The latter soon elected their own Monophysite patriarch. The foundation of the "Jacobite" Church (named after Baradai) was laid, and it exists today. Copts and Syrians thus established their national Church, and the first permanent division between the churches was complete.

After this neither Justinian nor his successors ever retreated from Chalcedon, and the empire joined its fate with Orthodoxy forever. But is it not tragic that one of the main reasons for the rejection of Orthodoxy by almost the whole non-Greek East was its hatred for the empire? A hundred years later the Syrians and Copts would greet their Mohammedan conquerors as saviors; this was the price the Church paid for the inner dichotomy of the union of Constantine.

Recurrence of Origenism

Justinian revealed the real extent of his absolutism in the obscure and lengthy history of the Fifth Ecumenical Council. The outward reasons leading to it may seem fortuitous, and it is not easy to discern its inner congruity with the gradual crystallization of Orthodox dogma, a congruity which, despite its sad historical appearance, has still preserved ecumenical authority for it in the mind of the Church.

The council arose from a new dispute over the theology of Origen, who, as we have already seen, was the first to attempt a synthesis between Christianity and Hellenism. In spite of the immense influence of the great Alexandrian teacher, certain points in his thought aroused doubts very early. Even at the end of the third century, Methodius of Olympus was writing against his doctrine of the pre-existence of souls and the nature of resurrected bodies. A hundred years later, at the end of the fourth century, Epiphanius of Cyprus, a celebrated exposer of heresies, regarded Origen as the source of the Arian subordination of the Son to the Father; at the same time St. Jerome was also writing against him; and finally, in 400, a council led by Theophilus of Alexandria in that city solemnly condemned the errors of Origenism. For in it Hellenism had fundamentally distorted Christianity, and the struggle against Origen was one aspect of the critical and difficult Christianization of Hellenism in which, as I have pointed out, we find the historical meaning of the patristic period. The Church "revised" Origen, discarding from his teachings what seemed incompatible with its faith and perfecting what seemed valuable and useful.

But the problem of Origen had not been posed on an ecumenical scale, and had been overcome primarily in theological disputes about the Trinity and God-Manhood, through gradual refinement of the theological language and hence by a clear theological mastery in Church tradition. Thus the sudden relapse into Origenism at the end of the fifth century and the beginning of the sixth was not a matter of chance; it revealed all the strength of Hellenistic themes that had not been overcome, even in the mind of the Church itself—a constant temptation to rationalize Christianity. The revival of Origenism must be interpreted in this connection.

It is not accidental that these disputes over Origen, which became so acute under Justinian, were limited almost exclusively to the monastic environment, which had arisen as a way or method of "practical" incarnation of the evangelical ideal. But very early the ascetic experience began to be interpreted and to grow into a definite theory. In this, Origen's influence was a decisive factor, and not Origen alone, but the whole Alexandrian tradition with its interest in mystical and spiritual interpretation of the Scriptures, and its ideal of *gnosis* as a higher way, and "deification." Disputes over Origen arose very early among the monks. According to tradition, St. Pachomius the Great had forbidden his followers to read his works. On the other hand, his influence may be felt in the *Life of Anthony* composed by St. Athanasius. Origen attracted Basil the Great and his friends, founders of monasticism on Greek soil; and without doubt the ascetic works of Evagrius of Pontus, which were distributed throughout the East on a vast scale and strongly influenced all later ascetic writing, were directly derived from Origenism. Along with the adoption of much that was valuable in Alexandrian tradition, its danger too might be discerned more and more clearly: it lay in the "spiritualization" of Christianity, the very subtle and innermost "de-incarnation" of man. This was a danger from Greek idealism which had not been overcome—the desire to replace "salvation" by contemplation.

At the beginning of the sixth century these disputes and doubts about Origen, which had never really died down among the monks, overstepped the desert boundaries and attracted the attention of wider Church circles. In 531 St. Sabas, founder of the famous monastery of Palestine, went to Constantinople to obtain government help for Palestine, which was torn by a Samaritan rebellion. He was accompanied by the monk Leontius, one of the main defenders of Origen's theology in the monastery. In Constantinople Sabas participated in the disputes with the Monophysites. The Origenism of Leontius was exposed and Sabas was forced to part with him.

Shortly afterward another convinced Origenist, Theodore of Raïthu (a monastery on what is now the Gulf of Suez), arrived in the capital. He became intimate with Justinian and was appointed to the important see of Caesarea in Cappadocia. With such protection at court, the Origenists everywhere raised their heads. But just then there came to Palestine on other business an ecclesiastical delegation from Constantinople which included the scholarly Roman deacon Pelagius, the pope's representative or "apocrisiary" in the East. He could not overlook the disputes among the monks over the name of Origen. In the West Origen had long been considered a heretic, and Pelagius raised an alarm. At his insistence, Patriarch Ephraim of Antioch solemnly condemned Origenism. The disturbances arising from this condemnation finally reached Constantinople. Despite all the efforts of Theodore of Raïthu, the emperor, when he had reviewed the whole matter, issued in 543 in the form of an edict a lengthy and well-grounded condemnation of Origenism, or rather of those aspects of it which were obviously contradictory to the doctrine of the Church. All five patriarchs signed this condemnation unconditionally, and there were still disputes only among the Palestinian monks. Despite the unusualness of a theological definition by state edict (apparently no one protested against this), Origenism, or its extreme assertions in any case, had been overcome in the mind of the Church.

Fifth Ecumenical Council

Paradoxically, the condemnation of Origen was the reason for much more important events, however. Although he had signed the edict, Theodore of Raïthu had never forgiven Pelagius for his interference in these disputes, which resulted in the condemnation of his beloved teacher. He gave Justinian the idea of condemning also the three late Antiochene theologians who had been chiefly connected in some way with Nestorianism: Theodore of Mopsuestia, Theodoret of Cyrrhus, and Ibas of Edessa. All three leaders had been absolved at the Council of Chalcedon as a result of the Alexandrian accusations, and had died at peace with the Church. The Council of Chalcedon had been a victory from the theological point of view for Pope Leo the Great, and through him for the whole West. Thus in attacking the three "heads" (or "chapters," as the three condemned teachers began to be called, in confusion with the three headings or chapters of the imperial edict against them), Theodore was insulting the West.

The plots of this dark intriguer are not quite clear to us— did he want a break with Rome as revenge for its interference with Origenism, or was he trying to strengthen his own position? Whatever the case, in the same court theological circle which had prepared the edict against Origen a new document was composed around 544, again in the form of an imperial edict, which solemnly condemned Theodore of Mopsuestia and those works of Theodoret of Cyrrhus and Ibas of Edessa in which they had disputed with Cyril of Alexandria. The emperor liked the idea, since the edict might furnish additional proof to the Monophysites that the Orthodox rejected Nestorius, and might bring them back into Orthodoxy at a time when administrative measures against the Monophysites were growing in strength.

While the condemnation of Origen had not aroused any opposition, the edict of 544 raised a storm. The papal representative Stephen, who had replaced Pelagius, refused outright to sign it. The four Eastern patriarchs signed only under threat of deposition and exile, and then on condition that if the Roman pope would not sign it they might revoke their signatures. The emperor had decided to get what he wanted, however. Pope Vigilius was arrested in Rome during a Church service and placed on a ship for Constantinople. En route, in Sicily he met the archbishop of Milan and representatives of the African churches; all were extremely opposed to the edict, regarding it as an open defiance of Chalcedon. He did not reach Constantinople until 547, where he was met with due solemnity.

Now began a long, sad story which cannot be passed over in silence. At first Vigilius adopted an uncompromising position and refused communion to the patriarch and to all who had signed the edict against the "Three Heads." Then Justinian began his theological brain-washing. It must be said that the arguments of the Byzantine theologians were essentially correct. Theodore of Mopsuestia, as we have seen, was undoubtedly more the father of Nestorianism than his disciple Nestorius himself. On the other hand, if the Church recognized Cyril's orthodoxy, the violent and obviously unjust attacks on him by Theodoret and Ibas

undoubtedly merited condemnation. The pope referred to
their absolution by the Council of Chalcedon. The Council
of Chalcedon, he was answered, had absolved them on the
basis of their rejection of Nestorius and had not discussed
their theological writings.

Finally the pope gave in and agreed to condemn the
Three Heads. But now a further storm arose in the West,
where Pope Vigilius was regarded as an apostate and be-
trayer of Chalcedon. The well-known African theologian,
Facundus of Hermiane, published a book *In Defense of
the Three Heads* which produced a sensation. Locally council after council opposed the condemnation, and in Africa
matters went so far that the pope himself was solemnly
anathematized. Justinian realized that the pope's signature
decided nothing in this case. The frightened Vigilius begged
him to review the whole matter and to summon an ecumenical council for this purpose. After the emperor had
obtained from the pope a written condemnation of the
Three Heads, he ordered preparations for the council. All
that had taken place previously was officially annulled.

Justinian understood the preparation for a council in his
own way. In Africa, for example, where opposition to the
edict was particularly strong, the main bishops were arrested
at the emperor's order, including the archbishop of Carthage, and replaced by others. Still the outcome of the
council seemed unclear. The emperor decided to alter the
initial plan. Instead of reviewing the whole matter again,
as he had promised Vigilius, it was much simpler to demand of the assembled bishops their signatures on a document already prepared. A new edict, with detailed theological argumentation, was issued and distributed to all the
churches. The patriarch of Alexandria, who refused to accept it, was immediately exiled and replaced by a new one.

Vigilius refused to recognize this edict, by which the emperor had broken his promise. Justinian was beginning to
lose his temper; sensing the danger, Vigilius and Datius
of Milan decided to seek sanctuary in an inviolable refuge,

the Church of St. Peter in the papal Palace of Hormisdas. Here a disgraceful scene took place. On the emperor's orders the police broke into the church to arrest the pope. He resisted so energetically that the columns over the altar collapsed and almost crushed him. The assembled crowd began stormily to express their outrage, and the police were obliged to withdraw ineffectively. Again there were threats, slander, and petty but hourly insults and humiliation. In the end several years passed in this way, in the course of which a vacuum developed around the pope; Datius of Milan died, and the circle of Western clerics melted away. Still the pope had apparently achieved his goal, the emperor's rejection of the edicts and a free solution of the question.

After endless wavering, the council finally opened in Constantinople on May 5, 553. It began with a solemn condemnation of Origenism, which still continued to disturb Palestine. The pope informed the council that while he would not be personally present at the deliberations, he would send his opinion on the problem of the Three Heads in written form. This lengthy document, filled with detailed argument, opened with an unconditional condemnation of the theology of Theodore of Mopsuestia. As for the man himself, the pope referred to an ancient practice of the Church not to condemn those who had died at peace with it, leaving this to the judgment of Christ. The pope refused to condemn Theodoret and Ibas, who had been defended by the Council of Chalcedon.

This document never reached the bishops. Instead, Justinian presented to the council Vigilius' written condemnation of the Three Heads, which he had given the emperor at the beginning of the dispute. Caught in a contradiction, the pope was excluded from the diptychs (his name no longer mentioned in the liturgy). On June 2 the council finished the condemnation of the Three Heads by signing fourteen anathemas. No one really defended the documents concerned, and the Eastern Church painlessly

accepted the decree of the ecumenical council as something self-evident.

In the end Vigilius, too, signed. He was not destined to
return to Rome, but died on the way in Syracuse in 555. In
the West the council was accepted with difficulty. The
main role in its acceptance was played by Vigilius' successor, Pelagius, who had been for many years one of the
main opponents of the condemnation of the Three Heads.
His long stay in Constantinople had taught him much,
however—perhaps most of all to penetrate behind the historical covering to the essence of things, and to distinguish
the temporal from the eternal.

Underlying Gains

Temporal aspects of these events were the disgraceful use
of force, which revealed what Justinian meant by "symphony" and how he carried it out; the obsequiousness of too
many of the bishops, which made force almost a legitimate
form of imperial administration of the Church; and the
quick resort to excommunications, curses, and schisms on
the surface of Church life.

The eternal aspect was the meaning nevertheless revealed
in these disputes, which outwardly appeared almost fortuitous or even imposed from above. In returning to problems that seemed already solved, the fathers of the council
indeed finished the work of Chalcedon and for the first time
freed its decisions from possible reinterpretation, placing it
in its truly Orthodox theological perspective. It was not
accidental that the council condemned simultaneously
both Origen and the most extreme representatives of the
school of Antioch. This was the judgment of the Church,
not only of heresy but also of its own past; it revealed completely the defects of both trends and their one-sidedness
within Orthodoxy itself. Neither Antioch nor Alexandria
alone could give an integral, catholic description of the faith

of the Church. Chalcedon had been a formula for synthesis, but the formula by itself was inadequate. It had to
be revealed in appropriate concepts, and the whole system
of thought and terminology had to be realigned in accordance with it. This work was performed deep in the mind
of the Church.

Justinian had behaved rudely, and much in the history
of his reign is darkened forever by this rudeness and violence. But there was a genuine dispute within the Church
about the Eastern Fathers; their writings were really sharply
contradictory to the tradition of Chalcedon. Again, the dispute about Origen was genuine, not forced on the Church
by Justinian. The truth in the solution of these questions
was not Justinian's, but the truth and rightness of the decisions and achievements of the period. This is the only
truth the Church recognizes in considering the Council of
553 as one of the ecumenical councils. And the whole future development of Orthodox theology confirmed it.

The historian inevitably generalizes. But Justinian's reign
should not be reduced to a mere triumph of caesaropapism
in its Byzantine form. This appears on the surface of
Church life, while behind the seething tumult of events it
is sometimes hard to discern the creative processes developing in the depths. We see monks rioting in the churches
and squares of a city, crushing the Church en masse. From
this it is so easy to draw conclusions about their lack of
culture, their fanaticism, their intolerance, as many historians do without hesitation. But we need only open the
monastic literature of these times to find a world of spirituality—such amazing refinement of the human mind, such
perception and holiness, such an all-embracing, wonderful
concept of the final meaning of our life!

Can even Justinian be fitted into his own plan "with
nothing left over" beyond his political schemes and calculations? Do we not see evidence even today in St. Sophia—
a church dedicated to wisdom, or meaning, whose very
cupola floods the world with an unearthly light—of some-

thing completely different in his dreams and visions? One point is beyond question: it was in just these decades that Christian culture began to be outlined and filled in. While Justinian's synthesis of Church and state would soon reveal its weakness, this culture of the Incarnate Word, the summit and symbol of which St. Sophia has remained throughout the ages, prevents us from oversimplifying that complex period.

Finally, we must not forget that in speaking of Church and state Byzantine historians usually confuse the relations of the state to the Church with those of the Church to the state. While in practice it is of course very difficult to make a precise distinction between them, it is extremely important to keep it in mind. The distinguishing feature of those ages was that two logics, completely different in origin and inspiration, clashed and were kept in precarious balance; from this came crises, breakdowns, and interruptions. The logic of the Roman theocratic state we have seen. The other was the Church's attitude toward the state, as at once "this world"—fallen, limited, and destined to be overcome in the final triumph of the kingdom of God—and the world of God's creation, man's dwelling, bearing the reflection of heavenly Reason and sanctified by the grace of Christ. These two logics met and clashed, not on an abstract plane but in living reality, with all the complexity and variety of factors operating within it. Moreover, they clashed in the mind of man, splitting it and introducing into it a tension it had not previously known. As the same people now composed both the world and the Church, conflict and tension were moved inward and became a problem of human thought, reason, and conscience.

On no account can all this be reduced to a victory of the state and its acceptance by the Church. Servile bishops leave on the surface of history a larger trace and echo than do Christians who really reveal the profundity of the Church's judgment of the world and the state, but do it gradually. Yet an attentive eye will perceive the Church's struggle for its inner freedom, even in the years when the empire outwardly triumphed. The emperor could do much, but not everything; a limitation was imposed on his absolutism from within.

This limitation was Christian truth. The abuse of power by the state was largely linked with the fact that a crystallization of the Church's experience and doctrine was going on within the Church itself, inevitably combined with divisions, disputes, and conflicts. But those who seemed on one day crushed by state absolutism were glorified on the next as saints, and the empire itself was obliged to revere the heroism of their opposition and their indomitable freedom of spirit. It is enough to mention once more the names Athanasius, Chrysostom, Euphemius, and Macedonius. Whatever the pressures of the state in their time, we are able to study and restore the evolution of Orthodoxy and all the profundity of the faith and experience of the Church —even if we forget these pressures and do not take them into account. Nicaea and Chalcedon were triumphant despite the state, which did everything to erase them from the mind of the Church; they triumphed only by force of the truth immanent in them. When Justinian, just before his death, indulged once more his personal passion for theologizing and attempted to impose, again by state edict, the dogma of the incorruptibility of Christ's body (a subtle question which divided the Monophysites at the time), the overwhelming majority of the bishops firmly and decisively declared that they preferred exile to acceptance of heresy. He died without taking further measures.

It is true that the problem of limitations on imperial authority within the Church was not raised in the mind of the Church. It had accepted the embraces of the Christian empire with hope and faith, and was destined to be crushed in them. The dream of a sacred empire was the dream of the Church as well for many long centuries. The grandeur of this concept constantly overshadowed its danger, limitations, and ambiguity in the Christian mind.

Yet this was not fear or servility, but faith in the cosmic destiny of the Church and the desire to render unto Christ the kingdom of the world. Therefore the Church never once betrayed or yielded its ultimate truth, for the sake of which it had accepted union with the empire.

Breakup of the Empire—Rise of Islam

Although Justinian's dream of empire was briefly realized, it was still only a dream; almost immediately after his death in 565 the empire began to fall apart. In 568 the wave of the Lombard invasion swept over Italy, the pressure of the Moors in Africa increased, and war never ceased in Spain. Islands of Byzantine influence would long be maintained in the West, but one could no longer speak of a Western empire. The eternal war with Persia, from which Justinian had ransomed himself in order to free his hands in the West, was renewed in 572. In about twenty years the Persians conquered part of Asia Minor, Syria, Palestine, and Egypt. In 619 the Persian fleet appeared before Constantinople and a hostile army occupied Chalcedon. From the north came invasions of Slavs, who were to be one of the main military and political problems of the empire in later times. In 626, when the Emperor Heraclius was gathering forces far from the capital to fight against Persia, the Avars, whose empire included the Slavs, surrounded Constantinople, and the Byzantines were to regard their deliverance from this siege as a miracle. The last favorable turn of events was Heraclius' victorious campaign against the Persians in 626–29, which brought the Byzantine army as far as Ctesiphon and liberated the whole East. In 630 he ceremoniously returned the Cross of Christ, which had been captured by the Persians, to Jerusalem.

But this was only a breathing spell. That same year, in remote Arabia, which had never previously been of interest, a band of fanatics around Mohammed conquered Mecca, united the scattered Arab tribes through the new religion of the one God, and created a source of inspiration, faith, and religious dynamism that became for many centuries the chief and most terrible rival of Christianity. Mohammed died in 632, and ten years later the empire of his followers included Persia, Palestine, Syria, and Egypt. When Heraclius, the last emperor of the still great empire, was dying in 641, the empire had already lost the whole East forever.

Thus the fate of Byzantium itself in the seventh century was finally decided in the East, and the emergence of Islam marks the borderline that divided the early empire, which was still Roman and universal in concept and thinking, from later Byzantium. The empire was becoming an Eastern state with a population homogeneous in cultural tradition, if not in blood, which lived under the unceasing pressure of alien worlds. Heraclius began the governmental reform, completed in the next century, which would enable Byzantium to survive for eight more centuries. This was the militarization of the state and its adaptation to its new situation as an island surrounded by enemies on all sides.

Still more important was the psychological and cultural evolution of the empire at the time. It has been defined as the "Hellenization" of Byzantium, but it would be more accurate to call it a second Hellenization. Rome itself, when it was building its empire, was quite Hellenized, and its climax in a cultural sense was also the climax of the Hellenistic period of world history. The Roman Empire performed a sort of synthesis here, and it was truly a Greco-Roman world. This is quite clear from the history of the Church in the time when it was spreading throughout the empire. Until the seventh century the state tradition of the empire remained this final Roman tradition. Although its center was gradually transferred from West to East, and however clear it became year by year that the West was lost, the empire still continued to be the direct heir of the principate of Augustus, the Antonines, and Diocletian.

The historians who attribute the final division of the Church wholly to contradictions between East and West, as a result of a supposed primal and absolute dualism between its Greek and Latin elements, are not only "naturalizing" Christianity but simply forgetting that it is impossible to derive any such dualism from the facts. For example, until the third century the language of the Roman Church was Greek; the father of all Western theology, St. Augustine, simply cannot be understood if we forget that he was rooted in Greek philosophy. And finally, the theology of the Eastern Fathers—Athanasius, the Cappadocians, and Cyril —was accepted and adopted in the West as completely as the theology of Leo the Great was accepted in the East. On the other hand, while Latin secular literature and Roman art were born under the influence of Hellas, Justinian's Code was still written in Latin, and Latin was still the official language of the Byzantine chancellory.

The unity of the Roman world was not destroyed by an internal division between East and West but by external catastrophe; the movement of peoples who flooded the western half of the empire and tore it from the East. This split, at first chiefly political and economic, led indeed to the obvious if gradual individualization of each world and its transformation from a half of an integrated whole into a self-contained unit, each increasingly inclined to interpret its tradition and development as a break from the original Roman universalism.

It was at this time that the second Hellenization of Byzantium took place, the beginning of a development which would finally transform it into a wholly Greek world. It can be traced in the change in official terminology, when Greek terms were replacing Latin; in the appearance of Greek inscriptions on coins; and in the change of legislative language from Latin to Greek. Though the Byzantines styled themselves officially "Romans" up to the downfall of the empire, the term acquired a completely new meaning. While the break from the West would never be complete or final, the triumph of Islam defined forever the boundaries of Byzantinism in the East. All that was not Greek, or was insufficiently Hellenized, fell outside the Byzantine orbit and opposed it as something alien and hostile.

Decay of the Universal Church

This evolution of Byzantium was immensely significant in the history of Orthodoxy. First, it meant a transformation of Orthodoxy into something like a national religion for a politically and culturally limited world. This "national" quality of Byzantine Christianity was still remote from the much later religious nationalism we shall see presently. It meant only a perceptible narrowing of the Church's historical horizon and orthodox way of thinking. In viewing the contrast, one may leave aside the truly universal conception of Irenaeus of Lyons, for example, and his joy in the unity of the Church throughout the world; and the awareness of the universal connection between all churches so forcefully revealed in the second and third centuries in the writings of Cyprian, Firmillian of Caesarea, Dionysius of Alexandria—and in Rome, of course, where ecumenical interests were never to disappear, although they assumed a new form.

Let us take only the example of the fourth century. This was a time when the union with the empire stimulated the mind of the Church, which regarded it as the source of a world triumph of Christianity. We need only recall the promising buds of Syrian Christian literature, mention the names of Jacob Aphraates, St. Ephraim the Syrian, and later St. Isaac the Syrian, and indicate the possibilities of Coptic Christianity, so tragically cut off from Orthodoxy by Monophysitism; or the missions to the Abyssinians, Goths, and Arabs. Even in the difference between trends and schools, between the psychological profiles of Antioch,

Alexandria, and Edessa, so unfortunately erased by the Christological dispute, were great possibilities for further development and mutual enrichment of the catholic tradition of the Church.

This is particularly apparent from the large number of Eastern and Egyptian liturgical rites that have come down to us from the period when the liturgy was not completely uniform according to the Byzantine style. With its victory over the empire, the Church was really beginning to express itself in various cultural traditions, making them part of the Church and in turn uniting the whole Mediterranean world. This by no means implies, of course, any absolute pluralism of traditions; Syrian and Coptic theologians remained within the framework of the same Christian Hellenism that had been the historic flesh of Christianity itself from New Testament times. Still, it made possible the enrichment of this Hellenism, as did the later injection of the Slavic element and its development into Russian Orthodoxy and Russian culture.

The expansion of Islam cut off all these developments. But it is important to keep in mind that the psychological decay of universalism had begun even before this—that in the Christological dispute the East was torn from Byzantine Orthodoxy, preferring the historical and theological dead ends of Monophysitism and Nestorianism to enslavement under the Orthodox empire. From this point of view the victory of Islam itself must be seen in relation to the first deep religious and political crisis in the Christian world: the first break on the historic way of Orthodoxy.

Last Efforts: Monothelitism

On the plane of the state and politics, therefore, the last imperial attempt to restore the religious unity of the empire by bringing the Monophysites back into the fold of the Orthodox Church was ineffective and too late. This was

"Monothelitism," a dispute over the will of Christ which the Emperor Heraclius had raised and which was a source of new disagreements and violence. It finally resulted in a new victory for Orthodoxy—the final step in the Christological dialectic. Although it was brought up for political reasons, the controversy essentially concerned comprehension of the Chalcedonian doctrine of Christ's God-Manhood. It may seem more than ever that this was a dispute over words and formulas, but again we must conclude that behind the words was revealed a difference in realization or understanding of Christ. It seemed to many Orthodox that the divergence between them and the moderate Monophysites, followers of Severus of Antioch, was in appearance only. The Monophysites rejected Chalcedon because they still thought that in the Chalcedonian concept of "two natures" Christ was divided and the unity of His Person, work, and sacrifice denied.

Monothelitism was an attempt to interpret Chalcedon in a way acceptable to the Monophysites. It was not a rejection of it but an explanation and adaptation. From the metaphysical sphere the question was shifted to psychology; in Christ there were two natures but a single action, one will. In other words, the two natures were not "expressed" in any way existentially, and the unity for the sake of which the Monophysites had split off was saved. All previous attempts to overcome Monophysitism had been excessively mechanical; they were directed toward enticing the Monophysites back into orthodoxy by concealing the real difference of view on both sides. This new attempt promised not to be mechanical. Its supporters did not cloak the meaning of orthodox doctrine, but really intended to clarify it and demonstrate that there were not two natures in the Chalcedonian doctrine, which would be equivalent to two *hypostases* or personalities.[8]

In all likelihood the initiator of this view was the patri-

---

[8] V. V. Bolotov, *Lectures in the History of the Ancient Church* (in Russian, St. Petersburg, 1907), Vol. 4.

arch of Constantinople, Sergius. He had suggested it to
Emperor Heraclius as a possible basis for religious unification with the Monophysites just at the moment when
Heraclius was mobilizing all the forces of the empire to
liberate the Eastern provinces from the Persians. In 622
the emperor met the head of the Severian Monophysites,
Paul the One-Eyed, in Karin (Erzerum), and in a theological discussion there used for the first time the expression
"one action"; hence the first stage of the dispute is usually
called "Mono-energism."

The emperor again assumed the initiative in this theological solution; the unfortunate lessons of the past could
not entirely cure this fundamental flaw of Roman theocracy. After a first attempt to feel out the ground, events
began to develop, and the result in 632 was a *unia* signed
in the form of nine anathemas and enforced by state edict.

Its success was only apparent; neither the Monophysites
nor the Orthodox accepted it. Although Cyrus of Alexandria, one of the chief participants in this attempt, wrote,
"Alexandria and all Egypt are delighted," only the leaders
recognized it. Most of the Copts did not follow the conciliatory hierarchs, and the same was true in Armenia,
Heraclius' main target in view of its strategic position between Byzantium and Persia. But since it was outwardly
successful, the document remained the official doctrine
of the empire, and Patriarch Sergius began to carry it out
within the Church.

At this point there was a reaction from the Orthodox
side. The act of union had been couched in extremely cau-
tious terms, yet it was still obviously a compromise. Its
defenders insisted that they were not departing from the
Tome of Leo the Great but were merely restating his faith.
Yet "single action" meant much more than only "a single
person." The difficulty was that by "divine energy" or the
total subordination of the human nature in Christ to the
divine (since God is the source of all Christ's human
actions), the Monothelites, like the Severians, meant the

passivity of His human energy. They compared the operation of the divinity in Christ's humanity with the operation of the soul in the human body. This customary analogy became dangerous in the present instance, for it did not point out the most important point: the human freedom within this divine energy, whereas the body is not free in its subordination to the soul.

The human element was presented too naturalistically and its unique feature was not pointed out with sufficient force, precisely because it was not perceived. The Monothelites were afraid to recognize the "natural" vital capacity of the human in Christ, "confusing it with independence; therefore the human aspect seemed to them inevitably passive."[9] In brief, Monothelitism again cut away the completeness of Christ's humanity, although very subtly, and deprived Him of that aspect without which man remains an empty form: human operation and human will.

The scholarly Palestinian monk Sophronius raised the alarm, urging Sergius and Cyrus to repudiate the expression "one operation" as unorthodox. Sergius sensed the danger when Sophronius became patriarch of Jerusalem in 634. Anticipating the latter's written confession of faith by which each newly-elected patriarch informed his fellows of his election, Sergius wrote to Pope Honorius in Rome endeavoring to bring him over to his side. Aware of Rome's sensitiveness to its position in the Church, he set out his nets very cleverly, and Pope Honorius immediately fell into them by accepting Monothelitism as a genuine expression of the orthodox doctrine of Christ. But while Sophronius lived, Sergius had difficulty in implementing his agreement with Rome. In 637 the patriarch of Jerusalem died, and the next year Emperor Heraclius issued his own *Exposition of Faith* (*Ecthesis*), which was openly Monothelite, to be accepted by the whole Church. Shortly afterward both Patriarch Sergius and Pope Honorius died.

In Constantinople Monothelitism was accepted for a

[9] Florovsky, *op. cit.*, p. 37.

long time, but in the West it immediately provoked an uproar of protests. The real struggle against the heresy was begun during the reign of the grandson of Heraclius, Constantine—or Constas, the diminutive by which he has been known in history. The chief defender of Orthodoxy during these years was the abbot of one of the monasteries of Constantinople, St. Maximus the Confessor. In Africa in 645 he entered into a public dispute against a former patriarch of Constantinople, the Monothelite Pyrrhus, and the transcription of this dispute is a major source of information for us about the controversy. Subsequently a number of synods in Africa condemned the heresy, and the Church's opposition to the state's confession of faith became increasingly obvious.

In 648, a new theological edict, the *Typos*, in which the emperor attempted to impose the *status quo* upon the Church, forbade any discussion of one or two wills. In response Pope Martin convoked a great council of 105 bishops in the Lateran basilica, where Monothelitism was solemnly condemned, and this condemnation was accepted by the whole Western Church. Now the problem shifted once more from discussion to persecution; in July 653 Pope Martin was arrested, and after lengthy torture brought to Constantinople where a prolonged martyrdom awaited him. After a disgraceful trial in the Senate during which he was charged with absurd political crimes—after beatings, mockery, and imprisonment—he was exiled to the Chersonesus (Crimea), where he died in September 655.

Soon St. Maximus the Confessor followed him along the same glorious and painful road. Again there were the same trial in the Senate and the same political accusations. Maximus answered in simple terms, but each of his answers hit the mark. According to tradition, in response to the judges' assertion that even Roman clergy had taken communion with the patriarch, Maximus answered, "Even if the whole world takes communion, I shall not." Maximus was sentenced to exile in Thrace. His sufferings lasted an-

other seven years. He was summoned back to Constantinople, browbeaten, tortured, and mutilated. Maximus remained adamant to the end and died during his last exile
in the Caucasus in 662.

Sixth Ecumenical Council

Every opposition seemed to have been broken, and the
whole empire was silent. This does not mean that the
Church accepted Monothelitism, however. The West continued to reject it; the power of Byzantium did not extend
beyond the borders of Italy and often seemed only nominal
in Rome itself. The emperor supported the heresy, but
when he died his successor Constantine Pogonatus, wearied
by this new division, gave the Church freedom to decide
the question in its essence and summoned an ecumenical
council—the sixth—which met from November 680 to September 681 in Constantinople. Monothelitism was rejected
and the Chalcedonian definition supplemented by the doctrine of two wills in Christ.

We preach also, according to the teachings of the Holy Fathers,
that in Him there are two natural wills or willings and two natural modes of action, indivisible, unalterable, inseparable, un-
merged. And the two natural wills are not contrary (one to
the other), as dishonorable heretics have said—let it not be so!—
but His human will follows, not as resisting or reluctant but
rather as subject to His Divinity and omnipotent will.

The modern mind is again bewildered: what do "two
wills" mean? And how can this be disputed and anything
decided about it? Yet by overcoming Monothelitism and
affirming the human will as well as the divine in Christ,
the Church laid the foundation for a Christian anthropol-
ogy, for a concept of man that has given definition to the
whole humanistic inspiration of our world and our culture.
Christian humanism, faith in the whole man and his abso-

lute value, is the final result of the Christological disputes
and a genuine discovery of Orthodoxy.

The council anathematized the leaders of the heresy, the
four patriarchs of Constantinople—Sergius, Paul, Pyrrhus,
and Timothy—as well as Cyrus of Alexandria and Pope
Honorius, whose condemnation by an ecumenical council
has constantly been referred to by the Orthodox as proof
that the ancient Church ignored any doctrine of papal
infallibility. On the other hand, those mainly responsible,
the emperors Heraclius and Constas, were passed over in
silence. Nor was mention made of the two martyrs for the
truth, St. Martin the Pope and St. Maximus the Confessor;
formally they were political criminals. Both names were
added to the list of confessors and teachers of the Church
only later, and this silence gives a rather unfortunate color
to the final victory of Orthodoxy in the Christological dispute. The truth continued to conquer, but men were unfortunately becoming accustomed to the double bookkeep-
ing of Byzantine theocracy.

Changing Church Structure

While Monothelitism resulted in a fruitful reaction from
Orthodox theology and in further development of the *Horos*
of Chalcedon, it justified none of the political hopes that
had been placed in it. The problem was finally settled at a
time when both Monophysites and Nestorians, whom it
was designed to attract, were separated permanently from
the empire by Islam and consequently no longer represented a danger of internal separatism. Orthodoxy had
become the state and even the national, Greek faith of
Byzantium; but this meant also that Orthodoxy itself had
merged completely with its Byzantine outer covering and
had accepted it as its "historical" canon.

This was expressed primarily in the final triumph of the
seat of Constantinople as the center of the whole Eastern

Church. Justinian in his Code had called the Church of Constantinople "the head of all other Churches" and was apparently the first to call its patriarch "ecumenical." The title provoked sharp protests from Pope Gregory the Great at the end of the sixth century, but nevertheless became under Heraclius the usual title of the patriarchs of the imperial city. The Greeks, it is true, have always made the reservation that it does not signify that the patriarch of Constantinople is in any way superior to his brethren, and in the twelfth century one of the most authoritative Byzantine canonists, Theodore Balsamon, did not regard the patriarch of Constantinople as holding "any of the advantages which adorn the Pope of Rome." Indeed, the Greeks have never suffered from "papism" in the sense of claiming that the bishop of the capital held any divinely established primacy over other bishops.

Yet the structure of the Church, of which the patriarch of Constantinople became the central point, differed essentially from what we saw when the Church first united with the Roman Empire. Canonically everything remained as it had been; the universal structure of the Church remained as always a union of autocephalous (i.e., autonomous) patriarchs, the bishops of the large cities retained their pompous titles, and dogmatically speaking, every bishop remained what he had been in the doctrine of St. Cyprian of Carthage, St. Hippolytus of Rome, or—even earlier—St. Ignatius of Antioch: the image of God, the fully-empowered preserver of apostolic tradition, and the bearer of the unity of his bishopric. In fact, however, such local churches, which had previously felt themselves to be the people of God in all its fullness in a particular locality, were increasingly becoming eparchies or administrative subdivisions of a greater whole; and the head of the eparchy, the bishop, was accordingly becoming a representative or agent of the central, higher Church authority concentrated in the hands of the patriarch of Constantinople and the patriarchal synod.

The change in the practice of episcopal consecration is extremely indicative of this. According to the *Apostolic Tradition* of St. Hippolytus of Rome, a document of the first half of the third century, a newly-elected bishop was always consecrated amid the congregation of the Church to which he was elected—among the people whose spiritual father, first priest, and pastor he was to be, and with their prayerful participation. It was the bishop's marriage to the Church, according to St. Paul's teaching in the Epistle to the Ephesians. Immediately after his consecration he celebrated the Eucharist, and the bishops who had laid hands upon him participated in this Eucharist as concelebrants. Also the bishop naturally remained in his Church to the end of his days, so that a Church which had lost its bishop was called "widowed."

In the course of time, however, the significance of the local Church was progressively weakened, giving way to a centralized concept. By the fourth century we encounter bishops shifting from one see to another. At first the practice was generally condemned, but the protests dwindled, and the transfer of bishops from see to see became so usual that much later, in Petrine Russia, it had become the norm of Church life. Bishops were increasingly accepted as assistants, representatives, and executives of the orders of central power, and a new institution naturally developed which had been absolutely unknown in the early Church: the episcopal synod of the patriarch.

The early Church had known episcopal councils, but their significance had been that local churches were really represented; they participated in the person of their bishops. The bishop, uniting his flock, was its voice and the witness to its faith, and for it he was the voice of the Church Universal expressed at the council. The synod, on the other hand, was an administrative organ, and for a bishop to participate in it meant, however paradoxical it may sound, that he was in fact separated from his own flock and Church. The synod did not feel itself to be the "mouth of the Church" as a council would be, but a sort of permanent authority which the bishops represented in their local churches. We have seen that the synod of Constantinople was formed almost haphazardly, being composed of bishops who happened to be passing through the capital on various business. Once established, however, it soon became a permanent institution, and the obvious reason for this was the increasing parallelism between the structures of Church and empire. Later Byzantine documents, as we shall see, openly confirm the parallel between them: the patriarch corresponded to the emperor and the synod to the Senate. This is far removed from the sacramental root of the structure of the early Church.

When Egypt, Palestine, and Syria fell under the rule of Islam, Constantinople became the only patriarchal see in the empire, and naturally the see became "ecumenical," since the empire was called *oekumene*, the universe. During the Christological dispute, Constantinople was obliged to oppose the other Eastern centers: Alexandria, Antioch, and Ephesus. The capital was frequently the source of heresies and of compromise with heresies; but it assumed the whole weight of the struggle for Chalcedonian orthodoxy. From the time of Justinian and the separation of the churches, the orthodox Chalcedonian bishops of Antioch and Alexandria, competing with local Monophysite hierarchy, were not local men but appointed from Constantinople. This sort of control from the capital increased in the seventh century; to replace the patriarch of Antioch, Macarius (deposed for Monothelitism by the Sixth Ecumenical Council), the orthodox Theophanes was simply appointed and consecrated right in Constantinople. This practice became usual in the Orthodox Church for a very long time to come. The patriarchs of Antioch and Alexandria became leaders of small groups of Melkites, or Greek minorities in a Monophysite sea, and naturally came to regard themselves as representatives of the center, the powerful ecumenical patriarch.

The importance of the patriarch of Constantinople increased so much by reason of these various circumstances that he assumed the position of head of the whole Eastern Church, much as the Roman pope stood at the head of the Western Church.[10] The analogy must not, of course, be carried too far. The Roman pope in the West not only assumed the position of head, but the fall of the empire made him the bearer of secular authority as well—the source of imperial and state structure. The Byzantine patriarch, on the contrary, acquired his position because the theory of "symphony" demanded a parallelism between the structure of state and Church. While the empire was personified in the emperor, the priesthood must also have a single personification—which became the ecumenical patriarch of the new Rome.

Byzantine Theology

Following the development of ecclesiastical structure, a characteristically Byzantine evolution took place in Orthodox theological tradition. Here Constantinople long lacked a personality of its own—its own school, like Alexandria or Antioch. It was either under the tradition of one of the competing tendencies or obliged to occupy a position of compromise because of its imperial interests. Chalcedon was the first step in a theology specifically Byzantine, in that it overcame the extremes of the two main traditions and combined them in a creative synthesis. Byzantine theology developed further along this same road. The main stages were marked by the Fifth and Sixth Ecumenical Councils, the theme of which was the deepening, the more precise definition, and the assimilation of the Chalcedonian dogma.

Yet while Chalcedonian orthodoxy was at first a sort of

10 T. Barsov, *The Patriarch of Constantinople and His Power in the Russian Church* (in Russian, St. Petersburg, 1878), p. 104.

synthesis between Alexandria and Antioch, the conclusions resulting from this synthesis were a specific feature of Byzantine Orthodoxy. A reference to the past and to tradition has always had fundamental importance in the Church. Thus the early Christian writers made much use of the adjective "apostolic": for example, the *Apostolic Tradition* of St. Hippolytus of Rome, and the later *Apostolic Constitutions* and *Apostolic Canons*. This did not mean to convey the idea of original apostolic authorship, but only that the writer regarded the proposed doctrine as stemming from the apostles, as part of the same unchanging and eternal tradition of the Church. After the fourth century a similar meaning attended reference to the Fathers, those theologians and teachers whose teaching was finally accepted by the Church as an expression of its experience and tradition, and hence became normative.

After the Council of 381, Emperor Theodosius in a special law pointed out to his subjects certain bishops, communion with whom should be *de facto* an outward sign of orthodoxy. He did this to bring order out of the chaos that reigned as a result of the Arian dispute. In the fifth century St. Athanasius and the Cappadocian Fathers, St. Basil the Great, Gregory the Theologian, and Gregory of Nyssa, were recognized unconditionally by everyone, and the argument that something came "from the Fathers" acquired increasing importance. The Christological disputes again raised questions as to the orthodoxy of whole theological traditions; we have seen that the Fifth Ecumenical Council was forced to condemn theologians who had already died and had been revered in their regions as Fathers. The Fifth Council furnished a sort of review and re-evaluation of local traditions, and it was natural that a list of "Selected Fathers," undisputed bearers of orthodox tradition, should be composed there for the first time. It included St. Athanasius the Great, Hilary of Poitiers (a Western opponent of Arianism), Basil the Great, Gregory the Theologian, Gregory of Nyssa, Ambrose of Milan, Augustine, Chrysostom, Theophilus and Cyril of Alexandria, Leo the Great, and Proclus. Not one "Father" was from Constantinople. Proclus had been patriarch in the capital but expressed the Alexandrian tendency in his theology. Byzantine theology began by summing up, overcoming contradictions, co-ordinating words and concepts. Therefore it was in Byzantium that the cycle of tradition was first outlined and the "patristic testaments" defined which would forever remain the foundation of Orthodox theology. The pre-Nicene Fathers and almost all the "Eastern" teachers remained outside this cycle. In content Byzantine theology was limited to two themes: the doctrine of the Trinity and the doctrine of the God-Man. These were the themes of the great dogmatic disputes of the fourth and fifth centuries, and all the resources of the Byzantine ecclesiastical mind went into developing and assimilating them.

Quality of Life in the New Age

In the seventh century there was a perceptible coarsening of morals, a certain "barbarization" of the whole pattern of life. The centuries of invasion, impoverishment, and constant military tension had left their mark. One could already sense the approach of the Middle Ages, in the negative sense (which in no way excludes their positive aspects), and much even in the life of the Christian community reflected this coarsening. Christians had become used to Christianity and it had become an ordinary, everyday matter.

This is the main impression we receive from the decrees of the so-called *Consilium Quintisextum*, or Trullan Council, of 691, summoned by Emperor Justinian II to supplement by disciplinary decrees the work of the Fifth and Sixth Ecumenical Councils, which had been limited to purely doctrinal action. The life of the Church required clear regulatory principles, and the Trullan Council (so called from the pillared hall of the palace in which the sessions were held) provided them in the form of 102 canons. They give us a picture of the daily life of the Church in that period. The purpose of the Council was to heal infirmities, and its decrees, of course, reflect only the negative aspects and defects of the Church community, but these are interesting just because they indicate the extent to which the empire was Christianized after four centuries of the "age of Constantine."

So far as the social and political scene was concerned, Christianity had conquered beyond question. The defects in the Church community themselves resulted from this victory and its decisiveness. Christianity had entered into the flesh and blood of mankind, a large fraction of which had been unified by the empire, and in the depths it of course defined, evaluated, and judged life. This will be discussed presently.

Yet no victory maintains itself; it requires constant effort and tension, but inevitably the tension begins to slacken. For example, in the struggle against the pagans and its heroic conquest of the world, the Church had never hesitated in adapting many "natural" forms of religion, usual for paganism, to the service of Christianity. The pagans had celebrated the birth of the Invincible Sun on December 25; Christians allotted to this date the celebration of the birth of Christ, which taught men "to honor the Sun of Righteousness and to come to know it from the height of the East."[11] The pagans had celebrated an "epiphany" on January 6, which became the date of the Christian Epiphany as well. The ecclesiastical cult of "Unmercenary Saints" had much in common with the pagan cult of the Dioscuri; the forms of the Christian saint's life with the models of pagan eulogies of heroes; and finally, the explanation of the Christian sacraments to the catechumens with the mysterial terminology of pagan initiations.

[11] Hymn for Christmas Day.

However, all these borrowings were in fact only formal; the Church filled the mold that was customary for the time with all the novelty of its Gospel, the image of Christ and His followers, so that the mold itself was entirely converted to the Church and became a vehicle for the light, wisdom, and vital force of the Gospel. The central point, however, is that no conversion is in itself a guarantee of the purity of Christianity, and no form—even the most Christian in essence and origin—can magically save, if it is not filled with the Spirit and the truth by which it is justified and which it serves. One must keep in mind that paganism comprises not only the religions which preceded Christianity chronologically and were eliminated when it appeared; it is also a sort of permanent and natural magnetic pole of religion, and in this sense a constant threat for every religion. Christianity demands unceasing effort, continual filling of its forms with content, self-testing, and "trial of the spirit." Any divergence between form and content, or the emergence of form as a value and goal in itself, is paganism. It is a return to natural religion, to belief in form, ceremony, and sacred objects without regard to their content and spiritual meaning. In this sense even Christian rites and sacred objects may themselves become centers of pagan veneration and may overshadow what they solely exist for: the liberating force of truth.

This tendency becomes perceptible in the seventh century, appearing as a kind of price for the complete political victory of Christianity. In 530 a Byzantine monk, Barsanuphius, attacked "mechanical" religiosity which reduces the whole significance of Christianity to external forms. "If you pass by relics, bow down once, twice, thrice . . . but that is enough. Cross yourselves three times if you wish, but no more."[12] Other teachers attacked those who express their faith only by "covering crosses and icons with kisses." What are the Gospels and communion to them? If the Gospel is

12 J. Pargoire, L'Église Byzantine de 527 à 847 (Paris, 1923), p. 221.

too long and the prayers dragged out longer than usual, they display signs of impatience and displeasure. Even during short services, Christians fill the time talking about business or condemning their neighbors. Others simply stand on the street so as to run into church at the last moment and "take communion on the run," as St. Anastasius of Sinai expressed it. But they are perfect Christians, for have they not kissed the icons of Our Redeemer and the saints? In Byzantine society were many examples of the sins of superstition and a superficial attitude toward the faith. Behind them loomed something still more terrifying: under the Christian outer covering a most obvious dual faith continued to exist. Many of the canons of the Trullan Council are devoted to the struggle against open distortions of Christianity and its transformation into pagan magic.

Unfortunately the clergy themselves, supposed to be a model for the faithful "in word, life, love, spirit, faith and purity," were not beyond reproach. In many places the level of clerical education fell: the council assigned the bishops to preach every Sunday, and not to give way to their own ideas but to be guided by the Fathers. Many canons forbid presbyters to maintain hotels, lend money on interest, accept payment for ordination, or play games of chance. They portray a perceptible decay in the monastic life as well; the council especially insisted that monasticism is a way to salvation, not a means of avoiding military service or achieving a secure old age. Monks should not leave the monasteries, spend the night under the same roof with a woman, or arrange a celebration for their own tonsure.

All this does not mean that religious life in Byzantium consisted only of defects. The council mentions them because its purpose is to combat them. If only by their resemblance to the defects of almost all subsequent periods of Church history, they demonstrate that Christianity had ceased to be selective, had become the religion of the masses, and for too many was only a self-evident form the inner meaning of which was not even considered. For these it had truly become a natural religion, and they no longer heard its call for a "renewal of nature."

Church life at this period cannot of course be judged only by the canons of the Trullan Council. The effort to remedy defects and expose sins is evidence that spiritual leaders had preserved unsullied the genuine ideal of Christianity. Moreover, this ideal had truly grown into the human mind, fundamentally transforming not only individual lives but the whole spirit of the culture, all that composed its main value for each era. For the past must be studied and judged from its concepts and from the treasures toward which its heart strives—not only by its failures. In other words, we must discover not only how far this society realized its ideal, but just what the ideal was.

Development of the Liturgy

From this point of view, nothing expresses the spirit of the age better than the Byzantine Church services, which began to be arranged just at this time into a sort of system, a structured world of forms and modes which has remained the permanent and unsurpassed pinnacle of Eastern Orthodoxy. Many varied factors affected its development and establishment in the services of the Orthodox Church, and even today we may distinguish the strata of various periods, each of which had its own liturgical key. The first was the synagogue and the Old Testament foundation of the early Christian cult, which the Sacrament crowned and filled with new meaning. Second, there was the development of a daily cycle in which the features of monastic psalmody were reflected. Later came the swift growth of the cult of saints and the influence of dogmatic disputes, expressed mainly in the increased number of Church feasts. Finally, the characteristic features of the Church's new position in the state and in society caused various aspects of human life to be sanctified by the Church. We shall see some of these details in the next chapter.

After the evolution of ecclesiastical structure noted earlier came that of other forms of Church life, primarily the liturgy. Here also the triumph of a specifically Byzantine tradition, that of Constantinople, is visible and gradually grew in strength. The early Church had a number of local liturgical traditions. In the Acts of the Apostles the Eucharist was defined as an assembly "of all together for one and the same purpose"—for the eternal realization of the sole and unique Supper—but each Church expressed this fundamental uniform content in its own form, which was the fruit of genuine liturgical creativity.

Almost a hundred anaphoras, or eucharistic prayers, have come down to us from ancient times, ascribed to different names, but each essentially expressing long liturgical experience and revealing the basic and unalterable meaning of the Eucharist in human words. Thus modern liturgical scholarship distinguishes types of eucharistic prayers—the Jerusalem, the Alexandrian, the Roman, the Syrian, the Persian, and so on—each of which combines in turn a whole group of liturgies having their own characteristics. Even more forcefully than purely theological literature, here each Christian tradition expresses its spirit, its ethos, its interpretation of the universal truth of the Church.

The Church of Constantinople, however, not being an ancient one, had no such clearly expressed tradition as Egypt or Syria. For a long period there was a struggle between various influences—that of Antioch, expressed by St. John Chrysostom and Nestorius, and that of Alexandria, expressed by Anatolius, who was elected patriarch at the Synod of Robbers—and each was naturally reflected in the development of the liturgy. We know, for example, that Chrysostom brought into Constantinople much of Antiochene liturgical practice, and Nestorius protested against the use of the term "Mother of God" in the liturgy.

On the other hand, the permanent link with the court,

the constant presence of the emperor at the liturgy, and the imperial concept of the Church of St. Sophia inevitably carried weight. The tradition of Constantinople came to include elements of court ritual which expressed the theocratic concept of imperial authority and made everything surrounding the emperor "divine."

Finally, through Constantine, the influence of liturgical customs in Jerusalem was very perceptible. In the fourth century Jerusalem was a center of general interest; majestic churches were built there, pilgrims came from all over the world, and there, in the Holy Land, steeped in memories of the earthly life of the Savior, the services became increasingly dramatic. This is well demonstrated in the diary of Etheria, a pilgrim from Gaul who visited the Holy Land at the end of the fourth century and left a detailed description of its Church customs.

Thus the liturgical pattern that gradually formed in the capital was naturally a synthesis of various traditions and influences. Its basic features were formed in the seventh century, when the see of Constantinople was elevated permanently to the central position in the whole Orthodox Church of the East. Once formed, it not only influenced the other "local" traditions but soon became the only form of divine service for the whole Eastern Orthodox Church. Thus the Byzantine liturgy in its dual form, that of Chrysostom and of Basil the Great, gradually squeezed out the ancient Alexandrian liturgy known by the name of St. Mark, as well as the Antiochene liturgy of St. James, brother of the Lord. This triumph of the Byzantine rite applied not only to the Eucharist but to the whole cycle of divine services. The "Byzantine rite" in the end became the only rite of the Orthodox Church.

Late Byzantium furnishes the definitive system of services. In the seventh century, the basic tone of liturgical creativeness may already be sensed. It was founded, of course, upon Holy Scripture. The language of the Bible became and remained the language of the Church, and this not only because it was permeated with religion and full of rich images, or corresponded strikingly to religious feelings in all their variety. The faith and experience of the Church are inseparable from the Scriptures, which are its source. Everything the Church believes and by which it lives took place "according to the Scriptures" ("For I delivered to you first of all that which I also received, how that Christ died for our sins according to the Scriptures; And that he was buried, and that he rose again the third day according to the Scriptures: . . ." (I Cor. 15:3–4). But this "according to the Scriptures" means much more than fulfillment of prophecies and predictions; it means first of all the inner link between what Christ did and what the Scripture relates—aside from this link neither Scripture nor the meaning of Christ's acts can be understood. The unfolding and deepening reflection of this link is precisely the content of the Christian service, of Church poetry, and even of the rite itself.

Veneration of the Virgin Mary

Since it is impossible to illustrate this development in all its complexity, let us take one example with very particular meaning for the Church: the gradual growth in the services of the veneration of the Mother of God, which plays such an important part in the liturgical life of the Church. This example is significant also because most historians of religion regard the cult of the Virgin Mary as indubitable proof of a metamorphosis within Christianity, the penetration of an ancient, almost primeval cult of the fertility forces in nature. Their main argument is that in the first centuries we see no special singling out of Mary, let alone a cult, which did not arise until the fifth century— just the period when Christianity became "reconciled" with the world.

Other historians, while they establish historical reasons

for each of the Mariological feasts, the time it appeared, and the authors of the texts, still miss the main point: that what gives significance to the flourishing of these feasts of the Virgin is the growing strength of the Mariological theme in the content of the Church services. Finally, the Protestants, as is well known, simply reject veneration of the Mother of God because it lacks "biblical basis."

Yet it was precisely because of the biblical basis that this veneration arose; it is linked first of all with the Bible. This biblical basis is the reflection of the Old Testament in the New, as I have just shown, and on the other hand, the discovery of even more profound meaning in the Old Testament in the light of the New. For example, the Feast of the Entrance of the Virgin into the Temple, which probably arose at the end of the seventh century and for which hymns written by St. Andrew of Crete have been preserved, has no formal biblical basis; the Gospel tells us nothing of any such event. Yet we need only read the liturgical texts of this feast in their original form (they have been significantly altered since then) to see the genuinely mystical insight or reflection that lay behind the feast.

If we constantly and prayerfully read Scripture, our attention is drawn continuously to new depths of meaning in it. Thus, the Temple at Jerusalem occupies an important position in both the Old Testament and the Gospel, and Christ compares Himself to this unique and sacred center of Judaism, the meeting point of all its religious life: "Destroy this temple, and in three days I will raise it up . . ." He is speaking of the temple of His Body. But even from this it is clear that Christians could not help but regard the Old Testament Temple as a prefiguration of another religious meeting point, another unique and all-embracing center. The whole positive significance of the Temple was fulfilled in Christ—He was the new Temple, and this Temple is Man, his body and his soul.

We have already noted the significance of this contrast between the two temples—the Temple at Jerusalem and that of the Church "not made by hands": the Body of Christ—for Christian Church buildings. The Christian reflection did not stop with this, however. In a time when the Church was growing in its understanding of Christ's humanity, amid the tension of all its spiritual forces, it inevitably included in its reflection the Person from whom Christ had received His humanity, His Body. If God had chosen a Man to be His Temple in the future, then the Virgin Mary was such a temple of God in a most particular and literal sense, "for what was born from Her is holy." Her body was a temple erected by the Old Testament itself, by all its sacredness, its expectation of salvation, its faithfulness to God, which made possible the union of God with Man, and in this sense She is the fruit of the Old Testament Temple, of that link with God which the Temple expressed. If this is so, then reflection reaches out to the relationship between this living temple and that other one whose significance, as the only center and source of salvation and union with God, Christ came to "fulfill" by His Incarnation: "The all-pure Temple of the Savior . . . today is led into the Temple of the Lord,"[13] and in this entry the final meaning of the Temple is revealed and it in turn is transcended.

One may object that this would be a feast for an "idea" which had become encrusted with "myth." This is both true and false. The concept is based on an undoubted historical fact, the entry of the Virgin Mary, like every Jewish girl, into the Temple at Jerusalem. True, the fact has not been documented, but it is beyond doubt, since it is self-evident: clearly in any case Mary entered the Temple and was in the Temple. While the liturgical formulation of events narrated in the Gospels is guided of course by the narrative itself, here in the divine service the historical fact is gradually surrounded with poetic or symbolic details that

[13] Kontakion of the Feast, cf. I. F. Hapgood, *A Service Book of the Holy Orthodox Catholic Apostolic Church* (3d ed.; Brooklyn, N.Y., 1956), page 172.

emphasize the significance the Church has found in it. Fundamentally this is just a theological unfolding of the Scriptures and of all the meanings inherent in them—a reflection of the realities of Christianity.

The same may be said of the other feasts of the Mother of God, which gradually developed into a whole *Theotokos* cycle, paralleling the liturgical cycle of John the Baptist. There was no "metamorphosis," only the development of the original experience of the Church. It is enough to read the very earliest texts of the services for the Mother of God to be convinced that veneration of her not only did not eclipse the Christocentrism of the early Church, or introduce any neopagan elements into Christianity, as certain scholars—even Christian ones—assert; but is on the contrary wholly rooted in the Church's reflection of the image of the Savior as God and Man.

Veneration of the Mother of God quickly colored the whole Church service, and this perhaps reveals one of the most profound aspects of the Christianization of the world at that time. From those centuries when the Christian seed was only beginning to grow, and few changes for the better were outwardly apparent in morals, in society, in social and governmental ideals—when, on the contrary, a pronounced barbarization of the world might even be observed—the image of the Mother, from whom all humanity gained sonship on the Cross, an image of complete purity, meekness, love, and self-abnegation, reigns forever over this world. The Church's experience of the Mother of God is profoundly Christian, or more accurately, it is human in a Christian way. In this experience dogmatic understanding is permeated with a sympathy utterly delicate and personal—in it attention is focused for the first time on the meaning of one's personal life, and it penetrates into the depths of the human image and elevates it to divine radiance. The veneration of the Mother of God, the first fruit of the Church's exploration of the dogma of Christ's God-Manhood, is the source of the tenderness and sensitivity that Christianity introduced into human consciousness. And the world which sensed so palpably the protection of this maternal love, which could sing of it and deck it in such beauty, was a world already profoundly Christian regardless of all its sins and imperfections.

Reflection of Theology and Asceticism in the Services

A characteristic feature of the period must be recognized in the gradual permeation of theological experience into liturgical poetry and the Church services. While the Bible remained the basic content and framework of the services, as it had always been—the Psalms, the Old Testament hymns, the reading—this framework increasingly included the creations of Church hymn-writers: *kontakia, stichera,* and canons. First comes St. Romanos Melodus, who died probably in the middle of the sixth century. The rise of the so-called *kontakion* form of liturgical poetry, later pushed aside by the canon, is linked with his name. What has reached us from him (the *kontakion* of Christmas, "Today a virgin bringeth forth the Super-substantial"; for Easter, "Though Thou hast descended into the grave, O Deathless One"; and so on) [14] indicates his immense poetic talent, and in his works we fully sense what one may call the miracle of Byzantine liturgical writing: the striking combination of plastic literary form and genuine poetry with a profoundly theological, penetrating content. In comparison with later Byzantine works, which contain so much watery rhetoric, the early strata of our service books reveal real treasures. This is already great Christian poetry, which of course bears witness to the maturity of Christian culture. Another amazing monument from this same period is the *Akathistus* or "not-sitting hymn" (it was always sung standing), long ascribed to Patriarch Sergius the Monothelite,

[14] Cf. Hapgood, *op. cit.*, pp. 178, 230.

and composed, according to tradition, after the miraculous escape of Byzantium from the siege of 626.

A somewhat different note is introduced by the works connected with ascetic experience: the Great Canon of St. Andrew of Crete, who died in the first half of the eighth century, is the finest of these and is still read on the first days of Lent. While the heritage of Melodus contained in poetic form the revelation of the Church's dogma and doctrine, particularly the Trinity and the doctrine of the two natures, the Great Canon is dedicated wholly to repentance. Monasticism had from the first been a road of repentance, but it is characteristic that in the liturgical handling of this theme there is an almost exaggerated self-incrimination and self-blame. Again one must be aware of the whole significance of this element; it emphasizes the defects in the Church previously discussed. The monastic community is not reconciled with evil and does not minimize Christianity. Most important of all, the deep sigh of repentance we now hear in Orthodox Church services as a constant theme expresses again how deeply the image of the Man revealed in the Gospel, and assimilated in the experience of holy men by fasting, prayer, and vigil, had entered into the mind of the Church. Behind the customary images of the Psalter and the all-embracing sense of God's majesty, before which everything seemed trivial, there now sounded forcefully a longing for man's "primeval beauty." It is repentance coming not only from a recognition of broken commandments or from fear or worship of God, but from a human being who recognizes an "image of inexpressible glory" within himself and is therefore able to measure the full depth of his downfall. This was a real longing for divinity, a constant view of oneself in the light of the God-Man.

There were many sins and much evil in the Byzantine ecclesiastical community, but self-satisfaction was not one of them. Toward the end of the early Byzantine period it was as if the whole Church were decked in black monastic garb and had taken the road of repentance and self-condemnation. The stronger the outward victory of the Church and the more solemn, rich, and magnificent the outward forms of Christian Byzantinism became, the more strongly sounded this outcry of repentance, the entreaty for forgiveness: "I have sinned, I have transgressed, I have been unrighteous in Thy sight, nor have I done nor have I observed what Thou hast commanded us."

The surpassing beauty and splendor of St. Sophia; the holy rhythm, seeming to measure eternity, of the liturgical mystery that revealed a heaven upon earth and transformed the world again and again into its pristine cosmic beauty; the bitter sadness and reality of sin, the awareness of constant downfall—all this was the ultimate profundity of this world and the fruit of the Church within it.

Thus outwardly the Byzantine cycle describes Orthodoxy at the end of the first four centuries of the "period of Constantine." In the seventh century this cycle was only perceptible as yet. The real climax of Orthodox Byzantium would come in the next era, and it is there that we must consider the Seventh Ecumenical Council, since that period overlaps the title of this chapter.

Like every historical form, Byzantinism was of course limited and imperfect and had a number of defects. In the final account, however, unlike other forms, it alone would express the unshakable historicism of Christianity, its link with the fate of the world and of man. Though this marriage between Church and empire was the source of so many weaknesses and sins, all that rejected it in the East at the time became a blind alley, an exit from history, doomed to gradual decay in sterile sands. In the story of Orthodoxy, however, a new time was beginning which would bring new pain but new victories as well.

4 BYZANTIUM

Significance of the Byzantine Period

It is strange that the Orthodox mind has had so little interest in Byzantium. As a field of study, Byzantium has been the domain either of secular historians—among whom, of course, Russian scholars have held and rightly still hold a leading position—or of specialists on specific problems. Despite the abundance of monographs in which Orthodox historical scholarship may take a confident pride, there exists no history of the Byzantine Church in the full sense of the word, which would both describe and try to comprehend this phenomenon in its totality. Somehow entire centuries have slipped from the Church's memory, and this makes every attempt at a rapid survey of Byzantium extremely difficult. The only thing that can be done is to try to give some sense of the meaning of the Byzantine problem.

Byzantium can in no way be considered merely a completed and outlived chapter of Church history. Not only does it continue to live in the Orthodox Church, but in a sense still defines Orthodoxy itself, constituting its historical form. Just as modern Catholicism crystallized in the Middle Ages and in the era of the Counter-Reformation, so—perhaps to an even greater extent—did Orthodoxy acquire its present form, its historic canon, in Byzantium. Simple inquiry will

198

soon show that any aspect of modern Orthodox Church
life to which one might refer found its present-day form in
the Byzantine period in particular. The development of
the Rule of worship was completed in Byzantium, a Rule
which makes of it a system permitting almost no progress
or change. The Byzantine *typicons* and *euchologia* of the
thirteenth and fourteenth centuries differ hardly at all from
our own missals and rule-books. The Orthodox icon is
painted in accordance with the Byzantine tradition; our
canonical tradition was fixed in both volume and interpretation by Byzantine canonists. The patristic heritage, which
has until now been the basis of Orthodox theology, was
given final shape in Byzantium, and there first flowered the
manner and spirit of Orthodox piety which is best expressed
in Russian by the word *tserkovnost*. In a sense the Byzantine
period must be acknowledged as decisive in the history of
Orthodoxy, as the age of the crystallization of Church life.
The modern Orthodox Church is—from the viewpoint of
history—the Church of Byzantium, which has survived the
Byzantine Empire by five hundred years.

All historians of Byzantium declare in unison that a new
period in her history opened with the beginning of the
eighth century. The seventh century had ended in anarchy
and the almost complete ruin of the empire. In the year 717
the Arabs besieged Constantinople, and internal disorder
made her an easy prey for any conqueror. Leo the Isaurian
—one of those soldiers from the eastern border country, numerous in the Byzantine army, who often rose to the highest ranks and by whom the empire was actually held
together—saved her. Leo was proclaimed emperor and thus
began the new Isaurian dynasty. In a series of victorious
wars, he and his son Constantine Copronymus (717–45,
745–75) retrieved the situation and added internal strength
by a profound military, economic, and administrative reform of the state. This reform, completing the evolution
already begun under Heraclius, concluded the metamorpho-

sis of Byzantium from a world empire into a comparatively small state in which all was subordinated to the need of withstanding pressure: that of Islam from the east, the Slavs from the north, and—soon to come—the Normans from the west. The Roman *oekumene* had finally been transformed into Byzantium.

Background of Iconoclasm

For the Church this period opens with a new disturbance, one that has branded the names of the Isaurian emperors in its memory forever. This was iconoclasm, cause of a prolonged struggle lasting almost half a century. There has been much scholarly dispute as to its origins. Some have seen in it the influence of the Mohammedan East, with its ban on human images, and an attempt at a certain psychological compromise with Islam; others, the first revolt against the Church of a secular culture inspired by the emperors, and a struggle for the liberation of art from the Church; while a third group has detected a new outburst of the perennial Hellenic "spiritualism," for which the veneration of icons was a manifestation in religion of the artificial and material.

At any rate, it has been customary since the tenth century to lay all responsibility for the rise and spread of heresy at the feet of the emperors. But new research shows that the dispute over icons first arose in the Church itself, and that state authority interfered in a peremptory way only later. It has also been shown that there were sufficient grounds for the dispute.

The veneration of icons has had a long and complicated history. It, too, is the fruit of men's gradual assimilation of the Church's faith. The early Church did not know the icon in its modern, dogmatic significance. The beginning of Christian art—the paintings of the catacombs—is of a symbolic nature. It is not the portrayal of Christ, of the saints, or of the various events of sacred history as on an icon, but the expression of certain ideas about Christ and the Church: first and foremost, the sacramental experience of baptism and the Eucharist—that is to say, the twofold Mystery through which salvation is granted to him who believes.

In art of a signitive kind it is not the interpretation of its subjects—for *how* they are interpreted makes no difference to its aims—but their selection and combination that are important. It is not so much inclined to depict divinity as it is to portray the function of divinity. The Good Shepherd of the sarcophagi and the catacombs is not only not an image, he is not even a symbol of Christ; he is the visual signification of the idea that the Saviour saves, that He has come to save us, that we are saved by Him. Daniel in the lion's den is likewise not a portrait of even the most conventional sort, but a symbol of the fact that Daniel was saved and that we have been saved like Daniel. This art cannot be called art in the real sense of the word. It neither represents nor expresses; it signifies, and it signifies that fiery core, that living sun of faith in the "mysteries" to which the martyrs and pastors of those centuries, the newly-baptized pagans, the rite of their baptism, and the enemies of the Christian Church themselves all bear witness.[1]

But, although it renounced art for the sake of something else, this painting of the catacombs actually proved to be a cause of the rise of

that new, medieval art, religious and Christian throughout, which gradually consolidated itself both in the east and in the west of the Empire. In order that it might arise, corporeal and mental forms and images had to become spiritual, a naturalistic art had to become transcendental. So as to come to life and be reborn, art was obliged to renounce itself and plunge, as though into a baptismal font, into the pure element of faith. It accepted "penitence for its life" and was washed "in the

[1] V. V. Weidle, *The Baptism of Art* (Westminster, England, 1950).

waters of everlasting life" that it might become "a new creature."[2]

The icon is also a fruit of this renewal of art and its appearance is inextricably connected with the unveiling in
the Church's consciousness of the meaning of the Incarnation: the fullness of the Godhead that dwells corporeally
in Christ. No one has ever seen God, but the Man Christ
reveals Him in full. An image of the Man Jesus is therefore
an image of God, for Christ is the God-Man. If the material
universe and its matter can be sanctified by grace of the
Holy Spirit, and in feeding our bodies also feed the "whole
man" in God's conception of him as an incarnate spirit; if
the water of baptism grants us forgiveness of sins; if the
bread and wine of the Eucharist make present to us the
Body and Blood of Christ, then a portrayal of Christ, the
product of human art, may also be filled with the grace of
His presence and power—may become not only an image
but also a spiritual reality. In the icon there is at once a
further revelation of the profundity of the dogma of Chalcedon and the gift of a new dimension in human art, because Christ has given a new dimension to man himself.

Icons in the Seventh Century

By the seventh century many literary remains give evidence of the veneration of icons; it is a well-established fact
of Church life. Writes Leontius of Neapolis:

I sketch and paint Christ and the sufferings of Christ in
churches, in homes, in public squares, and on icons, on linen
cloth, in closets, on clothes, and in every place I paint so that
men may see them plainly, may remember them and not forget
them . . . And as thou, when thou makest thy reverence to
the Book of the Law, bowest down not to the substance of
skins and ink, but to the sayings of God that are found therein,

[2] *Ibid.*

so I do reverence to the image of Christ. Not to the substance of wood and paint—that shall never happen! . . . But, by doing reverence to an inanimate image of Christ . . . I think to embrace Christ Himself and to do Him reverence. . . . We Christians, by bodily kissing an icon of Christ, or of an apostle or martyr, are in spirit kissing Christ Himself or His martyr.

In this perspective, every saint is a witness for Christ, showing forth all the power of union with Him, being His living icon. And from this Chalcedonian interpretation of the icon came the method of painting them prescribed by the eighty-second decree of the Trullan Synod (692):

In venerating the ancient icons and the saints who were devoted to the Church, as symbols and prototypes of the Truth, we especially venerate grace and truth as the fulfillment of the Law. Therefore, that what has been accomplished may be represented to all men's eyes through the art of painting, We decree that henceforth there are to be imprinted upon the icons of Christ our God—Who took on the guise of humanity that in this semblance men might discover the depth of God's humility—His Words, to bring to mind His life in the flesh, His Passion, His saving Death, and the redemption of the whole world which has proceeded therefrom.

In this text the fundamental meaning of icons is given: they are testimonials to the Incarnation, reminders of it, images whose subject has been filled with power.

As is almost always the case in the Church, acceptance and definition preceded the path of understanding; experience came before revelation in thought. Moreover, because the line dividing the Chalcedonian essence of icons from real idol-worship is exceedingly fine, the veneration of icons very soon became perverted in many places and took on improper forms. The seventh century, as already indicated, was simultaneously the time of astonishing fruits of Orthodox spirituality and of an indisputable coarsening of the mass of Christians. Among the latter the veneration of icons was sometimes marked by crude and sensual superstition. "Many think," wrote St. Anastasius of Sinai, "that he sufficiently reveres his baptism who, entering the church, kisses all the icons without paying any attention to the Liturgy and the divine service."[3]

We hear of the custom of taking icons as godparents for one's children, of adding paint scraped from icons to the Eucharistic wine, of laying the Sacrament upon an icon so as to receive it from a saint's hand, and so on. Obviously, many practices involved a fundamental distortion; the honor paid to icons was often close to idol-worship, and the honoring of their material substance was permitted. In other words, the same thing occurred with the veneration of icons that had often happened earlier with the cult of the saints and the veneration of relics. Arising from sound Christological foundations as a product and revelation of the Church's faith in Christ, too often they lost touch with this foundation and, changing into something self-contained, lapsed back into paganism.

But these distortions alone were not sufficient to create the profound and long-lasting iconoclastic movement. A subtle and theologically considered rejection of the whole concept of the icon developed, which forced the Church to further creative effort and theological contemplation.

Iconoclastic Movement

Iconoclastic sentiments appeared at the very beginning of the eighth century among the bishops of the eastern borderlands of the empire. They at once proved so strong that Germanos, patriarch of Constantinople, was obliged to defend the ancient practice of venerating of icons in a special epistle. The ferment soon reached the Emperor Leo and immediately took on an imperial dimension; Leo openly sided with the iconoclasts, and in the year 730

[3] Migne, *Patrologia Graeca*, LXXXIX, 829.

published a decree against icons. The patriarch, who had not submitted to him, was removed and replaced by Anastasius, who was sympathetic to iconoclasm. Shortly thereafter the first blood was shed. In a skirmish between the mob and soldiers who, at the emperor's command, had taken down from the Chalcopratian Gate a revered icon of Christ, several persons were killed. In Greece opposition to the new movement took the form of a political uprising; the entire West condemned iconoclasm, again unanimously; all this poured oil upon a blazing fire. But it was Leo's son, Constantine Copronymus who set in motion real persecution of the icon-worshipers. A brilliant general and statesman, he also showed himself a remarkable theologian; fragments of his works against icons that have been preserved display deep, well-reasoned conviction.

Constantine pursued his iconoclastic policy systematically. Carrying out in the space of a few years a purge of the episcopate, in 753 he summoned a council in Constantinople at which icons and the veneration of icons were condemned. The active minority, the convinced opponents of icons, had triumphed. The majority were unprepared, for they had never thought through the theological question of the veneration of icons.

Having secured the council's approval, Constantine put its decision into practice with fire and sword. Many names of "new martyrs," as the Church entitled them, have remained in our calendar from that decade of blood (762–75). It must be admitted that the Church's first reaction was rather feeble. Among the martyrs of this period we find almost no bishops, secular clergy, or laymen. Many continued to revere icons secretly, but did not state publicly their convictions. Even St. Tarasius of Constantinople, who was to be a future hero of the Seventh Ecumenical Council, at which the dogma of the veneration of icons was promulgated, pursued a brilliant governmental career under Copronymus. In fact, only the monks resisted the emperor's policy and it was upon them that the weight of persecution fell.

It will be appropriate later to show that in this struggle with the monks another implication of the iconoclastic conflict comes into view, no longer purely a theological matter. Here one need only stress that the monks proved to be the chief witnesses to truth; indeed, the lives of St. Stephen the New or St. Andrew Kalivitus are illumined by an early Christian spirit. Along with the attack on the monks, there was also a widespread destruction of icons themselves, which were replaced by worldly art: hunting scenes, decorative designs, and the like. No one can guess how the persecution would have ended, if the aged emperor-fanatic had not died in 775. Under his son Leo IV the Khazar—though he, too, was a convinced iconoclast—the persecution died down. A further shift took place when, after Leo's death, authority passed to his wife Irene (780–802) because of the minority of his son, Constantine VI. She had always been a devotee of icons and the monks, and began the preparations for an ecumenical council. To this end she installed as patriarch Tarasius, the state secretary, a wise and moderate Orthodox. But fifty years of iconoclasm had had a deep effect on Byzantine society. The first attempt to assemble the council in Constantinople was frustrated by the soldiers, who worshiped the memory of Copronymus.

Seventh Ecumenical Council

Only in 787, and not in the capital but in Nicaea, did the Seventh Ecumenical Council assemble, with Patriarch Tarasius presiding. Here the dogma of the veneration of icons was formulated and promulgated. The way had been paved for it by the reaction of Orthodox theological thought to the years of iconoclasm; first and foremost by St. John of Damascus, who died in all probability before the iconoclastic council of 753. John had lived in Syria under the rule of the Arabs; he then became a monk in the monastery of St. Sabas in Palestine. He derived his defense of icons directly from the Incarnation of Christ. Before He was made Man only symbols and "shadows" were possible. In a certain sense the whole world is full of natural images of God, but something completely new began from the moment that the Word became flesh.

When He Who is without a body and without form, Who has neither quantity nor magnitude, Who is incomparable with respect to the superiority of His nature, Who exists in Divine form—accepts a bond-servant's appearance and arrays Himself in bodily form, then do thou trace Him upon wood, and rest thy hopes in contemplating Him, Who has permitted Himself to be seen.

An image of the Man Christ is also an image of God; as Florovsky has said, everything that is human in Christ is now the living image of God. And in this union matter itself is made new and becomes worthy of praise. "I do not bow down to matter, but to the Creator of matter, Who for my sake took on substance and Who through matter accomplished my salvation, and I shall not cease to honor matter, through which my salvation was accomplished." This means that everything in the world and the world itself has taken on a new meaning in the Incarnation of God. Everything has become open to sanctification; matter itself has become a channel of the grace of the Holy Spirit.

This Christological definition of icons and their veneration forms the substance of the dogma promulgated by the Seventh Ecumenical Council. The whole Christological dispute, in fact, comes to a climax with this council, which gave it its final "cosmic" meaning.

We therefore, proceeding as it were along a royal road and following the God-revealing teaching of the saints, our Fathers,

and the tradition of the Catholic Church . . . with all cir-
cumspection and care do decree: that, like the image of the
glorious and life-giving Cross, there shall be placed in the holy
churches of God, on the sacred vessels and vestments, on walls
and on wood, in houses and along the roads, glorious and holy
icons, painted in colors and made from mosaic and out of
other substance expedient to this matter—icons of the Lord
Jesus Christ—and . . . of the Mother of God . . . and of all
saints and holy men.[4]

The reverence rendered to these images is different from
the "true devotion according to the faith which befits the
Divine nature alone"; the council defined it as a "worship
of reverence." In it the "honor rendered to the image
ascends to its prototype and he who reveres an icon is wor-
shiping the *hypostasis* of the one portrayed." In this way
the justification of the veneration of icons concluded the
dogmatic dialectic of the age of the universal councils,
which was concentrated, as we have already seen, on two
fundamental themes of Christian revelation: the Trinity
and the Incarnation. In this respect the "faith of the
Seven Ecumenical Councils and of the Fathers" is the everlasting and immutable foundation of Orthodoxy.

Persecution by the Iconoclasts

Although vanquisl.ed dogmatically, iconoclasm revived
with new strength after the death of Irene in 802. There
were still supporters of the heresy, chiefly in government
and military circles, where the glorious reign of Constantine
Copronymus was remembered with intense admiration. All
the misfortunes and failures of the empire that came at
the beginning of the ninth century—wars, invasions, revolts
—were blamed in such quarters on icon-worship. In 815

[4] B. J. Kidd, *Documents Illustrating the History of the Church,* Vol. 3
(London and New York, 1938), p. 73.

Emperor Leo V the Armenian demanded of the Patriarch Nicephorus that the icons in churches should be raised above human height, making it impossible to kiss them. From that instant all understood that a persecution was inevitable. But on this occasion the Church was not taken unawares: the decree of the recent ecumenical council and the writings of the defenders of icon-veneration had given it strength. The entire Church rose to the defense of Orthodoxy against the emperor. The Patriarch Nicephorus was the first to suffer, but he had time to announce the imminent struggle to the Church and summon it to resistance. He was deposed and exiled. The saintly Theodore, abbot of the famous monastery of Studios in Constantinople, took his place at the head of the Orthodox population. On Palm Sunday 815, thousands of Studite monks moved through the city in procession, carrying icons. The gauntlet had been thrown down before the state and a bloody persecution began. It produced more victims than the persecution of Copronymus: scores of bishops exiled, monks drowned in sewn-up sacks or tormented in torture chambers. Somewhat lessened in violence, this persecution continued under Leo's successors—Michael II (820–29) and Theophilus (829–42)—and after the year 834 the wave of terror gained fresh intensity.

The final victory of Orthodoxy once again came through a woman. The Empress Theodora, wife of Theophilus, halted the persecution immediately after her husband's death. In March 843, Methodius, one of the sufferers on behalf of icon-worship, took the patriarchal throne. On the first Sunday in Lent the reinstatement of icons was proclaimed in the Cathedral of St. Sophia, and this day has remained in the Church's memory as the "Triumph of Orthodoxy." Each year on this Sunday the Church celebrates its victory over the last of the great heresies and, solemnly proclaiming the truth, excommunicates all those who do not acknowledge it.

Church and State in the Eighth Century—
The Issue of Monasticism

But the dogmatic question of the meaning of icon-worship does not exhaust the significance of the iconoclastic upheaval. The vexing problem of Church-state relations became so acute during the controversy as to reach a breaking point, and the synthesis of Justinian collapsed. In itself the Church's conflict with a heretical emperor was nothing new, and St. John of Damascus was only repeating the words of St. Maxim the Confessor when he declared, "It is not the busines of Caesar to engage in definitions of the faith." The importance of iconoclasm lay in the fact that it thoroughly revealed all the ambiguity of the union of Constantine; it exposed the pagan and anti-Christian roots of the Byzantine theocracy in their fundamental form. The overthrow of iconoclasm, therefore, became the starting point of a new synthesis, a union of Church and empire which was to determine the subsequent fate of the Byzantine world.

I have spoken of the significance of monasticism in the preceding era: at the moment when the world was being Christianized, it embodied the eschatological aspect of Christianity as the overcoming of the world by the light of the Kingdom "not of this world," and by that very light saving Christianity from falling into worldliness. From this standpoint there is nothing more characteristic and noteworthy in the Church's relationship to the Christian world than the victory of monasticism in that world and its acceptance as a norm of the Christian way. Not only the Church, but even the empire yielded to monasticism: emperors vied with great noblemen in creating monasteries, so that at the outset of the struggle with iconoclasm the number of monks in Byzantium had reached a hundred thousand—an almost incredible percentage of the population.

But if the empire accepted this victory of monasticism unreservedly, and safeguarded it with every possible guar-' antee and privilege, monasticism in turn could not but become in the course of time a real burden. Above all, it lay like a heavy load upon the economic life of the state; tens of thousands of persons were lost to the army, the vast property of the monks escaped taxation, a whole section of the population was found to be outside state control. Rather early in Byzantine legislation we see attempts somehow to regulate this elemental fact and guide it into normal channels of activity. In addition, the very triumph of monasticism proved harmful to itself; from the beginning of the seventh century there are increasing, unmistakable signs of deterioration. The monasteries had grown rich, and privileges of every sort had now begun to attract some who had little interest in the pursuit of Christian perfection. The monks who had become the counselors, mentors, and confessors of the whole of Byzantine society were naturally often exposed to the temptation of abusing this confidence. The decrees of the Trullan Synod paint a rather disheartening picture in this regard.

But in the eighth century a spirit of heroism began to sweep abroad. The empire was perishing, and the Isaurian emperors saved it at the price of a terrible straining of all the forces of the state; in this stress a new patriotic consciousness was born. This total mobilization—similar to that of Russia under Peter the Great—was bound to give rise to questions about monasticism and the monks. It seems obvious that Copronymus' hatred for the monks was not based simply on their defense of icons. The division between two fundamental attitudes toward society, which had poisoned relations between Church and empire from time immemorial, was becoming clearer and clearer. For some, the state was called upon to be the mainstay and earthly receptacle of the Church, and therefore must submit to ecclesiastical values, even when such values were in conflict with state interests. For others, Christianity itself was in the final analysis a state cult, the religious support of the empire. The logic of the first attitude saw in monasticism a symbol of the supernatural role of the Church and the inner freedom of Christian personality from the all-absorbing utilitarianism of the state. The second attitude must sooner or later find monasticism useless, and therefore also harmful to the state.

Behind the revolt against monasticism could be seen the desire of the Isaurians to subject the Church entirely to the state and render it "useful" in every respect. In this regard the Isaurian emperors were well suited to perfect that theocratic logic which had essentially prevailed in Church-empire relations since the conversion of Constantine. Leo gave expression to that absolutist state-consciousness in the preface to a new code of laws which he published: "The Lord, having entrusted the realm to the emperors, hath likewise commanded them to tend Christ's faithful flock, after the example of Peter, the chief of the Apostles." Here is the final deduction from the Justinian "harmony."

Victory for the Monastic Principle

The victory of icon-veneration, therefore, was also a victory for monasticism, an inward triumph as well as an external one. Persecution had revived and renewed this aspect of the life of the Church, and at the start of the ninth century we see a genuine flowering of Byzantine monasticism, linked above all with the name of St. Theodore of Studios. It was he in particular who finally formulated that definition of monasticism's function in the Church which would consolidate its triumph forever. In his "system" it is clearly defined as a special ministry of the Church (it had started as a private, lay, and individual movement). The monks were the Church's "nerves and her support," they were the "salt of the earth and the light of the world," "a light for them that sit in darkness," "an example and a declaration." This was true because the goal of the monk was not different from that of the layman but the final goal of every Christian: the kingdom of Heaven, the soul's salvation—and one cannot save one's soul except by renouncing the world.

"To ask where it has been revealed to us that we should renounce the world and become monks—an echo of iconoclastic doubts of the value of monasticism—is simply to ask where it has been revealed to us that we should become Christians."[5] We must not think that St. Theodore saw salvation in monasticism alone; but he does assert that Christianity is impossible without what in the Gospel is called renunciation. And indeed, history confirms the fact that actually the Gospel's call to "the one thing necessary" has been realized only in the monastic life. Essentially, all Christians are summoned to completely dedicated devotion, but historically this completeness is always being turned into minimalism, into compromise and worldly laxity. Therefore, the monastic life is in its own way an historic shadow of Christianity which the Church will continue to cast until it is fulfilled. According to St. Theodore, the monastery must be the active inner kernel of the Church, a perpetual reminder of the Christian's ultimate calling and the Church's support and affirmation. In Constantinople itself he revitalized the ancient monastery of Studios, which soon became one of the chief centers of Byzantine Church life. Monastic life was finally established in the heart of Byzantium.

This triumph also spelled the failure of the iconoclastic attempt to destroy the independence of the Church, and simply to fit it into the theocratic framework. Historians have often misunderstood the meaning of this victory. "In the struggle for Orthodoxy," Harnack wrote, "the Church was victorious, in the struggle for freedom she was de-

[5] Quoted in A. P. Dobroklonsky, *St. Theodore* (in Russian, Odessa, 1913), p. 146.

feated."[6] But what sort of freedom is in question here? The monks were not fighting for the separation of Church and state—still less for a clericalist subjection of the state to the Church—but only for that conception of theocracy which, since the days of Constantine's conversion, had opened the arms of the Church so broadly to the empire. In opposition to Harnack and all historians who measure Byzantium according to Western criteria (which in fact did not exist in the West itself until considerably later), it must be affirmed that the Church, not the empire, was victorious in this struggle. Of course, there are no final victories in history; like the triumph over paganism under Constantine, this victory also had its negative aspects. But before mentioning them, we must try to pinpoint the essence and significance of this new, late-Byzantine conception of theocracy. Only then shall we have a reliable standard of judgment as to the success or failure of the Orthodoxy of Byzantium.

Late Byzantine Theocracy—The Church's Version

The theocratic conception of the Byzantine Church is expounded best of all in the *Epanagoge*, an introduction to the code of laws published at the close of the ninth century by Emperor Basil I the Macedonian, which was to remain until the end of the empire the fundamental law on relations between Church and state. A comparison with Justinian's ideas shows the change that had taken place in the state's understanding of itself. The *Epanagoge* also has as its starting point the parallel position of emperor and patriarch—"the most exalted and the most necessary members of the realm"—and the obligations of each are defined.

The task of the Emperor is to safeguard and secure the strength of the nation by good governance, to restore this strength when

[6] A. Harnack, *Lehrbuch der Dogmengeschichte*, Vol. 2 (Freiburg, 1888), p. 462.

it is impaired through watchful care, and to obtain new strength
by wisdom and by just ways and deeds. The aim of the Patriarch is first of all this—that he is to preserve in piety and purity
of life those people whom he has received from God; . . . he
must, where there is opportunity, convert all heretics to Orthodoxy and the unity of the Church . . . further, he must lead
unbelievers into adopting the faith, astounding them with the
splendor and the glory and the wondrousness of his own devotion . . . The Emperor must perform beneficial acts, wherefore he is also called benefactor . . . The aim of the Patriarch
is the salvation of the souls entrusted to him; he must live
by Christ and strive wholeheartedly for peace . . . The Emperor must be of the highest perfection in Orthodoxy and
piety . . . versed in the dogmas concerning the Holy Trinity
and in the definitions concerning salvation through the Incarnation of Our Lord Jesus Christ . . . It is natural for the
Patriarch to be a teacher and to treat high and low alike without restraint . . . and to speak of the truthfulness and safeguarding of dogmas before the face of the Emperor without
confusion . . . The Patriarch alone must interpret the maxims
of the ancients, the definitions of the Holy Fathers, and the
statutes of the Holy Councils . . . It is for the Emperor also
to support, first, all that is written in Holy Scripture, then all
dogmas established by the seven Holy Councils, and also selected Roman laws.[7]

Several scholars have inferred from the *Epanagoge* a full
and final blending of Church and empire into a single
Church-state body, the crowning of the process begun by
Justinian. Its text would appear to justify such an interpretation. But commentary usually goes no further than a simple statement of this fact, while the *Epanagoge* is equally
concerned about overcoming the harmful aspect of the
Justinian "harmony" of Church and state. In one sense a
fusion really did occur: all members of the Church were
subjects of the empire, the borders of Church and empire
coincided. But does this mean that they constituted a single

[7] Cf. G. Vernadsky, *The Byzantine Doctrine of the Power of the Emperor
and Patriarch* (in Russian, Prague, 1926), pp. 149 ff.

organism, headed by a diarchy of emperor and patriarch?

It must not be forgotten that the *Epanagoge* was political law, and spoke of the state, not the Church. This state, because it was Christian, was organically linked with the Church, and the same bond was exemplified in the diarchy of emperor and patriarch. The meaning of this diarchy lay in the fact that, apart from his position in the Church as defined in the canons, the patriarch now had a special position in the governmental structure: his place was analogous to that of the emperor. He was in some sense the Church's representative in the state, the guardian of its Orthodoxy and faithfulness to Christianity, a guarantee of the empire's Orthodoxy. He alone, therefore, had a right to teach and interpret Church doctrine, and the state itself charged him with the defense of the Orthodox faith before the emperor himself.

Of the emperor the *Epanagoge* required only fidelity to Orthodoxy—to her doctrine concerning Christ and the Trinity. One must emphasize that in the Byzantine vision of the ideal, Church and state were not connected by a juridical definition and delimitation of their spheres of action, but by the Orthodox faith: the faith and doctrine of the Church, which the empire had accepted as its own. And the fountainhead of this doctrine, its custodian and interpreter, was the Church and not the empire.

Outward Signs

Hallowed by its Orthodoxy, the empire was of course no longer an object of indifference to the Church, and its special, sacred purpose was manifest in the position which the emperor, for his part, held in it. This was symbolized in his coronation ceremony, which from the ninth century on can be considered as in its own way a liturgical expression of Byzantine theocracy. A vital moment was the emperor's profession of faith and his oath to maintain the faith in its entirety. The imperial power had finally ceased to be the one reflection in the world of divine power and was now itself subject to the truth preserved by the Church.

In all probability the ceremony of Anointing became in the ninth century the fundamental, operative moment of the coronation. This conferring of a special charisma upon the emperor by the Church for the governance of the empire did not signify the politicization of the Church, but—even if only symbolically—the clericalization of the empire. The emperor bowed his head, and the patriarch with his own hand placed the crown upon him, saying, "In the name of the Father and the Son and the Holy Ghost"—to which the people would answer, "Holy, Holy, Holy! Glory to God in the highest, and peace on earth!" The Byzantine emperor's special part in divine service is often mentioned as though he had a particularly sacred or even a sacerdotal position in the Church. Those who discuss this point most are apt to know least about it. As the Russian Byzantine scholar, D. F. Belyaev, has skillfully demonstrated, this participation was actually quite unimportant and devoid of any priestly significance.[8] He kept the right, which had once belonged to all laymen, of entering the apse so as to bring his offering to the altar. The sixty-ninth decree of Trullan Synod, sanctioning this right, speaks of the exception made in this case for the emperor, but stresses that the right belongs to the lay status in general.

It is clear that one cannot simply equate Byzantine theocracy with either the subjection of the Church to the state, or the subjection of the state to the Church (for which the medieval popes struggled), although both tendencies too often appear as its sinful distortions. If the empire had received the faith from the Church and was consecrated by that faith, the Church in turn, without being false to its mystical and sacramental independence, had entered into the empire, had charged it with protecting and safeguarding the Church and even with its earthly

[8] Cf. D. F. Belyaev, *Byzantina* (in Russian, St. Petersburg, 1891–1908).

organization. In this sense it is true that henceforth Church and empire would comprise a singe whole: "unmixed and inseparable." This did not occur through a confusion of ideas, since confusion, along with iconoclasm, had been surmounted, but on the contrary, out of the perfectionism of the Church, which felt itself to be an "icon of Christ" for the world, but did not assume earthly power, nor take upon itself the organization of man's life.

Nothing testifies so convincingly that the empire had now overcome the old poisons of pagan theocracy as the breakdown in official imperial art during this period.[9] Until the eighth century the forms of the ancient imperial cult were still predominant in likenesses of the emperor. Always he was the same emperor-conqueror and sovereign, knowing no restriction to his power, the personification of victory as he had been in pagan iconography. But pagan symbols of victory were replaced after Constantine by Christian ones. The empire conquered now under the sign of the Cross—"In this sign conquer"—as it had conquered before under other emblems, but in its political consciousness it did not yet feel the victory of Christ over itself, and the old triumphal motifs gained ground in the official symbolism of the iconoclastic emperors. But now with the triumph of Orthodoxy we see a sudden change, almost a leap forward. "The overwhelming majority of the imperial portraits of this era," writes Grabar, "belong to the type 'The Emperor before Christ,' one that is very rare and exceptional in the pre-iconoclastic period. The triumphal cycle yields to a cycle which glorifies first and foremost the emperor's piety, and not his victory."[10] It is no longer an image of the absolute sovereign of an empire, but an icon of the Byzantine theocracy.

Thus the triumph of Orthodoxy was not a mere return to Justinian's formula, but represented an inner regeneration of it. The empire had been and remained holy, but

[9] Cf. A. Grabar, *L'Empereur dans l'Art Byzantin* (Paris, 1936).
[10] *Ibid.*

the source of this sacred character had previously been the ancient and absolute conception of the state as the reflection on earth of divine order. Now it became the recognition of the empire as a handmaiden of Christ. This was set forth and made manifest in a variety of ways in Byzantine liturgy. For example, the Eucharistic prayer of the Liturgy of St. Basil the Great includes the following:

Lord, think upon the mighty and Christ-loving Emperor whose reign upon earth Thou hast justified: gird him with the armament of truth and good will, shield him in the day of battle, strengthen his sinews, uplift his right hand, hold fast his realm, subject unto him all barbarous peoples that desire war, grant him a profound peace that cannot be taken away, declare to his heart the good of Thy Church and of all Thy people, so that in his peace we may live a tranquil and quiet life in all piety and purity . . .

It is evinced in the spirit of the Byzantine army, which now became the "Christ-loving" army defending the "domicile" of Christ—that is to say, defending the earthly mainstay of the Church; it is reflected in the ritual of the court, which was wholly directed toward expressing the mission of the empire. Christ was Pantocrator, Creator, and Lord, and before Him knelt with upraised hands and bowed head the Byzantine emperor—here was something new in the image of the empire, which became the spirit of its consciousness in the final epoch of its history.

One must not think this was only ideology; in its own way, it was very deeply reflected in psychology and everyday life—in the entirety of that genuinely Church-centered atmosphere in which Byzantine society lived and breathed. Of course, so many sins are connected with this Orthodox way of life and so much falsehood was hidden beneath its outward guise, that a modern reader of history, looking back, is tempted to see in it only hypocrisy—only the stifling atmosphere of an external ecclesiasticism and faith in ritual. But he would be forgetting the goodness and light that were thus introduced into Byzantine life in an age when, politically and socially, the world was still only beginning to discover the explosive force of the Gospel. The ideals of mercy, love of poverty, and charity are not as sharply reflected in Byzantine chronicles as are the crimes by which political history was often made, and have therefore been ignored by historians. But one may speak, nevertheless, of a special sort of Byzantine humanism, linked undoubtedly to the feeling of Christ's constant presence in the world in all His aspects: as King, Savior, Teacher, and Judge.

Inherent Weaknesses

The dimensions of the victory, of course, should not be exaggerated. Against the background of this theory, in its own way great and beautiful, all the countless retreats and distortions that took place in reality now seem too ugly. True, no emperor will again dare to impose heresy on the Church as Byzantine emperors from Constantine to Theophilus had done (with the exception of the question of union with Rome, but this sore subject we shall explore later), and the Church's voice was to sound stronger than it had before. Like the state in the Church, the Church in the state would now acquire a new and more important position. Such patriarchs as Photius or Nicholas the Mystic were statesmen who did not confine themselves to the ecclesiastical sphere but took a fully qualified part in the solution of important matters of state, including dynastic and even military problems.

But the completely arbitrary nature of state authority always remained an incurable sore in Church life; still worse was the almost equally complete acceptance of this arbitrariness by the Church hierarchy. It was as though, having isolated its dogmatic doctrine in an inviolable holy of holies, protected by vows and with the empire itself subjected to it, the Church no longer felt any limit to imperial

authority. It was as though, having become completely
Orthodox, the emperor could now do anything that suited
him in the Church.

There are too many instances during these centuries of
this arbitrary use of power, of capitulations of the Church,
for even a simple enumeration to be possible. Their tragic
series began almost immediately in the clash between the
patriarchs Photius and Ignatius, which may serve as something of a symbol for all ensuing crises.[11] Each twice
ascended the patriarchal throne and on both occasions was
driven from it by a simple command of the emperor. Each
in his own way offered opposition, met arbitrary power
with a passive firmness. Each was personally virile and reflected in himself a certain truth of the Church. Nor did
the entire hierarchy submit; many had the strength to prefer exile to surrender. Nevertheless, the Church as a whole
accepted all this manipulation almost as if it were equitable.
Not a single voice rose in defense of the Church's essential
freedom; apparently no one now felt keenly its mystical
independence of the state, in whose name so much blood
had been shed a hundred years before.

We have seen already the quite exceptional importance
achieved by the patriarch of Constantinople in the Eastern
Church by the end of the seventh century. But the further
time progresses, the fewer traces does he leave in history;
little by little these traces are reduced to the mere listing
of names. Of course exceptions are encountered. But it is
enough to compare, for example, the tenth century—the
era of the Macedonian dynasty—with the twelfth, the age
of the Comneni. The remarkable patriarchs of the iconoclastic epoch—Germanos, Tarasius, Nicephorus, Methodius
—are followed by no less eminent men: Ignatius, Photius,
Nicholas the Mystic (who was victorious over Emperor Leo
VI in the question of the latter's fourth marriage), and
Polyeuctus. In the eleventh century we still meet with

[11] Cf. F. Dvornik, *The Photian Schism: History and Legend* (Cambridge,
England, 1948).

such princes of the Church as Michael Cerularius (under whom communion with Rome was finally severed). Of course not all patriarchs in these centuries can be compared to these figures of the first rank. One may point to the scandalous Patriarch Stephen (a brother of Emperor Leo VI—elevated to the patriarchate at the age of nineteen), and in particular to Theophilactus, son of the Emperor Romanus Lecapenus, who for thirty years shamed the Byzantine Church with his disgraceful behavior. But after 1081, when Alexius Comnenus ascended the throne, the patriarchs seem to withdraw into the background. We find very meager information about them in the Byzantine chronicles through which we establish their names, their chief "acts," and the years in which they were appointed or died. A curve could be traced, showing a gradually fading image of the patriarch side by side with the ever-increasing splendor of the *basileus*, as the Eastern emperors were called. And this is not accidental. It gives proof that the scales of the unattainable harmony were inclined in the direction of imperial power.

It is important to emphasize that this painful weakness cannot be explained solely in terms of the government's coercing the Church—in terms of the superiority of physical force, so to speak, as at the beginning of the Constantinian union. This was an inner, organic weakness of the representatives of the Church. Their dual situation made them not just the victims but also the agents of their own destiny. The thirst for a sacred theocracy, the desire to illumine the sinful stuff of history with the light of Christ; everything that could justify the union of Church and empire—this ideal required for its attainment a very subtle but very clear distinction between the Church and the world. For the Church is thoroughly fulfilling its mission to transform the world only when it completely feels itself to be a kingdom not of this world.

The tragedy of the Byzantine Church consisted precisely in the fact that it became merely the *Byzantine* Church, that it merged itself with the empire not so much ad-

ministratively as, above all, psychologically, in its own self-
awareness. The empire became for it the absolute and
supreme value, unquestioned, inviolable, and self-evident.
The Byzantine hierarchs—like the Russian, later on—were
simply incapable of going beyond the categories of the
sacred empire, of appraising it in the light of the life-giving
freedom of the Gospel. Everything became sacred and
everything was justified through this sacred character. One
could shut one's eyes to sin and evil—these things were simply the result of "men's frailty"; there remained a heavy
embroidery of sacred symbols which converted the whole
of life into a solemn ritual, lulling and gilding over conscience itself.

Theoretical perfectionism, completeness of dedication,
led in an ironic way to a minimizing of morality. On his
deathbed the black monk's robe shrouded all the emperor's
sins, the outcry of conscience found relief in the liturgical
confession of impurity. Everything—even penitence, even
the conviction of sin—had its order, and in this Christian
world with its pall woven of gold, frozen in a kind of motionless ceremonial, there no longer remained any place
for the simple, bare, incorruptibly sober judgment of the
most artless book in the world: "For where your treasure
is, there will your heart be also." The real tragedy of the
Byzantine Church lies, not in the arbitrary rule of emperors,
or its own sins, but in the fact that the real treasure that
filled its heart completely, and subjected everything to
itself, became—the empire. It was not force that van-
quished the Church, but the temptation of "flesh and
blood." The Church's consciousness came under the spell
of an earthly illusion, an earthly affection.

The Conservative Trend

With this assimilation of the Church to government and
empire—not only external but internal and psychological—
was linked a certain polarization of thought that charac-

terized this period: a dichotomy between two basic tendencies in theology and religious experience.

First, there is no doubt that the era of the ecumenical councils, the time of creative tension in ecclesiastical thinking, ended with the iconoclastic controversy. The desire to fix Othodoxy in some precise and final formula is intrinsically connected with the relations between Church and state. One need only recall the after-effects of the theological disputes of the fourth and fifth centuries, as a result of state interference. This does not mean that theological development within the Church came about by the initiative of the state. But the state tried to turn to its own advantage themes which had been developed in the speculations of the Church. From the very start we can sense in these disputes a state motif, as it were—a principle of requiring religious unanimity for the peace of the state. This had been the point of view of Constantine himself, for all his personal devotion. As time went on, the motif became stronger. The fevers of dispute and heresy that shook the body of the Church shook the organism of the state as well. The government was increasingly determined to reduce all differences of opinion to a common denominator, not so much from disinterested love of truth as for preservation of the integrity of the multinational empire, where any religious discontent immediately flared up into a fire of ethnic and political passions and separatisms of all sorts. From this drive to control the troubled waters of racial elements came all the endless attempts to find a compromise with Monophysitism which led the state into religious relativism. Too frequently it did not seek the truth, but rather peace and unanimity at any cost.

The victory over iconoclasm marked the turning point in this respect. While previously the emperors had been mainly concerned with finding a confessional minimum acceptable to all the diverse sections of the empire, the necessity of seeking such a minimum now disappeared of itself; religious unity was achieved at the price of the loss of all dissidents and the diminution of the empire. State authority had finally become Orthodox. In addition, it was fully aware of its mission, entrusted to it by God: the meticulous preservation of Orthodoxy in all its inviolability and purity. Previously, the emperors had shown initiative in clarifying the faith, and theologized in order to obtain general consent; now the consent was achieved, since all protesting masses were outside the imperial borders.

This new situation required a new policy. Bitter experience had shown that each religious divergence brought a threat of shock within the state as well. Now the basic concern of the emperors became the desire not to allow any religious disturbance, but to foster a sort of religious *status quo*. Orthodoxy coincided with conservatism down to the very letter of tradition. Iconoclasm revealed for the last time the dangerous fact that religious passions could turn into political discord. This experience was crucial. Naturally the Church, which had always longed for dogmatic unanimity and harmony with its "external bishop," joyously accepted the conservative policy of the state; here were rooted all the preconditions for its whole subsequent theological life.

Official Theology

The time had come in the history of Byzantium when both Church and state took the past into account—when this past had changed from something recent and familiar into antiquity, had become hallowed by age, and had developed psychologically into a sort of eternal ideal—not so much an inspiration to future creativity as a demand that the Church should constantly return to it and submit to it. With the silent consent of Church and state, a sort of psychological full-stop was now placed at the end of the account, and the total summed up. Each new reference to theological themes and each posing of new questions now had to be referred to the past. The tradition of the holy Fathers, confirmation by their authority even if only outwardly by means of references and quotations—sometimes even torn out of context—became a kind of guarantee of reliability. In the work of the last great Father of the Church, St. John of Damascus, we perceive this concern to refer everything to the past and to the Fathers—to rely on a *consensus patrum*. "His *De Fide Orthodoxa* has remained the summation of Greek theology, to which nothing was added and in which little change was made in subsequent centuries," writes one historian. Later Byzantium tacitly acknowledged that the catholic truth of the Church had been formulated, once and for all, by the ancient Fathers and the seven ecumenical councils. Even new misunderstandings, new false doctrines or questions, must be answered from the same storehouse; in the treasure chests of the writings of the Fathers must be sought the answers to all questions.

This backward-looking tendency was fundamental to the stream of Byzantine religious thought which may be labeled "official" or "school" theology. Its basic assignment was to prove that everything had been decided, and that reference to the past was the sole guarantee of Orthodoxy. But there is no reason to minimize the significance or contributions of this official theology; it bore witness to the undoubtedly high level of Byzantine ecclesiastical culture, to spiritual and intellectual interests that had never been extinguished, and to the constant concern for enlightenment, schools, and books that made medieval Byzantium the cultural center of the world—to which we are indebted for the transmission of all ancient Christian tradition.

The beginning of this official current of Byzantine theology may be attributed to the cultural renaissance that occurred in the second half of the tenth century and was centered in the university in Constantinople. From this circle of scholars and theologians, assembled by Caesar Bardas, came the "father of Byzantine theology," the Patriarch Photius. He combined genuine theological talent, shown in his polemic against the Western doctrine of the

Holy Spirit, with the academicism that was typical of his followers. His knowledge was universal and legendary, and he created a whole galaxy of scholars and theologians; from among his associates came St. Constantine the Philosopher, brother of Methodius, the apostle to the Slavs. His *Amphilochia* was a typical example of theological writing, entirely based on patristic quotations.

In the tenth century, under the emperors Leo the Wise and Constantine Porphyrogenitus, the palace at Constantinople was a center of intense intellectual activity, but the dominant interests were antiquarian, archeological, and bibliographical. "In this period we know of no authoritative name nor any original composition," writes an historian of the reign of Leo the Wise. From the point of view of transmitting tradition and culture, the contributions were enormous, but from the creative point of view they were weak.

A Vital Liturgy

Most important for the Church was the liturgical work that marked these centuries. First come the names of St. John of Damascus and St. Theodore of Studios. In Church tradition John is considered the composer of the *Octoechos*, the collection of hymns divided into eight tones or melodies. An immense number of contributions are ascribed to him, not all correctly. His liturgical poetry is very remarkable in form and content, and its influence was decisive for the writing of Byzantine hymns. Characteristic features are the Damascene's effort to fix the service in a definite pattern, and the almost complete dependence of his theological themes on the tradition of the Fathers. The Byzantine service, as already observed, is a blend of the dogmatic achievements of the preceding period in liturgical form. It is almost entirely adorned with the colors of the Trinity and of Christology.

The same sense of completion and fixedness may be

remarked in the liturgical activity of the center at Studios, headed by St. Theodore. This produced the *Triodion*, the hymns and orders of service for the periods of Great Lent and Easter. Here the *Typicon*, or service manual, was gradually put together in an effort to fix the services more and more securely. Each Byzantine generation would only have to fill in the empty places in the pattern.

The liturgical heritage of Byzantium is so immense that we cannot expect it to contain only masterpieces. There were a great many rhetorical exercises, repetitions, and imitations. As a whole it was a magnificent structure, with much of surpassing beauty and profundity of thought. In the *Typicon* itself—or rather the *Typica*, since there were a great number of them—if one can decode their secret language, a whole philosophy of Christian life emerges, and very fine, well-thought-out Christian concepts. We need only point to the luminous beauty of the Easter service, the abundance of liturgical cycles, those for Christmas, Lent, and the feasts of Mary, or to the theological profundity of the *Triodion* or the *Octoechos* (the book of liturgy for the variations in service during the rest of the year).

For centuries these liturgical riches were to be the main source of knowledge and religious life and inspiration in the Orthodox world, and in the darkest ages, when traditions were broken and education became rare, people in the Church would rediscover again and again the spirit of universal, all-embracing, and inexhaustibly profound Orthodoxy in its golden age. All spiritual culture, all theological erudition of a Byzantine or of a citizen of Holy Russia, was acquired in the Church and in the living experience of the divine service. There were no seminaries, academies, or theological faculties; but devout monks and Christians drank the living waters of divine knowledge from hymnology. During the all-night vigil services, matins, and vespers, to the sounds of the ancient chants, there developed a reverence that was strong and unshakable, and an Orthodox outlook that was expressed in life and action and did not remain only a misty philosophical theory.

These treasures were gathered in the churches, and men and women, experiencing them reverently, arranged their pattern and way of life accordingly.

Without doubt the liturgical contributions were the highest achievement of Byzantine Orthodoxy; they indicate the profound understanding and assimilation of the dogmatic insights of the preceding age and the inner continuity of life and tradition. Nevertheless, this theology is only the expression in beautiful forms of the experience of the past, fixing it in a system of divine services. Everything really new that was introduced into this pattern in the Byzantine period was usually very much weaker and more rhetorical, or only decoration in a certain sense—the luxuriant flowering of liturgical symbolism, the elaboration of ceremonies, the sometimes unnecessary prolongation of prayers and hymns of an earlier period which had been classic in their succinctness and expressiveness. *Mutatis mutandis*, later Byzantine liturgical contributions were baroque by comparison with the transparent simplicity of pure Byzantinism.

An analogous effort to systematize tradition may be seen in the work of Simeon Metaphrastes of the tenth century, the codifier of the lives of saints; or that of Oecumenius, a well-known Byzantine exegete. Here everything is Orthodox and traditional, very frequently beautiful and ingenious, but nothing is added to what has already been said by the ancient authors. Still more typical is the celebrated document of the twelfth century, era of the Comneni: the *Panoply* of Euthymius Zigabenus, a model of official theology. After that time such works became more frequent; they were theological collections of answers and arguments for all occasions. In the capital and at court there were many disputes on theological themes, but they were glitteringly poetic debates, not genuine discussions of "the one thing necessary." "It was the fashion to speak about theology," wrote an historian. "The court competed with the clergy, professional theologians were zealous in searching for new themes and in searching the Scriptures for problems with which to confound their opponents . . ."

New Hellenization

Official theology was characterized by this spirit until the end of the empire. There were periods when it flourished: the time of the empire of Nicaea (thirteenth century) or of the Paleologi (fourteenth and fifteenth centuries). It is even customary to speak of the "renaissance" of the Paleologi, reflected as we know in the Western Renaissance. Yet in this cultural renewal the Christian themes are weakest. Dying Byzantium would fertilize the West, not with the light of Orthodoxy but with Hellenic antiquity —with Plato and Plotinus! For in Byzantium itself in the last years of its existence we perceive a sudden return to pure Hellenism and to philosophical problems that once seemed to be solved in patristic theology. The connecting link between Byzantium and the West, just before the fall of the empire, was not their common Christian heritage but the neopaganism of Gemistus Plethon, the founder of the Platonic academy in Florence, the high priest of Hellenism for all Italy.

This was the price paid for official theology, the preservative spirit that triumphed in Byzantine Orthodoxy. When Church doctrine became state authority to which one must submit by obligation, the Greek mind began to seek new nourishment in pre-Christian philosophy, with which it had become familiar on the school bench. What had previously been only a subject for study in school—gymnastics for the mind—now again acquired independent interest and came to life as an arena for problems that could not be posed in religious terms. The faith remained, inviolable and beyond doubt, but intellectual interest in it disappeared; the urge to comprehend it intellectually was stifled.

Yet again, but in a new form, there arose a dichotomy between Christianity and Hellenism. This had earlier been a conflict from which Christianity by its creative efforts emerged the victor. Now there was no longer even a con-

flict; no one rejected or criticized Christianity. The Byzantine philosophical renaissance developed alongside
Christianity and parallel to it, as a completely autonomous
sphere. The cast of mind of Michael Psellus, a pioneer
in philosophy at the end of the eleventh century, is characteristic of the new humanistic spirit. He taught about
the nature of God according to Orpheus, Zoroaster, Am-
mon, Parmenides, Empedocles, and Plato; the break with
theology seems complete. Yet this did not prevent him
from writing theological tracts in the most reverent and
classic spirit. As with Gemistus Plethon, the neopagan
philosophy he created did not prevent him from defending
Orthodoxy at the Council of Florence in 1438–39. The
practice, if not the theory, of a double truth developed in
Byzantium, and this was the strongest symptom of the
theological crisis. Christianity had failed to satisfy the needs
of the Byzantine; its spiritual integrity had been violated,
and a certain part of it—the creative part, indeed—drew it
to another, non-Christian world.

The Byzantine Church responded to this philosophical
renaissance more than once by interdictions and anathemas,
but official theology proved incapable of overcoming it from
within, by a new creative synthesis. Whatever the contributions of this theology, they could not of course replace
the creative enthusiasm by which "the ancient books are
forever animated," the books of the great Fathers and
Doctors, memorials to the theological spring of Church
history. Knowledge and assimilation cannot replace experience.

Monastic Theology

Everything so far discussed refers to the upper stratum
of the Byzantine Church, which was in direct contact with
the empire and firmly bound by the political-ecclesiastical
ideology that prevailed after the triumph of Orthodoxy.

Yet it would be as historically incorrect to judge Byzantium by this aspect alone as to evaluate the synodal period in the history of the Russian Church, for example, solely on the basis of minutes of the sessions of the Holy Synod, or by seminary textbooks copied from Latin models. For while Latin scholasticism predominated in the Russian seminaries, St. Seraphim of Sarov was revealing in his talks with Motovilov his profound doctrine of the Holy Spirit; and a fugitive from the Kievan seminary, Paissy Velichkovsky, by his life as an elder was preparing the way for the renaissance of Russian monasticism. So in Byzantium, while official theology became more and more a scholastic commentary on the texts of the Holy Fathers, another genuine tradition, eternally alive and creative, continued to survive in the monasteries. It is usually called Byzantine mysticism, but was in fact only a continuation of the original trend of theological speculation: the disclosure of the content of faith in the experience of life.

This was the case in the theology of St. Simeon the New Theologian (949–1022), whose life has been described by his disciple, Nicetas Stethatos. He has left us hymns, letters, and ascetic and theological treatises. It was of course a specifically monastic theology, dedicated wholly to the description of illuminations and mystical contemplation—to that "communion with the Divine Light" which had been the purpose of monastic asceticism from the start. "Being in a state of illumination, the holy man is completely on fire with the Holy Spirit, and even in this anticipates the mystery of his deification." Grace appears with all possible stillness and joy, and this light is the preparation for the Eternal Light, the radiance of eternal bliss. The mind plunges into it, is clarified, is itself made light, and unites completely with the Source of light Himself.

Although this is a theology of renunciation and solitary ascent to God, in the life of the Church it was even more important and influential than official theology. In these spiritual elders the Church experienced the extreme of freedom from the world—a freedom from the evaluation of all worldly things completely lacking in her close marriage to the empire. This was theology from experience, not from books, and through it the practical significance of Christianity was reanimated as a struggle for human reality.

A good illustration is the conflict between St. Simeon and the officials of the Constantinople patriarchate over his veneration of his deceased teacher and mentor, a conflict between spiritual freedom and the spirit of the consistory, which could not tolerate any departure from the routine of official ecclesiastical life. The solitary hermit was persecuted, sent into exile, suffered oppression; but in the final account he and not the consistory was victorious. The mind of Orthodoxy eventually recognized him as a real witness to its faith and hopes. Less than a hundred years after his death, St. Simeon was venerated by the whole Eastern Church.

Mt. Athos

Beginning with the tenth century, the "Holy Mountain," Athos, became the main center of Byzantine monasticism and also of this speculative tendency in Orthodox theology. So it has remained to the present day. The settlement of hermits on Athos began very early, possibly as soon as the fourth century. Here, too, monasticism passed through all the phases of its development: the life of the hermit; later the *laura*, which combined solitary asceticism with some community; and finally monasteries with a strictly regulated life. The founder of this regulated monasticism on Athos is considered to be St. Athanasius of Athos, in whose time the famous *laura* that bears his name was established (960). In the twelfth century, under Emperor Alexius Comnenus, Athos was finally sanctioned as the recognized center of Byzantine monasticism.

All the threads of speculative theology by which Eastern

monasticism had lived since the time of the desert Fathers converged here, and in the late Byzantine period Athos was the center of an intense theological life. Nothing so reveals the dichotomy in theological thinking of Byzantium—the whole difference between official theology and the theology of experience—as the disputes over "hesychasm" that began on Mt. Athos in the fourteenth century, associated with the name of St. Gregory Palamas. Outwardly the dispute concerned almost technical problems of ascetic practices, the so-called *hesychia* through which the "gathering of the mind" is achieved and the contemplation of the Divine Light is attained. Very soon, however, the basic question was asked: What does the holy man contemplate, see, and commune with? The opponents of Hesychasm felt that in the theology of "deification," or union with God, the bounds between creation and God were erased, that in its extremes the Hesychast doctrine of the uncreated Light on Mt. Tabor bordered on pantheism. The dispute came to concern the theological question of the nature of the light of the Transfiguration.

The Mystical Root of Theology

St. Gregory Palamas, a monk of Athos and later archbishop of Thessalonica (1296–1359), undoubtedly a very great Byzantine theologian, came to the defense of the Hesychasts. Catholic historians have frequently interpreted his doctrine as an unprecedented innovation in the history of Orthodox theology, expressing all the extremes and peculiarities of Eastern mysticism. As recent research has well demonstrated, however, in fact it only completes and renews in a creative way the most authentic and basic tendency in the Orthodox view of Christianity. This is the conception that God really is present in the world, that we perceive Him and unite with Him, not by abstract deductions or philosophically, but ontologically. In this defense of real union with God lies the meaning of the doctrine of Palamas on divine energies that permeate the world, through which the world, without merging with God—essentially impossible—is united with Him and can commune with Him, have Him within itself, and endlessly grow nearer to Him. The whole tradition of the Fathers of the Church was revived in the experience of Hesychasm and the theology of Palamas: in the image of the God-Man in Christ and the gifts of the Holy Spirit, Christianity is revealed as a vision of the fullness of God in the essence of man, and in this fullness, of the "communion with God" of everything in the world.

For St. Simeon the New Theologian and for St. Gregory Palamas—to limit ourselves only to these two pinnacles of Byzantine mysticism—the authority of the Fathers stood just as high as it did for the theologians of the patriarchal school in Constantinople. But they had no reason to question the tradition of the Holy Fathers. For them it was not an outward authority requiring blind submission. They lived in the tradition and perceived it from within as a unity of faith and experience; they were aware of it as the fruit of the same Spirit that had inspired the Fathers as well. For them, as for the earlier Fathers, theology was not abstract knowledge but "the work of life and the creative solution of vital problems." They were free, precisely because they had in themselves and their religious experience the criterion for their unity in faith with the Fathers and with tradition. Though the way of mysticism is a special one, set apart in a special sphere of theology, all genuine theology is mystical at the root, since it is primarily evidence of religious experience. In the course of spiritual endeavor, creativeness, and effort the strength of true tradition is revealed. Otherwise it turns into a dead historical document, binding the mind with abstract and meaningless formulas.

Thus the limitation imposed on official Byzantine theology by the external authority of texts resulted in a re-

newed outbreak of "dechristianized" Hellenism on the one
hand and of conflict with the Hesychasts on the other.
Prof. F. I. Uspensky has attempted to reduce all these
controversies to a struggle between two fundamental philosophical positions which, he alleges, define the history
of Byzantine thought: Aristotelianism and Platonism.[12]
The philosophers and mystics, he maintains, stem from
Plato, while the official doctrine of the Church, including
that of St. John of Damascus, is expressed in the language
of Aristotle. The fallacy of such a pattern has been demonstrated a number of times. For example, one of Palamas'
main enemies, Nicephorus Gregoras, was by philosophy a
convinced Platonist. Actually the question of whom to
follow in the structure of Christian dogmatics—Plato or
Aristotle—could not arise for Palamas or St. Simeon. For
them the primary reality was Christian revelation and that
theory of contemplation which they attempted to fix in
words, but for which of course neither Plato nor Aristotle
could be completely adequate. Palamas could refer to both
Plato and Aristotle and criticize both, because neither had
defined his religious experience, yet both are evaluated on
the basis of it. Christian theology by its very essence was
necessarily eclectic in its relation to pre-Christian philosophy, however highly it might honor it and boldly utilize
the language to express its own "inexpressible mysteries."
Therefore the synthesis with Hellenism and the absorption
of it into the Church which had taken place in the writings
of the Fathers was naturally revived in Byzantine mysticism.

The latter was the chief and most valuable tendency in
Byzantium's spiritual heritage, and down to the present day
it has continued to fertilize the religious consciousness of
Orthodoxy. The Councils of 1351 and 1368 in Constantinople, which confirmed "Palamism" as a true expression
of the faith of the Church and consecrated to sainthood
Palamas himself (to whose memory the second Sunday in

[12] F. I. Uspensky, *Studies in the History of Byzantine Education* (in Russian, St. Petersburg, 1892).

Great Lent is dedicated), therefore represent the spiritual
peak of Byzantine Orthodoxy.

Basic Church Unity

In Church history the late Byzantine period is still known
as the "era of the division of the churches," and the label
is of course appropriate to the full significance of this great
tragedy of Christian history. In a certain sense the whole
life of Byzantium inherited the stigma of this event, and the
experience of the division which took place at that time still
colors the relations between the Orthodox East and Rome.
One may study the division of the churches in two aspects: the historical and the dogmatic. Historically it was
a very complex matter, and only by approaching it dis-
honestly or from a partisan viewpoint can one place the
whole guilt on either side and justify the other accordingly.
Dogmatically it does not matter so much just how the
churches came to be divided, as what essentially divided
them: those assertions of the Roman Church—first about
itself (the dogma of papal infallibility), and then about
the faith of the Church (the doctrines of the Holy Spirit
and of the Immaculate Conception of the Virgin)—which
the Orthodox regarded as contradictory to the basic truth
of Christianity. But for good understanding we must first
investigate the history of this division.
I have spoken of the unity of the early Church, and how
it was perceived in the psychology of early Christians as not
only the form but in a very real sense the *content* of Christianity. Christ had come to gather the scattered children
of God into one, to unite those who had been separated by
"natural" causes into a supernatural unity of the new people
of God, in whom "there is neither Jew nor Greek, there is
neither bond nor free, there is neither male nor female:
for ye are all one in Christ Jesus" (Gal. 3:28). This unity
was embodied in the unity of each local Church, which in

its assembly headed by the bishop showed forth the form of one Body, with Christ as its head; and also in the unity of all churches, which were linked by one faith, one apostolic succession, one life. The joy in this unity, the constant sense of the victory of grace over all natural divisions, is the most inspiring theme in documents of the early Church. The Church was really one in history, in the facts of its life; unity was for it not a mere unattainable idea. The whole extent of the sin and tragedy of divisions within it can only be measured by the standard of this unity.

We have seen also that the basic structure of the Church was that of a universal union of local churches bound by the unity of apostolic succession; each Church community was both an image of the unity of Christ and the Church, and organically a part of the universal unity of all Christians as one people of God. While the structure of the local Church and its bond with other churches derived directly from the very essence of Christianity, the outward forms of this bond between churches changed and developed, depending on historical conditions. For example, in the apostolic era the unquestioned center of unity of all the churches was the Jerusalem community, the Mother Church in the full and absolute meaning of this word—the source and model for all other communities. With the end of Palestinian Judeo-Christianity, we already see within the Church several such centers, each consecrated by apostolic authority but also a center because of the number of Christians and the importance of the city. At first such centers— Antioch and Ephesus in the East and Rome in the West— had no jurisdictional or canonical rights connected with them; but as the source of preaching and dissemination of Christianity to the areas around them, they naturally enjoyed particular respect and authority. For example, at the end of the first century the Roman Church sent an epistle to the Church in Corinth, where disputes had arisen; while Bishop Ignatius of Antioch on his way to martyrdom exhorted the churches of Asia Minor in the faith. There is no

mention of "rights" or "subordination," but the more ancient churches were naturally more concerned for the universal unity of Christians and the welfare of the Church.
Among them the Church of Rome, the Church of the apostles Peter and Paul—the Church of the capital of the empire
—undoubtedly enjoyed special recognition from the very
first.

There was also some friction, even at a very early stage,
as we have seen; the Roman bishops were inclined at times
to confuse their authority with certain formal rights, and
more and more to interpret the tradition of "presiding in
love" in juridical terms. Yet each time such claims ran into
the concerted rebuff of the whole Church—both in the
West and in the East. Toward the beginning of the fourth
century, however, Rome's first place was not denied by
anyone in the Church. On the other hand, the universal
structure of the Church had been defined in its basic features: it would find its final expression, as we know, in the
patriarchates or extensive regional unions of churches
around one great center.

Elements of Misunderstanding with Rome

Such was the situation at the beginning of the age of
Constantine. But from that time, the fundamental misunderstanding between the Eastern and Western halves
of the Church became deeper, ending in final separation.
On the one hand, in Rome it was increasingly apparent
that a firm conception of the papacy had developed according to which special God-given rights had been granted to
the bishop of Rome over the universal Church. This point
of view became increasingly strong after the fall of the
Western empire, when the Roman Church became the only
light in the approaching chaos. In the works of Pope Leo
the Great in the fifth century, this theory was expressed
with great clarity. It is equally clear that it sharply contra-

dicted the idea of the structure of the Church which the whole East had always held. In other words, in the fifth and sixth centuries we see within the Church two ecclesiologies—two doctrines of the Church—which were not only distinct but in fact mutually exclusive.

At this point we must also emphasize the East's essential fault in the division of the churches: namely, an almost complete insensitivity in the thinking of the Eastern Church to the underlying ecclesiological conflict, the lack of any consistent reaction to the growth of the papacy. The theory of the "power" (*potestas*) of the Roman primate was openly proclaimed in Rome in the era of the ecumenical councils, and the Protestant canonist Theodor Zahn has formulated it as follows: "Rome is the head of the Church, without it the Church is not the Church, and only through union with Rome do the separate communities become part of the Catholic Church." But the East did not perceive, or did not want to perceive, how this theory clearly contradicted its own doctrine. Rome always clearly followed its own policy, but the East, without ever really accepting it, until the ninth century never once expressed its nonacceptance or rejection of it in any clear way. They always tried to conceal disagreement in diffuse and ambiguous phrases. When Catholic scholars now assert, on the basis of the councils of Ephesus and Chalcedon, that the East recognized the primacy of Rome at that time but later rejected it, it is rather difficult to answer the charge on the basis of formal historical evidence, since one may in fact conclude from the history of those two councils that the Greek bishops admitted the special prerogatives of the Roman bishop.

By interpreting these events in the context of the whole Eastern way of thought, comparing them with other facts and viewing the Eastern Church as a whole, we know this is not so, but the East made no formal answer either to Celestine at Ephesus or to Leo at Chalcedon. When Pope Celestine's legate at Ephesus declared that "Peter, to whom our Lord Jesus Christ has given the keys of the Kingdom and the power to bind and loose sins, now and forevermore remains and judges in the person of his successors," the Greek bishops remained silent. The protest of Pope Leo the Great against the twenty-eighth canon at Chalcedon (which made the see of Constantinople a "new Rome") was answered by Patriarch Anatolius with a cowardly renunciation of responsibility for the canon, assuring the pope that without the latter's approval not one of the decrees of the ecumenical council could be in effect. Even more characteristic of this eternal compromise with Rome was the signing of the formula of Pope Hormisdas by the Eastern bishops in 519, ending the thirty-year schism between Rome and Constantinople. The whole essence of the papal claims cannot be more clearly expressed than in this document, which was imposed upon the Eastern bishops.

According to Duchesne's calculation, in the period from Constantine to the Seventh Ecumenical Council, the Eastern Church was in schism with Rome for two hundred and three years in all;[13] but dogmatic problems and heresies— never the rejection of the papacy—were always the cause of the break. "The Easterners not only did not object in time to the growing mystique of papal dogmas," wrote a Russian historian, "they not only silently signed the papal formulations, but they themselves, by their appeals to Rome, heedless of the juridical implications, supported the sincere illusions of the Romans that the Greeks, too, shared the Western concept of the papacy."

Deepening Divergence

How can one explain this strange development? Catholic scholars usually allude to the lack in Byzantium of any clear doctrine of the Church, or to the "opportunism" of

[13] Cf. L. Duchesne, *Autonomies Ecclésiastiques, Églises Séparées* (Paris, 1905), pp. 164–65.

the Greek hierarchy, which recognized or repudiated the Roman primacy as necessity ordained. This is hardly an adequate account of the situation. The juridical and canonical aspects of the Church were less developed in the East than in the West, but the primary reason for this was that the Church and all it contained was felt to be based on a sacramental reality, the mystical essence of the Church as the Body of Christ. Another reason for the East's insensitivity to the papacy lay in its alliance with the empire, which has already been discussed at length. We have seen that one result of the conversion of Constantine was that the Church itself adopted his theocratic dream—that the empire became in a way an essential category in its earthly existence. For a very long time it seemed that the only earthly point where Christianity could adapt to the world and to history was in the idea of a single Christian empire, the universe founded by Constantine, who for the Church was a consecrated man, equal to the apostles. This "Roman idea" was held by the whole Church, in both East and West; but in the West the fall of the imperial state altered its form and was one of the reasons for the growth of the papacy. The great conflict between the popes and the German emperors was essentially a consequence of the split in this common Roman tradition, a struggle between two identical theocratic conceptions of world order.

In the East this idea gradually led to the development of a definite ideology of Church and state, an organic alliance. The danger of such an ideology was that it erased the boundary between ecclesiology (the doctrine of the Church's eternal essence) and the temporal adaptation of the Church to particular historical conditions, so that the empire became the earthly support of the Church. The doctrine of the Church merged, as it were, with the doctrine of its union with the empire—the ideology of Church and state. The question of Roman claims simply did not touch this ideology, which remained concealed from the consciousness of the Byzantine Church. The Eastern Church solved all its problems of administration and canonical structure—successfully or unsuccessfully—by co-ordination with the structure of the state. Therefore the East did not react ecclesiastically to the Roman question, since the question seemed administrative rather than ecclesiological. With the division of East from West and the breakdown of constant communication, the Easterners simply could not comprehend the dogmatic significance the popes attached to their jurisdictional claims, and carelessly assumed it was simply a matter of administrative precedence and love of power. Such an administrative matter, the East assumed, concerned the sphere of Church and state rather than the Church alone. This governmental barrier prevented the Byzantine Church from understanding the real theological or ecclesiological significance of the problem of the papacy. For the same reasons for which the Church of Constantinople was "condemned" to promotion, all papal protests against the promotion were also condemned to failure.

On the other hand, the East, continually shaken by dogmatic disputes, concentrated all its efforts on solving them, and was frequently obliged to seek help in the West, which was less "theological" but also less susceptible to diseases of heresy. Eastern bishops called the pope their father and teacher, instinctively aware that this would change nothing in the imperial organization of the Eastern Church. Frequently the emperors themselves, concerned to get a quick solution to dogmatic disputes that were leading to political rebellion, urged the Eastern bishops to an inconsistent "Romophilia." This occurred in the elimination of the so-called Acacian schism in 515, and later, in the consecration of Patriarch Menas by Pope Agapetus at the start of Justinian's reign.

It is completely incorrect to imagine problems of Church structure as alien to an Orthodox East forever soaring in the heights of metaphysics. One need only point to the whole canonical tradition of Byzantium, adorned by the names of Balsamon, Zonaras, Chomatenus, and many

others. But the canonical way of thinking in the East was
unlike that of the West. From the time when the imperial
authority became Christian, it was held that all questions
concerning outward organization of the Church should be
solved in conjunction with that authority, and that therefore ecclesiastical canons should be sanctioned by the
emperor and become the law of the land as well. The
East's insensitivity to the depth of its divergence from
Rome in its understanding and experience of the Church
resulted primarily from the merging of Church and state
in the ecclesiastical cast of mind in Byzantium.

Sooner or later, of course, this divergence was bound to
be clearly exposed. But it happened that communication
between the churches, which alone could have restored the
policy of healing each other's illnesses, broke down increasingly with the succeeding centuries. The Roman *oekumene*
was falling apart into separate worlds, the link between
them was being lost, and each was beginning to live its own
closed and separate life. The bond between the two halves
of the empire—which had been strained by Diocletian's
diarchy, the transfer of the capital to the Bosphorus, and
the division of Theodosius—was further loosened by the
barbarian invasions. The basic aim of Byzantine politics
was now becoming defense from the Asiatic East, which
constantly threatened it. The West ceased to be necessary
to Byzantium, and the Eastern orientation of Byzantine
politics, conclusively adopted by the emperors after the
failure of Justinian's dream, assured the empire of several
more centuries of political stability and even power. This
"Eastern" period lasted as long as Byzantium alone was
capable of withstanding the pressure of Asia. It included the
Isaurian and Macedonian dynasties. The last upswing in
this Eastern autarchy of the empire must be considered
to have taken place under Basil Bulgaroctonus, in whose
reign (976–1025) the empire stretched from Istria to the
Euphrates and from the Drava to Cyprus. Even at that
time, it "was not closed off as much in any direction as in

the West . . . The face of Byzantium was turned toward the East."[14]

Loss of Communication

It must be admitted that the Church submitted to this pressure of history and made no effort to overcome it. After the break in political and economic communications came the severing of ecclesiastical relations. Officially the Church was one; true unity, however, is not nourished by "official" ties but by living communion, particularly by a constant effort to overcome natural division by the unity of grace. This universal cast of thought, which had so inspired Irenaeus of Lyons and Cyprian of Carthage, grew weaker, ecclesiastically as well as politically, and East and West became locked each within its own horizon. During the iconoclastic controversy, through the fault of the Byzantine emperors, the last bonds connecting the empire with the papacy gave way.

True, the conservative and equally "imperially oriented" thinking of the popes passed through many doubts and torments before they determined on a schism. Only the desperate situation of Italy and Rome and the impossibility of procuring help from Byzantium threw them into the embrace of the Frankish kings, and this was the point of departure for a new period in the history of the Western world. Yet at this period of maximum alienation between East and West comes the final crystallization of Byzantine Orthodoxy. Here were two worlds, two traditions, two ecclesiastical psychologies, which knew little of each other; and though the unity of the Church was not as yet formally destroyed, in living terms it no longer existed.

The question of Roman claims, which had never been answered or even really posed in the East in the previous

[14] C. Neumann, *La situation mondiale de l'Empire Byzantin avant les croisades* (Paris, 1905), p. 25.

period, because of broken relations with the West, now disappeared, no longer demanding a solution. The popes had no time for the East in the troubled and stormy era of the Dark Ages, and Byzantium, plunged in its own difficulties, stopped thinking about the West. The Eastern Church, which had previously at least consulted with Rome, now became accustomed to getting along entirely without it and was finally enclosed within its own imperialism. Everything outside the borders of the empire was defined as "barbarian," and relations with these barbarians were extremely vague. The new position of the bishop of Rome was similarly obscure for the consciousness of the Byzantine Church. They tried to clear up the obscurity by a theory which called for five patriarchs—related to the idea of the "five senses," but did not give much thought to whether the pope would recognize these theories.

The result of this long alienation was that when the two worlds met again, they seemed really alien to each other: unneeded, incomprehensible, and—finally—hostile. There are few sadder pages in the history of the Church than those that record the lack of love, the suspicion, the pettiness, and the stifling narrowness that both sides revealed.

We see the first attempt at such an encounter at the end of the ninth century in the notorious affair of the patriarchs Photius and Ignatius, which left extremely sad memories in the East. It would be difficult to imagine more misunderstanding, intolerance, and haughtiness than were shown by Pope Nicholas and his successors in their intervention in the internal difficulties of the Byzantine Church. This has recently been acknowledged in Roman Catholic scholarship by Father Dvornik, who has devoted a remarkable volume to the rehabilitation of Photius, previously considered by Catholics the father of the schism.[15] Photius was the first to point out clearly the innovations in the doctrine of the Western Church that constituted the real

15 Dvornik, *op. cit.*

essence of the schism: the exaggerated role of the pope
and the doctrine of the procession of the Holy Spirit. It is
true that, once he had posed these questions, showing a real
understanding of the situation and demonstrating theologically the unorthodoxy of the dogma of *Filioque*, Photius
himself removed the questions from the agenda by simply
being silent about them. Still, he furnished us with the
beginning of a genuine ecclesiological and Orthodox reaction to the Western errors.

After Photius there was again a period of alienation; the
next real encounter with the West did not occur until the
middle of the eleventh century, and was obviously conditioned by reasons of state. The period after the death of
Basil Bulgaroctonus (1025) was marked by the beginning
of a sharp decline for the empire. At the time of this internal crisis, all the threatening concern was suddenly shifted
to a new enemy in the East, the Seljuk Turks—news of
whom, as Gelzer has remarked, rang like a death knell for
Byzantium. Weakened from within, the empire by itself
was no longer in a condition to withstand the Eastern wave,
and the balance of forces which had previously been
achieved began to break down. The historical situation
again impelled Byzantine policy to seek help in the West.
At the same time the appearance of the Normans forced
the Roman pope to turn toward Byzantium. Then began
that prolonged and utterly joyless history of negotiations
and trading that lasted until the last day of the empire.

Schism of 1054

It is clear from the foregoing that the event usually designated as marking the beginning of this major division of
the Church—the schism of 1054—must be interpreted in
the context of the whole political situation. The encounter
between East and West was born of necessity. Emperor
Constantine Monomachus was negotiating with the pope

on the mutual defense of Italy (the southern part of which belonged to Byzantium) against the Normans, and on this account promised Pope Leo IX to give back the south Italian dioceses then under the jurisdiction of the patriarch of Constantinople, for they were a part of the empire. This pact was concealed from the patriarch, Michael Cerularius; who, however, found out about it. Cerularius himself, an outstanding figure in the long line of Byzantine patriarchs, had become a monk against his will after participating in a political plot that failed. He was wholeheartedly devoted to the service of the Church, but brought a politically-minded, power-conscious temperament to the task. For a brief instant the delicate balance between Church and empire tipped in favor of the Church; Cerularius' career shows what the possibilities might have been for the Church if another psychology had been dominant within it. He decided to prove to the weak and indecisive emperor the independence and strength of his position.

Paradoxical as it may sound, the churches did not separate in the eleventh century over what really divided them then and continues to divide them today. At the time of the final schism the subjects of dispute were not the questions of the papacy and the Holy Spirit, but ritual divergences between East and West as to the use of unleavened bread, fasting on Saturday, the singing of Alleluia at Easter, and so on. This reflected a narrowing of the universal horizon of the Church; what was secondary, external, and ceremonial was overshadowing the importance of the truth. Almost all the Byzantine arguments against the Latin rites have long since become unimportant, and only the genuinely dogmatic deviations of Rome have remained. Yet nothing was said of them in the years when the final bonds were broken.

At the patriarch's instruction one of the leading Byzantine hierarchs, Leo of Ohrid, wrote a tract against the Latin rites. Of course, behind the argument over ritual, Cerularius was concealing his defense of the Eastern

Church from the capitulation to Rome imposed upon it by the emperor. It was so understood in Rome. Leo IX responded with an extreme assertion of papal authority: "No one can deny that, just as the whole door is directed by its handle, so the order and structure of the whole Church is defined by Peter and his successors. And just as the handle pushes and pulls the door while itself remaining stationary, so Peter and his successors have the right to pronounce judgment on any local Church. No one should resist them in any way or try to usurp their place, for the supreme seat is not to be judged by anyone." In proof of his special authority the pope referred to the *Donation of Constantine*, a document according to which the first Christian emperor had allegedly granted Rome to the popes. Today everyone recognizes its spurious character. The pope concluded by stating that the Church of Constantinople was in error, sinful, scandalous (even ruled by women!), and that Rome granted second place after itself to it only out of indulgence, not because it was deserved.

Such an outlook naturally precluded any hope of unity between the churches. The Greeks may legitimately be accused of pettiness, lack of love, or loss of a universal cast of mind, but these things would not have been enough to divide the Church. Papal pretensions, however, excluded all who did not agree to its spiritual monarchy. Whatever the errors of the Eastern hierarchs of the period, it was the papacy itself that was the real reason for the separation; whatever the Greeks may have done, it was the popes who acted to cut off the East.

Subsequent correspondence could not change anything in the developing events. In the summer of 1054 papal legates arrived in Constantinople—Cardinal Humbert, Bishop Peter of Amalfi, and Cardinal Deacon Frederick of Lotharingia, the future Pope Stephen IX. They were all leaders of papal reform, who later prepared the way for its flourishing under Gregory VII (Hildebrand). The emperor was still relying on his political agreement with the pope, and received the legates with due ceremony and rendered them every protection. In order to placate them, Nicetas of Stethatos, disciple and biographer of St. Simeon the New Theologian, who had also criticized Rome, was obliged by imperial order to condemn publicly and burn his writings against the Latin innovations. The patriarch received the papal epistle from the legates in silence, showed them no respect, and afterward refused to meet with them. For five weeks the legates sought an audience in vain. The rupture had grown ripe. In vain the scholarly patriarch of Antioch, Peter, one of the clergy of Constantinople, urged Michael and the Western hierarchs to place the unity of the Church above ceremonial rites. His appeal came too late; he did not perceive that the papacy had actually already divided the Church. Losing patience, the legates resolved on a demonstration against the patriarch. On the morning of July 16, 1054, when the people were assembled in St. Sophia for the liturgy, they entered the sanctuary and placed on the altar the bull of excommunication against Cerularius and his supporters. "Wherefore we, not tolerating the unprecedented neglect and insult against the first holy and apostolic throne and making every effort to support the Catholic faith, by the power of the holy and indivisible Trinity and of the apostolic seat whose mission we represent, sign the anathema against Michael and his followers if they do not repent."

The legates overestimated the strength of the emperor, and thought by this act to gain decisive support against Cerularius. They did not know the might of the patriarch; a popular rebellion began to develop in the capital and the emperor was forced to think of his own safety. He capitulated. It was officially declared that the Greek translators had distorted the sense of the Latin bull, and it was ceremoniously burned. On July 20 a council headed by Cerularius and composed of two archbishops, twelve metropolitans, and seven bishops solemnly excommunicated in turn those who had been responsible for the action of July 16.

The patriarch's epistle brought this to the attention of the whole Eastern hierarchy. So ended one of the major dramas in the history of the Eastern Church.

Alienation Completed

The schism of 1054 was only the beginning of the separation of the churches. At first it was experienced more as one of those temporary schisms between the two major sees of which there had been many in the past. Ecclesiastical bonds were not broken everywhere at once. The schism developed into final separation and into racial and religious hatred only in the following era, and here a fatal role was played by the Crusades, which revealed Byzantium's "Western problem" in all its complexity.

The emperors of the eleventh century, turning toward the West in response to increasing pressure from Asia, still did not perceive where this must inevitably lead. By calling the West to its aid, Byzantium revealed its weakness and involved the West in all its difficulties. It did not realize that the West to which it had appealed had long since emerged from anarchy and partition. Byzantium had overlooked the birth of a new world, strong in its youthfulness and still unused energy; the Crusades were an outlet for that energy and the first expansion of medieval Europe. So the West, which Byzantium had been regarding as a temporary support against the Asian East, immediately acquired a threatening, independent significance.

It is only too well known how the Fourth Crusade ended, in 1204, with the capture of Constantinople, the barbarous sacking of the city, the profaning of Orthodox sacred objects, and the sixty-year Latin empire in the East. But this was only the high point, the most vivid of the manifestations of hatred crowded into this prolonged encounter between the divided halves of the Christian world. The separation of the churches ceased to be a dispute between hierarchs or a theological controversy; for centuries it was part of the flesh and blood of the people of the Church, a constant source of anguish in their state of mind. "Latinism" in the East and "the Greeks" in the West were synonymous with evil, heresy, and hostility, and became terms of profanity. Now not the hierarchs but the masses of the people confronted each other, and in their thinking separation changed into an elemental hatred, in which loyalty to their faith and a sense of injury because of the desecration of their holy places were mingled with a basic rejection of everything strange, without distinguishing what was good in it from what was bad.

The worst part of the separation of the churches lies in the fact that through the centuries we find hardly any sign of suffering from it, any longing for reunification, any awareness of the abnormality, sin, and horror of this schism in Christendom. There was almost a satisfaction with the separation, and a desire to discover darker and darker aspects in the opposite camp. It was a separation not only in the sense that these two churches were in fact divided, but also in the sense of a continually deepening and widening gulf in the state of mind of the total Christian community.

This psychology gave an intolerable superficiality to the attempts at union that stretch like a crimson thread from the period of the First Crusade at the end of the eleventh century to the fall of the empire in the fifteenth. The reasons for their persistent renewal are only too clear. In the West they represented the theocratic drive of the papacy, which reached its maximum power under Gregory VII, to bring all Christendom into complete subjection. It was, in a way, a thirst for the unification of the Church, but very remote from that unity which had inspired the early Church, which was conceived primarily as a unity of faith, love, and life. Now, for the West, the whole problem of unity was reduced to a single point: submission to Rome and external recognition of its absolute primacy. Rome responded to every appeal from Byzantium for aid with the demand that they recognize the power of the pope, and then the whole Western world would become their ally. Because Rome had become the undisputed spiritual center of the West, each time Byzantium lay gasping from the embraces of Islam, which hugged her more and more closely, she had no one to turn to except Rome. The shameful chain of unending negotiations, disputes, promises, and falsehood, went on and on, containing everything but the most important factor: the real wish for unity, the longing for a genuine fulfillment of the Church of Christ.

It is impossible to enumerate all these attempts. In Byzantium they were almost entirely due to political problems. The Church actually rejected them all, despite the pressure of the emperor; more than anything else, this theme of union demonstrated that the emperor in Byzantium was not all-powerful. Michael VIII Paleologus, who through his intermediaries had signed the union of Lyons in 1274 despite the opposition of the Church, died excommunicate and was deprived of Church burial. In Byzantium itself, starting with the thirteenth century, a group of "Latinizers" sprang up, partisans of unity and supporters of Western ecclesiastical doctrine—a certain sympathy for Rome can be found even in the highest circles. But like the attraction of some Russian aristocrats of the nineteenth century to Catholicism, this was not a movement *within* the Orthodox Church, but simply the conversion of certain Orthodox to Catholicism, and rejection of union in the mind of the Orthodox Church itself remained unchanged.

The series of attempts culminated in a spiritual catastrophe for the Byzantine Church, the Council of Florence in 1438–39, which ended with the Greek hierarchs subscribing one and all to a complete capitulation to Rome. To understand the event, we must read the proceedings of this unlucky council, and feel some empathy for the torment of the Greeks, who were fearful of the destruction of the empire by Islam and persecuted by financial pressure from the Latins—since they even lacked funds to return home. They were under great psychological pressure from the emperor and subjected to the intrigues of the Latinizers, who were determined to achieve union at any cost. All this must be recognized in order to comprehend in human terms, if not justify, their cowardly error. The celebration by Catholics in 1939 of the jubilee of the union in Florence is evidence of profound misunderstanding of the real ecclesiastical conception of the Orthodox Church. Pope Eugene IV showed greater penetration at the time when he asked, on being joyfully informed by his bishops that all the Greeks had signed the union, "Did Mark of Ephesus sign, too?" Receiving an answer in the negative, he is traditionally supposed to have said, "Well, that means we have achieved nothing." In fact, all signed except one, but that one, St. Mark of Ephesus, became the expression of faith, experience, and tradition for the Eastern Church. When the Greeks returned to Byzantium, they immediately repudiated with horror the union that had been forced upon them, and the fall of the empire fourten years later tragically eliminated the very reason the council had been held. The empire, for whose sake some had been ready to sacrifice Orthodoxy, ceased to exist.

Such attempts at union were, in fact, especially responsible for reinforcing separation; the question of the unity of the churches was long confused by falsehood and calculation and poisoned by nonecclesiastical and debased motives. The Church recognizes only unity and therefore cannot recognize any "union." The latter implies a lack of confidence in unity, a denial of the unifying fire of grace which can make all that is "natural"—all historical insults, limitations, gulfs, and misunderstandings—nonexistent, and can overcome them by force of the divine power. The Byzantine period in the history of Orthodoxy began with the alienation between East and West. It ended with complete separation; from then on the Orthodox East was divided from the Roman West by an impenetrable wall. Orthodoxy became "Eastern" once and for all.

Cyril and Methodius

At the time the empire fell, a new factor had long since entered into Eastern Orthodoxy, had grown strong within it, and had acquired an independent significance. This was the Slavic element. The swift growth of Slavic Christianity out of Byzantine roots begins a new and extremely important chapter in the history of the Orthodox Church. The Slavs appear early in the life of Byzantium, illumined by the glow of conflagrations and caught up in the ravages of war. Until the end of the sixth century the empire was successful in throwing them back beyond the Danube, but in 580 almost a hundred thousand of them overflowed into Greece. In the seventh century, liberated from the Avar empire of which they had hitherto been a part, the Slavs gradually settled the ancient Roman provinces they had devastated: Illyria, Moesia, Thrace, and Macedonia. The whole century was spent in combating these still savage hordes. Gradually, however, the Slavs entered the Byzantine orbit inwardly as well as by external penetration, and the sons of their princes, like the Germans before them, gladly accepted minor court titles from Constantinople. The first Christianization of the Slavs began.

At the end of the seventh century came a new invasion from a Turkic people, the Bulgars, who asserted their authority in provinces settled by Slavs and began a struggle against the empire that lasted many years. As occurred later with the Varangian conquerors of the eastern Slavs, they themselves became Slavicized. Almost at the very gates of the capital, a mighty Bulgar-Slavic state was gradually formed by a nearly uninterrupted war that lasted throughout the whole eighth—or "iconoclastic"—century. We do not know how this new and threatening Slavic problem would have been solved for Byzantium if a development had not taken place in the second half of the ninth century that marks the real beginning of the Slavic chapter in the

history of Orthodoxy: the "translation" of Christianity into
Slavic by two brothers who became Byzantine saints: Constantine (who later received the monastic name of Cyril)
and Methodius.

There is an immense literature on the first teachers of the
Slavs. Historical research on their activity is complicated by
confessional hostility. Which holds the honor of first en-
couraging Slavic Christianity—Constantinople or Rome?
There are disputes on these matters, but the answers are
unimportant by comparison with the immense significance
of the heritage of Cyril and Methodius in the destiny of the
Eastern Church.

They belonged to the intellectual elite of Byzantium,
which was grouped around Patriarch Photius in Constantinople in the second half of the ninth century. Constantine
was a philosopher, scholar, and linguist, and important
missions to the Arabs and Khazars, who lived in southern
Russia on the near side of the Dnieper, had been entrusted
to him. Natives of Thessalonica, a city with a large Slavic
population, the brothers had in all probability known the
local Slavic dialect from childhood. In 862 the Slavic Prince
Rostislav of Moravia sent a request to Constantinople for
missionaries who could help him strengthen Christianity
among the Slavs. (It must be stated that the motives im-
pelling him were not solely religious, but also political. By
strengthening Christianity among the Slavs he was fortify-
ing his own national independence against the new historical colossus of Germanism, which was forming at the time.)
The choice, probably made with the help of Patriarch
Photius, naturally fell on the two brothers, and in the
middle of 864 they arrived in Velehrad, the capital of
Moravia.

Here, along with their purely missionary activity, they
began their great work of translating Christian writings into
Slavic. From a legalistic point of view, they were working
in a region that had been part of the sphere of influence
of the Roman Church from ancient times. These were years

of intense struggle between Pope Nicholas I and Patriarch
Photius. To regularize their situation, or perhaps because
of a summons from Rome, which had become disturbed
at the growth of Greek influence among the western Slavs,
the brothers quickly went to the Western capital, where
Nicholas' successor Hadrian greeted them ceremoniously
and affectionately. The Slavic Gospel was placed on the
altar of St. Mary as a sign of papal blessing, and the Slavic
liturgy was performed in many Roman Churches.

The mission to the Slavs, beginning under the dual blessing of Byzantium and Rome, promised quick success, but
the story of Constantine records the beginning of opposition as well, against which the brothers were obliged to
defend their work. He was not destined to return to Moravia but died in Rome in 869, becoming a monk just before his death and obtaining his brother's promise to continue the work he had begun.

Methodius was also unable to return to the scene of his
first labors. While the brothers were in Rome, German
pressure on Moravia had increased, and after 870 it became
part of the Western empire. Methodius stayed farther south
with the Pannonian Prince Kotzel, who shared Rostislav's
views on strengthening Christianity among the Slavs as a
defense against Germanism. Here, in all probability, he
introduced the Slavic liturgy for the first time, and this
caused many of his troubles. In 794 one of the Western
councils had forbidden the celebration of the liturgy in
any language but Latin, Greek, or Hebrew; technically,
Methodius had broken this law. Besides, although Latinism
was weak in Moravia, Pannonia had been under the administration of the Latin archbishopric of Salzburg for seventy-
five years, and conflict was inevitable. The missionary to
the Slavs was obviously "out of bounds."

Both Kotzel and the archbishop of Salzburg appealed to
Rome, which again supported Methodius. He was made
head of a separate diocese of Pannonia, subordinate to
Rome. But his enemies were not pacified. Methodius was

accused of flouting the Church canons, condemned by the *Sejm* in Regensburg (an assembly of secular and ecclesiastical notables), and forced to languish in prison for two and a half years. All his complaints to Rome were intercepted. Under Pope John VIII he again received firm support for a while. Understanding the full significance of the Slavs, the pope appointed him archbishop of Moravia and stood by him, despite never-ending intrigues. So in ceaseless struggle, defending his own rights, betrayed by his enemies but supported by the people, Methodius lived on until 885.

During this time immense work was accomplished, which was to fertilize the whole Slavic world. But the immediate work of the brothers fell to pieces among the western Slavs after Methodius' death. They could not hold off German pressures, and Pope Stephen, who could not understand the policy of his predecessors, simply liquidated the whole Slavic mission. The disciples of Methodius were driven out of Moravia, and only in the nineteenth century, during a time of Slavic renewal, did the work of Cyril and Methodius again become a rallying point for national liberation and western Slavic culture.

Rise of the Bulgarian Empire

In Bulgaria, however, there were more immediate fruits of their mission. This was the first great Slavic state, the first conscious effort to build an empire and to repeat the Byzantine experience among the Slavs. This Bulgarian prologue was destined to define the whole future course of Slavic Orthodoxy in one way or another. Until the middle of the ninth century, territorial consolidation proceeded and the Slavic tribes were united under the Bulgar khans. When Boris began his reign in 852, this territorial amalgamation was complete and the problem of baptism had arisen in turn.

It must be emphasized that from the very start the acceptance of Christianity had a political significance in the history of the Slavs, as well as a religious one; this may be explained by their relations to Byzantium. Although weakened and without its former halo of invincibility, the empire remained the golden dream of all barbarians throughout these centuries—a center of culture and political tradition, the true center of the world. Constantinople was a fabulous capital, full of treasures and riches, the symbol of strength, beauty, and glory. In the thought of the "barbarian" nations we can trace the paradoxical dualism of their relations with Byzantium. On the one hand, they had a military dream of conquest—to live off the riches of the empire, tear off bits of territory, and finally conquer it— this was the constant goal of the Slavic "empires." On the other hand they had a profound, almost religious respect for it, wanted to imitate it in every way and participate in its glorious and ancient tradition.

This tradition, however, was inseparable from Christianity. Only the acceptance of Christianity could bring culture within the reach of the barbarians and include them among the great families of the human race. Therefore baptism became an inevitable stage in the political development of the Slavs, a sign of their historical maturity.

Christianity had of course existed in Bulgaria even before Boris; it was imperial territory, Christianized in ancient times. But he was the first to make of it an instrument of political growth and crystallization for his empire; in brief, he transplanted into the minds of the Slavs the Christian theocracy by which Byzantium had lived since the conversion of Constantine.

His political calculations are also apparent in the fact that he wavered for a long time between Byzantium and Rome as the proper auspices for baptism. He was obliged to take into account those around him, his bodyguard, who were closely tied to the national pagan tradition. These nobles must regard Christianity, not as the faith of their enemies the Byzantines, but as the basis for Bulgaria's national and political independence from Byzantium. Yet according to Byzantine theocratic ideology, which linked Church and state in indissoluble union, baptism meant entry into the state as well—entry into the Byzantine world. In other words, it threatened to absorb the young Bulgar state. The basic ecclesiastical policy of Boris and his successors, therefore, became that of obtaining at any cost their own independent, "autocephalous" Church, which could become the same religious sanction for Bulgaria that the Church of Constantinople had been for the empire. This was an extremely important moment in the history of Orthodoxy and must be particularly stressed. Christianity came to the Slavs in its Byzantine, theocratic aspect, and immediately became the source of the same inspiration as in Byzantium. In this case, however, such a vision inevitably came into conflict with its Byzantine prototype, and introduced into the Orthodox world the poison of inevitable divisions and combat.

Boris continued to waver, apparently inclining to a Western solution, which was a matter of life and death for Byzantium to prevent. A military campaign in which the Greeks were victorious obliged him to capitulate: baptism was made a condition for peace. The Bulgar khan was immediately baptized, almost on the battlefield (869), and his godfather was the Emperor Michael III himself. But what Boris had feared indeed came to pass: the bodyguard began to rebel. The newly-baptized prince inundated them in blood, but understood the omens and immediately took measures to procure ecclesiastical independence from Byzantium. For him this marked the first step toward empire, the dream of all barbarians who in warfare against Rome had absorbed forever the Roman-Christian idea.

Byzantium had no notion of granting this autonomy, however. The political basis for the baptism of the Bulgars was the precise opposite of Boris' plan; Byzantium was striving to hold subject as far as possible a strong and dangerous Bulgaria, and to include it within the sphere of its theocracy. Once more we see all the magic that the concept of theocracy held for the Byzantine mind and its incapacity to judge events from a purely Christian or purely ecclesiastical viewpoint. According to this theory even baptism became not only admission into Christ's flock and the beginning of the reign of grace, but to a great extent it also meant acceptance of Byzantine citizenship. Itself poisoned, Byzantium, to its great shame, also poisoned those who received the Christian Gospel from it.

Now Boris began his manipulations. Not securing independence from Byzantium for his Church, he appealed to Rome. The dramatic conflict between Bulgaria and Byzantium was complicated by the separation of the churches, then in process. Nicholas I, enemy of Photius and one of the founders of the medieval papacy, seized joyfully on this opportunity to establish his power in the East. He sent two bishops with books, presents, and letters to Bulgaria; whereas the Byzantines had limited their delegation to archimandrites, a lower rank. Boris, delighted, drove all the Greek clergy out of Bulgaria, and a vigorous Latinization began. In his letters the pope tried in every way to discredit the Greek faith.

This did not last long, however. Boris wanted a patriarch and religious autonomy. The papacy was even less favorably inclined to this than Byzantium had been, for in the West the last trace of the independence of the ancient churches had now been eliminated. Boris broke with Rome as firmly as he had broken with Byzantium and once more appealed to Constantinople. Wiser for their experience, the Byzantines were forced now to agree to a semi-autonomous Bulgarian archbishopric. The later unfortunate history of relations between Bulgaria and Byzantium shows plainly that they made this concession out of necessity, not because they had rejected one iota of the idea of Byzantium's ecclesiastical monopoly. But Boris was for the moment placated since he could turn to strengthening his own empire, now Christian.

Bulgarian Orthodoxy

All this political coloring must not conceal from us the positive significance of Boris' work. Acceptance of the heritage of Cyril and Methodius in Bulgaria had immense subsequent meaning. The disciples of Methodius who had been driven out of Moravia came to Bulgaria and were received with honor. The wise khan inevitably perceived the value of the Slavonic Church service for his dream of a Slavic empire shored up by an independent Church. To avoid opposition from the Greek hierarchy, he sent Clement, leader of Methodius' disciples, to the region of Ochrida in the west of the kingdom, where the work of Cyril and Methodius had found it first fertile soil, and the bright image of St. Clement of Ochrida illumines the beginning of Slavic Christianity. Not limiting himself solely to religious enlightenment, he tried in every way to improve the economic conditions of his backward flock. Numerous members of the Slavic priesthood were trained, Christian Orthodox writings in Slavonic were accumulated, and the beginnings of an Orthodox Slavic culture laid down.

The personality of Boris himself was not limited to political calculations and dreams. As time passed, his political interests were increasingly replaced by purely religious ones. Christianity really developed within his soul; while he did not put aside his work or change his theories, "the one thing necessary" held increasing sway in the depths of his mind. A Western chronicler states that by day he appeared before the people in imperial robes, but passed the night in prayer. After ruling for thirty-six years, he abdicated the throne in 888 in favor of his son and withdrew to a monastery. State disorders summoned him back to power once more, but when order was restored and he had passed the empire on to his grandson Simeon, he withdrew permanently into a life of prayer.

Under Simeon (892–927) Bulgaria achieved its apogee. He had himself been educated in Byzantium, where he had studied "the rhetoric of Demosthenes and the syllogisms of Aristotle." All his life he was captivated by the beauty and majesty of the Byzantine court, the like of which he created in his own new capital, Great Preslav. This did not make him neglect Bulgaria, however; on the contrary, he carried Boris' dream to paradoxical extremes. Had not the time come when Bulgaria should assume the place of the decrepit empire and become the heir to Christian theocracy, and a Bulgrian khan crown his head with the sacred diadem of the Byzantine basileus? Thus Byzantine theocratic ideas, which had shaped the barbarians, had given them a weapon against Byzantium itself and shown them what program to follow. Their aim, and the limit of their desires, was St. Sophia, heaven on earth, the sole heart of the Christian universe. Simeon was the first of a long line of Slavic competitors for title to the Orthodox empire, which the Greeks had guarded so jealously and monopolistically.

Almost his whole reign was spent in warfare against Byzantium—the first great civil war in the Orthodox world. Bulgarian troops stood under the walls of Constantinople; but the time had not yet come for the empire to yield. Failing to conquer Byzantium, like his grandfather, Simeon appealed to Rome, and received the title of "Emperor" for himself and of "Patriarch" for his archbishop. True, this was pure fiction; there was no acceptance of Rome in Bulgaria at the time. But the fiction is an eloquent indication of the strength of the theocratic dream that possessed him.

The main significance of Simeon's reign was as a golden age in the history of Church Slavonic writing, a genuine flourishing of Slavic Christian culture. He spared no resources for its creation; he built schools and libraries and assembled whole armies of translators. The store of Church

Slavonic writings composed in his reign was sufficient for the needs not only of Bulgaria, but later for the Serbian and Russian Churches. Of course this whole culture was not and could not be original. Simeon himself had been a pupil in Byzantium, and the work of Cyril and Methodius had also been nourished at Byzantine springs. In various ways Bulgaria was repeating and assimilating the Byzantine experience. One historian has correctly called this cultural blossoming under Simeon "the Hellenization of Bulgaria." Thus the Slavic element was shaped by Hellenism, and so Slavic Byzantinism arose.

First place in this cultural activity was taken by translations of Byzantine writers: the Fathers of the Church, historians, and hymn-writers. Clement of Ochrida himself composed a life of St. Methodius, following Byzantine models, and translated a whole host of liturgical texts, saints' lives, and works of the Fathers. Dependence on Byzantium is also reflected in the replacement of the Glagolitic (Slavic) alphabet, which had been invented by Cyril, by the Cyrillic (mistakenly attributed to Cyril), which appeared about the same time and more resembled the Greek.

Thus the young Bulgarian kingdom acquired a sort of encyclopedia of contemporary Byzantine culture, which defined forever the development of Slavic Christianity. Although politically and even ecclesiastically independent of Byzantium, Simeon's Bulgaria was completely nourished by the Byzantine spirit. The Slavic language itself, when it became Church Slavonic, was almost a copy of the Greek. Dvornik has said that Bulgaria was "Slavic by language, Byzantine by spirit, and became the bearer of Byzantinism to the other Slavs, the Serbs and especially the Russians."

After the death of Simeon the decline of the first Bulgarian kingdom set in. In the tenth century the military might of Byzantium rose again; it was the Byzantine epic era, a restoration of all its strength and glory. This inevitably brought on a struggle against the hated Bulgarian competitor. In 972 the whole eastern part of Bulgaria was conquered and Byzantine theory immediately put into effect: Patriarch Damian was deposed and the jurisdiction of the Bulgarian Church was simply placed under Constantinople. The western part of the kingdom, the Macedonian and Albanian regions centered at Ochrida, survived until 1018, and the autocephalous Bulgarian Church survived with it. But then, after thirty years of warfare between the Byzantine Basil II Bulgaroctonus and the Bulgarian Tsar Samuel—celebrated in Bulgarian tradition (he had taken the title of "Tsar" after dethroning one of the Russian tsars in war with Constantinople)—Bulgarian independence was destroyed and the Church shared its fate.

Reading the accounts of this war, unequalled in cruelty and ferocity, during which the pious Byzantine autocrat ordered the eyes of fifteen thousand captives put out and sent back to the aged Samuel, it is dreadful to think that this was a war between Orthodox, and that both sides were inspired and nourished by the same "theocracy," that terrible, ineradicable falsehood of Byzantium and of the whole age of Constantine.

Once he had eliminated his enemy, it is true, Basil showed magnanimity: Bulgarian nobles were given Byzantine titles and the archbishopric of Ochrida received an apparent autonomy, but in another, Byzantine sense. Actually, Bulgaria was subjected to a compulsory Greek influence for almost two centuries, and the spirit of the Greeks toward the Bulgars is seen in the writings of Greek pastors about their Bulgarian flocks. "He stinks of rot, as the Bulgarian stinks of sheep"—so someone was described by Theophylact of Bulgaria, a celebrated eleventh-century Byzantine hierarch, theologian, and expert on Homer—for him the Bulgarian nature was the "mother of all evils."

The Bulgarian Empire would rise again with new strength at the end of the twelfth century, when Byzantium grew weaker. This was the so-called Empire of Trnovo, linked with the names of the Asen brothers, fighters for national independence. It began with the now-familiar threat of an appeal to Rome. If Byzantium would not recognize it, Rome would; the main goal was to achieve empire and the condition necessary for it, an independent patriarchate. Johannitsa Kalojan (1197–1207), the younger of the Asen brothers, appealed to Pope Innocent III, greatest of the medieval popes, in whose time the theory that the pope was the head of all Christian peoples reached its apex. Just when Orthodox Byzantium was falling under the blows of the Crusaders (1204), Kalojan was crowned by a Roman cardinal "Emperor of the Bulgars and Vlachs."

Yet this did not prevent him from making war upon the Latin masters of Constantinople, capturing Emperor Baldwin, and, despite all intercessions of the pope, putting him to death. The unity of Christian peoples was becoming more and more a bitter parody. Later the orientation changed again and Ivan Asen II (1218–41) entered into an "Orthodox coalition" with the Greek emperors of Nicaea, receiving in return Greek recognition of the Trnovo autonomy. Again it was recognition by necessity, which the Greeks would repudiate at their first chance.

So it continued until the very end, when the Bulgarian Empire was destroyed by the Turks at the end of the fourteenth century. Rupture and ties, alliances and wars; no one could solve the dispute by force any longer. The Orthodox empires were drawing to a close, but even the approach of the end could not change anything in their passionate dream—"in Christ God the faithful Emperor and autocrat of the Bulgars and Greeks," title of the last of the Bulgarian emperors. If only nominally, they felt themselves bearers of a single theocratic tradition. This was its last triumph in the consciousness of the Orthodox, and the time of its decay in real life.

As in Byzantium, only in the hush of monasteries, far from the unfortunate theocratic decor, could a genuine Christian soul grow and mature, and the real fruits of baptism be produced. Such were John of Rila, the martyrs of

Trnovo, the disciples of the Hesychasts (the "little Athos" in Sofia); mention should also be made of the constant growth of theological interest, reflected in Church Slavonic writings. The theocratic dream of the Bulgarian Empire would perish like the dream of Byzantium, but the illumination of Bulgarian Orthodoxy would leave a deep trace, and would bear imperishable fruit in the later development of the Orthodox East.

The Serbian Empire

The history of the rise of the Serbian Empire in these same centuries is in many ways a repetition of the Bulgarian experience. Here, too, the story begins with a partitioned tribal life and passes through the first contact with Byzantium and early Christianization. Constantine Porphyrogenitus places this in the seventh century during the reign of Heraclius. In the ninth century the heritage of Cyril and Methodius reached the Serbs from neighboring Pannonia and Bulgaria and established Eastern Byzantine Christianity among them permanently. In the ninth and tenth centuries the first town representing a state capital was established at Rashka, where the grand *zupans* ruled. During the intense struggle between Byzantium and Bulgaria, the Serbs fell by turns into the sphere of influence of one or the other, and the see of Rashka was subject to Constantinople, Bulgaria or Ochrida, depending on the circumstances. Yet under all these changing influences a national Serbian self-consciousness grew and became established. It grew, of course, in proportion as the Serbs adopted Byzantine ideas, in either their Greek or their Bulgarian version. Here, too, the "Roman temptation" came to life; in 1078 the Grand Zupan Michael received a king's crown from Pope Gregory V. By the middle of the twelfth century Serbia already had all the elements of statehood, and the time was drawing near for her to take on the same Byzantine theocracy and enter the lists as a possible heir to Byzantium.

This was the work of the famous Nemanya. By a series of wars against other *zupans* and against Byzantium, he united the Serbs, and a theocratic theme immediately entered the situation. Stephen the First-Crowned, his son, began by flirting with Rome; this was the era of Innocent III and the first fall of Byzantium. Later the orientation changed, apparently under the influence of Stephen's younger brother. This was Sava, the monk of Athos, who there founded the famous Serbian monastery of Hilandar together with his father, the aged Nemanya, also a monk of Athos in his old age.

Soon afterward Sava went to Nicaea, where the capital of the Byzantine Empire had been transferred after the destruction of 1204. At this time the Byzantines were seeking allies against their Latin conquerors and it was very important for them to prevent the Slavs from passing into the Latin orbit. Therefore they agreed to the autonomy of the Serbian Church and to installing Sava as its first archbishop. When he returned to Serbia, he established the ecclesiastical center of the new empire at the monastery of Zica. He divided the country into dioceses and consecrated his disciples. Then he completed a solemn "revival" of Christianity in Serbia. A council of all the clergy was assembled in Zica, a special service performed, and after it the archbishop announced on behalf of the whole people a solemn confession of faith and a curse against all heresies. As the final act and logical consequence of all that had gone before, he again (1221) crowned his brother Stephen. After holding office for fourteen years, in which he established both Church and empire, Sava made his disciple Arsenius archbishop and himself set off for the holy places. He died in Bulgaria, at the capital of his relative, Emperor Ivan Asen, in 1236. The day consecrated to his memory has remained a national Serbian holiday, for St. Sava was the father of both Serbian Orthodoxy and Serbian statehood.

Subsequent history of the Serbian Empire only recapitu-
lates the familiar pattern: the same complex relations with
Rome, the same political question of union, the constant
shifts in orientation for or against the Greeks. The last
flourishing of Serbia was the reign of Stephen Dushan
(1331–55), when the country almost achieved the original
dream of the Slavs: establishment of a united empire under
the Slavic banner. Dushan's policy had a single aim, to
capture Constantinople, unite Serbs, Bulgars, and Greeks
under his rule, and eliminate the growing Turkish threat
by these combined efforts. In 1346 he was crowned in his
capital, Skoplje, "Emperor of the Serbs and Greeks," and
prior to this he had elevated the archbishop of Serbia to
patriarch in Pech. He flirted with Rome, however, and was
excommunicated for it by the Church of Constantinople.
In the autumn of 1355 he prepared for a final march on
Constantinople. Never had the dream of a Slavic replacement of Byzantium seemed so near realization. The empire
was saved by Dushan's unexpected death.

Early Slavic Orthodoxy

But the end of all empires, the Turkish Horde, was fast
approaching, and with it the destruction of the great theocratic dreams. Perhaps in this first flowering of Slavic Christianity, we can best discern the results of the late Byzantine
chapter in the history of the Orthodox Church—both the
intrinsic narrowness of its religious and political idea and
the spiritual vitality of Byzantine Orthodoxy itself. In the
Slavic version of Byzantinism, Church and empire sprang
from the same idea, the same outlook, originating from
the empire although directed against it. This hostility, the
basic distortion of the Byzantine heritage, survives down
to our own time. Yet it is characteristic that the mortal
antagonism of the Slavic empires to Byzantium, which
lasted for centuries and shed so much Orthodox blood, in

no way destroyed the unity of the Byzantine style of Orthodoxy itself, and Slavic Christianity was and remained primarily a precise reflection, repetition, and development of
Byzantine Christianity. If this Slavic Orthodoxy is seen distinct from its external political fate, we see a truly united
Orthodox world which has one personality and is nourished by the same roots, filled with the same spirit. This
unity proved stronger than political and national divisions.
Byzantinism simultaneously poisoned the Slavic world by
its theocratic messianism, and fertilized it forever with the
inexhaustible riches of its Chalcedonian striving toward
God-Manhood. In addition to its saints and martyrs,
the striking religious art of the Balkan churches, only now
beginning to reveal its spiritual beauty to the world, is a
silent witness to the profound Christianization of the Slavic
psyche, and its receptivity to the highest ideal of Christian
Byzantium.

The dark ages of Turkish control would not obliterate
this Orthodox seal upon the externally divided but fundamentally united Byzantine Christian world.

5 THE DARK AGES

Turkish Conquest

On May 29, 1453, after a two-day assault, the troops of Mohammed II took Constantinople. The last emperor, Constantine XI, had fallen in battle. The holy city became the capital of the Ottoman Empire. Bulgaria was overcome, Serbia was finally conquered in 1459, European Greece in 1459–60, Bosnia in 1463, and finally Egypt in 1517. The whole Orthodox East, except for Russia, was under Islamic rule, which was to last for more than four centuries. The era of the great eclipse of Orthodoxy had come, leaving a deep imprint on the mind of the Eastern Church.

In defining the nature of the Turkish yoke, one must first emphasize that it was not a persecution of Christianity. When Mohammed entered the city, after three days of pillage, outrages, and revelry after victory, he announced "law, mercy, and order." He was no barbarian; he had been in Constantinople before and knew Greek, and while conquering Byzantium he was attracted to it by his special sympathy for everything Greek. A historian has remarked that his entourage included "sympathetic Christians as secretaries, since the Turks were very poorly educated." The same historian wrote that "Christians administered his whole Empire." This was an exaggeration, but it is not without foundation; Mohammed undoubtedly dreamed of

271

strengthening and ornamenting his empire with Greek culture. In addition, although the Koran taught that Christians
were unbelievers, it recognized Christ as a prophet and
showed respect for Him. Therefore one of the first acts of
Mohammed after victory was an invitation to the Greeks
to elect their own patriarch.

They chose Gennadius Scholarius, who had participated
in the Council of Florence but had been converted by
Mark of Ephesus from sympathy to Rome to a fanatic hostility to union. The Turks also invited them to put Church
life in order and return to their accustomed occupations.
Later a *firman*, the highest state charter of the sultan, defined once and for all the legal status of Christians within
the empire. All Christians were obliged to pay an annual
head tax, the *haradj*, to the state treasury, but this was their
only obligation to the conquerors. In return the patriarch
was given complete freedom in administering Church affairs, and no one was permitted to interfere with his orders.
The persons of the patriarch, bishops, and priests were proclaimed inviolable; all the clergy were exempted from taxes.
Half of the churches of Constantinople were converted into
mosques, but the rest were at the disposal of the Christians.
In all matters pertaining to internal ecclesiastical administration the canons remained in force; the Porte did not
infringe in any way upon the independence of Church administration. Freedom of Church feasts and of public worship was recognized; marriages, funerals, and other Church
ceremonies were celebrated openly and without hindrance.
The solemn celebration of Easter was permitted in all cities
and villages. The Church was allowed to remain the Church
and Christians were allowed to remain Christians.

But another basic element in the status of Christians
under the Turks was no less important. For the Turks, who
unlike the Arabs were not religious fanatics, Christianity
was the national faith of the Greeks, as Mohammedanism
was for the Turks. Like Judaism, Islam in general made no
distinction between secular and religious society. To the

extent that the whole civil structure of Mohammedan society—state, courts, law, and everything else—was defined
by Islam, it was inapplicable to non-Mohammedans. Therefore the Christians in the Ottoman Empire received the
"rights" of a national as well as religious minority, and these
concepts were merged into one. The patriarch became the
milet pasha or leader of the people, and the Church hierarchy were given the rights of civil administration over the
Christian population. It judged Christians according to
Greek laws, its court was recognized by the Porte, and
sentences were carried out by the Turkish authorities. Christians could have their own schools, their own programs,
and their own censorship. Theoretically the Church became
a sort of state within a state.

Christians Under Turkish Rule

The position of the Church in the Turkish empire might
therefore be considered as firmly established. This was only
its outward aspect, however. Actually its position was very
often a terrible one, and it is impossible to describe all the
suffering, humiliation, and outright persecution the Church
was obliged to undergo in this age, which was dark indeed.
The "rights" just mentioned were not rights at all in our
sense of the word, but represented the mercy of the sultan.
The Turkish cast of mind was no less theocratic than the
Roman, which had however been mitigated by an ancient
and well-constructed juridical tradition. The Turkish sultan
was the source of all rights and of mercy, as well as of the
lack of it, and he was accountable to no one for his actions.
According to Islam, Christians were *rayah* or cattle, the
conquered, the unbelievers, and they had no real rights or
citizenship. If all sultans had been on the same high cultural and political level as Mohammed II, his firman might
have been observed, but it was broken even by Mohammed
himself, when he took away from Patriarch Gennadius the

Church of the Twelve Apostles, which he had previously granted to him.

Shortly after, a period of political decline set in for the Ottoman Empire, and arbitrariness, unscrupulousness, and corruption became the rule. The sultans fleeced their pashas, who in turn fleeced the Christians. There was no one to whom one could complain. The situation worsened perceptibly in the seventeenth and eighteenth centuries, the bleakest in the history of the Church. As the Russian historian, Kartashoff, has remarked, Turkey could have been swept away by any of the European powers in this period, but Europe supported her for fear of Russia, and closed its eyes to the scandalous sufferings of the Christians. In some places every Christian was slaughtered. Russia alone intervened on their behalf, but this frequently resulted only in a worsening of their position.

The rights of the patriarch were gradually reduced to nothing; all that was left to him was the "right" of being responsible for the Christians. In the course of seventy-three years in the eighteenth century, the patriarch was replaced forty-eight times! Some were deposed and reinstalled as many as five times; many were put to torture. The rebellions of the Janissaries were accompanied by terrible bloodshed. Churches were defiled, relics cut to pieces, and the Holy Gifts profaned. Christian pogroms became more and more frequent. In the nineteenth century Turkey was simply rotting away, but the "sick man of Europe" was supported at all points by other nations in opposition to Russia. There was, it is true, a series of reforms by which the sultans attempted to Europeanize Turkey and thus improve the position of the Christians; actually their situation grew worse, especially as national self-consciousness and dreams of freedom arose within the empire. Greeks in Turkey and Constantinople paid for the Greek uprising of 1821 by terrible slaughter.

That year was marked by the martyrdom of Patriarch Gregory V. He was not saved even by the decree of excommunication he brought himself to issue against the rebels, his own fellow believers, and later he redeemed this cowardice by his faithfulness to Christ at the hour of death. When it was suggested to him that he recant his faith, he answered, "You are laboring in vain; the Christian patriarch will die a Christian." This was on Easter Sunday, 1821. In the morning the patriarch had performed the Easter liturgy and had called on all, on this great feast, to forget all earthly cares. After distributing an Easter egg to everyone, he was arrested and hanged that same day at the gates of the patriarchate.

None of the laws promulgated by the Turkish Government to placate European public opinion helped the Christians. After the Crimean War, for example, during which the Turks were allies of England and France, and after the Peace of Paris of 1856, Sultan Abdul Medjid "out of ceaseless concern for the welfare of his subjects," issued the well-known *Gatti-Gamayun*, or decree written by his own hand, according to which the Christians were granted equal rights with the Moslems. What joy there was then in Europe! Actually, as Professor Lopukhin has pointed out, it meant

. . . that the Christian subjects of the Sultan, whatever oppression and humiliation they were suffering, were now unable to rely on any outside help but were obliged to count solely on their own resources . . . Since Turkey remained in the same disorganized, elemental state, the deliberate idolizing of her by European diplomacy in 1856 had never before been so sharply contradictory to the facts. This policy was shamefully exposed by the subsequent course of events during the last years of the reign of Abdul Medjid, when the Greeks, as a result of the *Gatti-Gamayun*, not only remained in a dreadful social and economic state, but even lost many of their former rights and privileges.[1]

[1] A. P. Lopukhin, *The History of the Christian Church in the Nineteenth Century* (in Russian, St. Petersburg, 1901), Vol. 2, *The Orthodox East*, pp. 47–48.

The whole second half of the nineteenth century was marked by Christian uprisings and bloody reprisals from the Turks. A period of open struggle and slaughter began, on a scale hitherto unknown—all at a time when benevolent European liberalism was triumphant in the West. The year 1861 was marked by uprisings in Bosnia and Herzegovina, in Serbia, Wallachia, Moldavia, and Bulgaria; 1866 by a rebellion on the island of Crete; and 1875 again in Bosnia and Herzegovina. These uprisings prepared the way for a new chapter in the history of the Orthodox Church.

Rise of Religious Nationalism

The era of the Turkish yoke was marked in the history of Orthodoxy by an unprecedented rise of religious nationalism. Its roots, as we already have seen, lay deep in the spirit of Byzantinism itself, which made an absolute value out of the concept of the "holy state." Yet this concept had arisen and developed at first in the context of Roman universalism. Rome had deified the state, not the nation. The multinational empire thought it had overcome all national limitations; it saw itself as a "universe" united by a single law, a single authority, a single culture, with faith in the same values, but had no racial features of any sort, or any exaltation of "flesh and blood." Any barbarian who accepted Roman citizenship and shared the cultural values of Hellenism would cease to be a barbarian and become a full member of that universe, a member of a united human society in which all the best elements lived according to values which were opposed to racial exclusivism of any sort. This universal spirit of Rome was its main point of alliance with Christianity, which was universal and all-embracing by its very nature.

The Church accepted alliance with the empire, placed itself under its protection, and gladly sanctified it by its blessing because the empire itself was aware that it was sum-

moned to a universal mission and that this calling was in
no way limited. It must be admitted that at first the empire really lived according to this inspiration. Constantine,
for example, considered himself responsibile for spreading
Christianity in Persia, and missions went out of early Byzantium to the Armenians, Georgians, Goths, Huns, and
finally to the Slavs. The inclusion of barbarian peoples who
had accepted Christianity within the empire was not dic-
tated by political imperialism alone but also by the conviction that the empire was the normal form for the Christian
world, which was united because it was Christian.

The first breach in this universalism was the division of
the empire itself, which ended with the separation of its
Western part. Still, the authority of the empire was recognized by the barbarians who came to power in the West,
even if only nominally, so that the Byzantine theory remained inviolate. The conflict with the West in the period
of the Crusades had tragic consequences, as we have seen.
Byzantine patriotism, which had previously fed upon the
imperial universal dream, was gradually transformed into
nationalism; from an affirmative feeling it became a negative passion, a rejection of everything alien and a morbid
sense of what was native.

This transformation became particularly obvious in the
period of the kingdom of Nicaea in the thirteenth century,
when the Latins ruled in the consecrated capital of the empire. Orthodoxy itself, which had consistently been accepted as the universal truth, able to subdue all peoples in
the period of the Fathers, was now emerging as something
Greek, in contrast to the Latin, Western faith. "Hellenism," which the Fathers had regarded as a synonym for
paganism, acquired a new meaning in the late Byzantine
period; it was conceived to be the source of national tradition, and the revival of it under the Paleologi was strongly
colored by nationalistic feelings.

Thus we may see that while the official ideology of Byzantium remained unalterably universal, despite specific his-

torical failures, the progressive geographical shrinking of the empire increasingly injected a national Greek element into its ideology, the final value of which was Hellenism and not the Christian empire. While Byzantium resisted any division into independent kingdoms and autocephalies on the grounds of its "universalism," in practice it imposed Greek culture on the Slavs—and this in the most concrete way, as we see from the domination of Greek bishops in conquered Bulgaria and their scornful attitude toward any native differences, even in language. This made the decay of the Orthodox world inevitable and forced the Slavs, like the Armenians and Syrians before them, to hate the Greeks. While the decay of Byzantine Christian universalism was an accomplished fact by the time of the Turkish conquest, the Turkish yoke, paradoxically enough, restored it. Since they made no distinction between religion and nationality, the Turks regarded the Christians primarily as a people, as a single whole led by the patriarch of Constantinople. (They would indeed be one people if they recalled the early Christian experience of the Church as a "new people," and the definition of the Christian as the "layman"—from Greek *laos*, the people, meaning one of them.)

Strangely, the Byzantines were relatively indifferent to the destruction of the empire, which had held such an immense and central position in Byzantine thought. The documents do not show that they felt it as a crisis or failure of their most treasured dream. Byzantine thought of the fifteenth century had already experienced the inward replacement of the imperial idea by that of Hellenism, and Hellenism was not only not eliminated under Turkish rule, but acquired an unprecedented authority in the person of the ecumenical patriarch. In the Turkish captivity the imperial power itself passed to the patriarch. The clear boundary between Church and state had disappeared long before in Byzantine thought, and now those who bore authority in the two spheres were also merged. This was possible because both Church and empire referred, as it were, to the same object: the Greek people, bearers of the eternal values of Hellenism, which were becoming increasingly independent values in themselves for the Greeks. The empire might narrow down to only the *rayah*; the task of its leader, the patriarch, then, was to preserve the faith and Hellenism (one was inconceivable without the other) until a future restoration. "The Patriarch sat down upon the throne . . . The bishops bowed down to him as their lord, as their emperor and patriarch." After quoting these words of a Greek historian, Professor Lebedev continued:

Their first thought in this case was that they had elected a new emperor, and the idea that they had obtained a legitimate patriarch in his person took second place. For them he was not patriarch because he was emperor as well, but rather, he was also the emperor because he was the patriarch. The Patriarch of the New Rome was, as it were, the Byzantine Emperor languishing in captivity, deprived of his freedom but not of his authority. His head was ornamented by a mitre in the form of a crown, depicting the two-headed eagle of Byzantium, but in his hand was the patriarchal staff, which he did not carry in vain.[2]

Greek Control of Outlying Orthodox Areas

When they received this power, not only ecclesiastical but national as well, the like of which they had not had in the last centuries of the empire, the Byzantine patriarchs did everything they could to establish permanently the triumph of the Greeks over all the Slavic minorities they had previously been forced to recognize. The Turkish period is marked by disgraceful internal struggle within the Orthodox *rayah* itself—and for what cause? Because of that same passionate nationalism which was stifling the awareness of the unity of the Church of Christ more and more with each century. Unfortunately, the Turkish concept of

[2] A. Lebedev, *The History of the Graeco-Eastern Church under the Turks* (in Russian, St. Petersburg, 1903), p. 29.

religion had long ago become the Christian concept as well.

The Christians painlessly and without embarrassment accepted the prohibition against converting Moslems, thus rejecting the universal calling of the Church; but they expended great effort—aided by the Moslems—in humiliating, subjugating, and subduing their own brothers in the faith. Themselves humiliated, exiled, and killed—so frequently only pawns in the hands of the Phanariots, Greeks who had grown rich in Turkish service—the patriarchs of Constantinople systematically endeavored not only to subdue all the Slavic churches which had previously been autocephalic, but also to make them Greek, eliminating any memory of their Slavic past.

The patriarchate of Trnovo was eliminated almost immediately after the Turkish conquest of Bulgaria. As early as 1394 a Greek metropolitan had been sent from Constantinople, and the patriarchate was changed into a division of the patriarchate of Constantinople. The other independent Bulgarian eparchy of Ochrida, established in 1018 when the Greeks destroyed the first Bulgarian kingdom, lasted until 1776, when the celebrated patriarch of Constantinople, Samuel I, completed the "unification" of the Orthodox Church. The year before he had succeeded in eliminating the Serbian patriarchate at Pech by paying its debts to the Turkish treasury. Everywhere former bishops who were native Bulgars and Serbs were deposed and replaced by Greeks. This canonical abuse of power was accompanied by forced "Grecizing," particularly in Bulgaria, where it later served as the basis of the so-called Bulgarian question.

The same sad picture prevailed in the East as well, in the patriarchates of Jerusalem, Antioch, and Alexandria, where Orthodox Arabs became the victims of this forced unification. All these offenses, stored up and concealed— all these unsettled accounts and intrigues—would have their effect when the Turkish hold began to slacken and the hour for the rebirth of the Slavic peoples drew near.

The Orthodox Church would enter this new period

deeply disunited by these nationalisms, having lost the consciousness of its universal mission. Broken up into little
worlds that treated each other with suspicion and hostility
and felt no need for each other, it submitted to what Solovyov called the "provincialism of local traditions."[3] Having
first become Eastern, Orthodoxy would now become thoroughly national.

The root of the evil did not lie in the national element
as such. The universal empire had long ago become a fiction,
and with the co-operation of the Church had been replaced
by these national states of mind, which found in Christianity a source of nourishment for their growth, establishment,
and national contribution to Christian truth. The nation
and the people are as much a natural fact as society; therefore the positive aspect of its Christian meaning could and
should be revealed within the Church. It was revealed in
its own fashion during the period of the Turkish domination, when the people merged entirely with the Church
and made it the bearer of all their best national ideals. The
tragedy, however, was that it also tainted national self-consciousness with hostility to other Orthodox peoples, and
thus the living unity of the Church was betrayed, replaced
by a theoretical unity. The Church became not only the
bearer of the Christian ideal but also a symbol of national
struggle—a source of religious nationalism that poisons the
Orthodox East down to the present day. Summoned to enlighten everything in the world by the Spirit and by truth,
in the final analysis the Church itself submits to "flesh
and blood," Christian patriotism mingling with pagan
nationalism.

Cultural Decline

No less tragic was the decline of ecclesiastical education
during the period of Turkish rule. True, even before the

[3] V. Solovyov (1853–1900), Russian philosopher and an acute critic of
Orthodox Byzantinism. Cf. his book, *Russia and the Universal Church*
(London, 1948).

fall of the empire education had been aristocratic, not available to the broad masses within the Church. The faithful were educated by the services, and our liturgical texts themselves bear witness to the high level of knowledge of the people of the Church. It cannot be said that education died out completely during the Turkish period, but it declined and, most important, its spirit changed. Its purpose now was to preserve the spirit of Hellenism in its most extreme nationalistic form. According to a Russian traveler in Turkey in the nineteenth century,

The academic love of Hellenism, without systematic study of it, satisfied with excerpts, leads only to a limited, onesided education which is next door to ignorance. The consequence of it is pedantry and pomposity, resulting from a ridiculous desire to apply ancient Hellenic phrases in simple conversation, and, finally, scorn for ordinary but useful knowledge. The teachers prefer to explain something about the state of the country two thousand years ago than to acquaint people with its contemporary situation. Byzantine arrogance, which acknowledges that a man is of value only if he is a Greek, continues to sow the most nonhumanistic concepts among Christians.[4]

School education in one form or another never ceased. The Patriarchal Academy in Constantinople lasted throughout the period of Turkish rule, while the school of Patmos, where its founder the priest-monk Macarius taught without compensation for twenty-five years, and the school of Janina have left illustrious and memorable traces. The Athenian Academy of Eugenius Bulgaris had a brief but brilliant history: "I have been told that the monks set fire to it intentionally," wrote Bishop Porphyry Uspensky, a Russian expert on the East, "for they thought that scholarship is not necessary for the life to come."

Yet the general level of education was very low. In the sixteenth century the metropolitan of Thessalonica claimed

[4] Quoted in Cyprian Kern, *Archimandrite Antonine Capoustine* (in Russian, Belgrade, 1931).

that "not one monk in the diocese knows ancient Greek or understands Church prayers," and at the beginning of the nineteenth century Constantine Oikonomos said that "simple reading of the service books, and often very badly at that, as long as it was done in a melodious voice, was the sole qualification for the position of priest or deacon." Only by the middle of the nineteenth century was the need for special theological education recognized, and the first seminary was opened on the island of Chalcis in 1844.

From this it is clear that the theological tradition was not maintained at the high level which was maintained, despite all internal difficulties, to the very end of Byzantium. One may note here a theme that persisted throughout the whole Turkish period: the polemic against alien ways of worship, particularly against the Latins and later the Protestants. The enslavement of the Greeks by the Turks had opened new perspectives to the papacy, of which it unfortunately had not hesitated to take advantage. The whole period was marked by constantly increasing Latin propaganda in the East, and such prosletyzing injected new venom into relations between the separated Christian worlds. Whole armies of skillful propagandists were sent to the East, prepared in special schools, the most famous of which was the College of St. Athanasius in Rome, opened by Pope Gregory XIII in 1577. A network of Roman episcopates covered the whole Orthodox East.

It must be admitted that the Greek polemicists were not able to respond to this well-prepared attack in any substantial way. In most cases they simply repeated old Byzantine arguments which had long since lost their point. "The Orthodox had hardly bothered to study the Latin Church, either its morals or its ideals," Lebedev has written, "and they retained the same antediluvian concepts of the Latins as they had of Egyptian torture chambers. The Latins had progressed in their ecclesiastical development, and when the Greeks were forced to answer them they

floundered about in a sort of vicious circle." However painful it is to admit, the deep-rooted hatred for the Latins
that led Greeks even to rebaptize Catholics was primarily
responsible for preserving Orthodoxy. Nicodemus the
Hagorite wrote in his *Pedalion*, "The fact that we have felt
hatred and repulsion for the Latins for so many centuries
shows that we think they are heretics, like the Arians, and
the Sabellians." The Turks, however, who disliked and
feared the Latins as "representatives of European imperialism," protected the Orthodox. When in the eighteenth
century the Orthodox in Syria complained to the Porte of
Catholic propaganda, the following decree was issued:

Some of the devilish French monks, with evil purposes and unjust intentions, are passing through the country and are filling
the Greek rayah with their worthless French doctrine; by means
of stupid speeches they are deflecting the rayah from its ancient
faith and are inculcating the French faith. Such French monks
have no right to remain anywhere except in those places where
their consuls are located; they should not undertake any journeys or engage in missionary work.[5]

The text needs no comment; here are the results of the
separation of the churches in the eighteenth century.

Silence of Orthodox Theology

Most important of all, during the Reformation, at the
most critical point in the ecclesiastical history of the Christian West—a period of review and re-evaluation of traditional values in the West—the Orthodox Church was mute,
and because of this the Western dispute was one-sided, deprived of any genuine universal perspective. The East could
only fence itself off, defend itself, preserve; it lacked resources to contribute its own experience or its uninterrupted
tradition as a way out of Western blind alleys. The first

[5] *Ibid.*

Reformers, convinced that in combating the papacy and medieval Catholicism they were returning to apostolic Christianity, made attempts to appeal to the Eastern Church as the arbiter of their dispute with Rome. Negotiations with the Protestants were particularly energetic under Patriarch Jeremiah II (1572–95), who subjected the Augsburg Confession, which had been sent to him, to a detailed analysis and exposed its obvious heresy from the Orthodox point of view. "You can never be in agreement with us, or rather, say with the truth," wrote Jeremiah, "And we beg you not to trouble us further, not to write us or appeal to us while you go on reinterpreting the guiding lights of the Church and its theologians in other ways, paying them respect in words but repudiating them in deeds . . . Go your way, and write us no more about dogmas."

The Orthodox Church could reject and condemn Protestantism, as it could fence itself off from Catholic advances, but unfortunately it could not perform its duty to bear witness to Orthodoxy and reveal its vital and creative significance. Moreover, from that time on Western Catholic and Protestant influences gradually began to penetrate into Orthodox theology itself, inculcating a sense of inferiority toward everything Western, and for a long while pulling it away from its own heritage. This influence came in through the young people who were sent to study in the West—in England, Switzerland, and Denmark—and who, lacking a firm foundation in their own faith, were easily infected with the latest Western theological fashions, absorbed its theological and spiritual atmosphere, and then became teachers of the Orthodox clergy. A clear example of this process is the well-known case of Cyril Lucaris, who as patriarch of Constantinople published his *Confession of the Orthodox Faith* in Geneva in 1629, a document which was completely Protestant in content and inspiration.

But this is far from the only example. As time went on, it became increasingly clear that even if the Orthodox Church managed to preserve its independence from the

Catholics and the Protestants, Orthodox theology had lost that independence and had changed into either a bare and sweeping denial of the West by means of dubious arguments, or a sort of compromise between Catholic and Protestant extremes.

After the fall of Byzantium only the West theologized. Theology is essentially a task of the universal Church, but it was only taken up separately, in schism. This is the basic paradox in the history of Christian culture. The West was theologizing when the East was mute, or, even worse, was repeating Western lessons without reflection. Until the present time the Orthodox theologian has been too dependent on Western support for his own constructive work. He received his primary sources from Western hands, read the Fathers and the acts of the councils in Western editions (which often were not accurate), and learned the techniques of dealing with the assembled material in a Western school.[6]

Our knowledge of the history of our own Church is primarily due to the achievements of many generations of Western scholars. This applies both to the accumulation and the interpretation of the facts . . . Western thought always lives in this past, with an intensity of historical recollection, as if to compensate for the painful gaps in its own mystical memory. The Orthodox theologian also ought to bear witness to this world, a witness drawn from the internal memory of the Church.[7]

Nationalistic feeling, the decline of education, the petrifaction of theology, the poison of temptations from other forms of worship—these were the negative aspects of this period in the history of the Orthodox Church. Its historical perspective was narrowed at this time, and unfavorable outward conditions were not solely responsible for this. Even today Orthodoxy has not fully recovered from all these illnesses.

[6] Ibid.
[7] G. Florovsky, The Ways of Russian Theology (in Russian, Paris, 1937), p. 516.

The Precious Core

Nevertheless, we must also try to see something else, less obvious but perhaps more significant in spiritual history, which cannot be measured by the usual historical instruments. Few are those who have been able to find the unfading treasures that lay behind this bleak exterior; the Russians, unfortunately, least of all, as they adopted the scorn of a great power for Eastern Orthodoxy in its early period. Yet those few who, at a time when the Russian Church was outwardly at its height, made genuine contact with the Eastern Church were inwardly converted and could no longer be satisfied with all the official splendor of imperial Russian Orthodoxy.

For alongside ignorance, chauvinism, avarice, and other sins, there continued to live in the East a genuine Orthodox sense of the Church which shone brighter in genuine spiritual beauty after it had shed the "squalid luxury" of the last period of the empire. One of the sensitive observers of the Christian East, Archimandrite Antoninus Capustin, whose diplomatic service in Constantinople, Athens, and Jerusalem brought him to recognize the universality of the Church at a time when no one seemed to remember it, wrote in the middle of the nineteenth century:

It is enough to see the Greek in the ruins of Athens or the Arab in the mud huts of the Levant, the Copt among the Libyan sands, or the Abyssinian . . . to become convinced that here there is another belt of spiritual geography, and other plants flourish here which have no need of our artificial fertilizers, nor waterings, nor graftings, nor our flowerpots or hothouses. God grant that our hothouse piety be equal to them. It is sad for me to speak against my own advantage, but what am I to do? As I stand in a wretched church in Suez and am possessed with the memory of so many of the splendid sanctuaries known to me, I would not be able to rise spiritually higher than the ugly and half-rotten rafters and boards of the roof above me. But the local inhabitant unquestionably prays here with an entirely Christian prayer to the heartrending sound of his native song. The wretchedness of the church does not signify the wretchedness of God for him, and it is a blessing for him.[8]

In a letter to Metropolitan Philaret he wrote: "When I examined the details of the religious life of the Greeks, I found in it so much of what we are taught in the *Menologion* and the *Prologue* that I would be repudiating my calling as an Orthodox priest and monk if I kept it from my Church." There in the poverty-stricken East he suddenly became aware of a longing for the unity of Orthodoxy, for a new period in its history—a call "not for partitioning the Body of Christ any longer according to countries, peoples, languages, passions, needs, governmental systems or schools, but a reunification of all in a life together of the spirit of love, peace and joy in the Holy Spirit . . ." and for the revival of "a single, organically alive, strong, ruling Orthodox Church of Christ."[9]

Once more behind the official history, which is filled with decline, sins, and weaknesses, another history is suggested, which contains the spirit of genuine Orthodoxy. In these years the *Philokalia* was completed, the peak of Eastern speculative experience, which by its profundity is now beginning to win over even the non-Orthodox.[10] The threads binding all these bearers of the age-old tradition into one family have not once been broken: the thirst for oneness with God, the longing for a perfect life. The great culture of the spirit, to which none of the refinements of the European nineteenth century can be compared in sensitivity, did not die. Only recently, when not only official documents of the period but the popular legends of Greece, Serbia, and Bulgaria began to be collected and studied, has

[8] Kern, *op. cit.*
[9] Cf. *ibid.*
[10] Cf. English translation in E. Kadlubovsky and G. E. M. Palmer, *Writings from the Philokalia* (London, 1951).

it been realized how what is most essential and elusive in Orthodoxy had entered the souls of the people.

Liberation

In the nineteenth century the dawn of freedom began to break over the Orthodox East. The Serbian uprisings of 1804 and 1815, the Greek uprising of 1821, and Russia's war of liberation against Turkey in 1877 resulted in the rebirth of independent Orthodox states. Yet while national liberation freed the churches of these countries from Turkish control, it did not free them from its tragic consequences: national hostility and proud self-assertion, infection with theories alien to Orthodoxy, the subordination of the Church to the state or complete merging with it. Eastern nationalism, born as we have seen out of the decay of the Byzantine theocratic consciousness, now merged with a new, Western type of nationalism whose spirit had hovered over Europe since the French Revolution. The Greek, Bulgarian, and Serbian kings of the Byzantine era had dreamed of a universal Orthodox empire; now the standard had become self-determination of nations, national culture, and disputes over border provinces. The Bulgaria of Simeon or the Serbia of Dushan might have dreamed of the conquest of Constantinople, but they breathed and lived by a single Christian-Hellenic culture and a universal tradition of the Church of the Fathers and the councils. Now what was "native," however partial, incomplete, or debased, gradually overshadowed the whole horizon of thought and became the idol for whose sake the great common past might be forgotten. If there was anything that could compete with this idol of nationalism, it would now be the West, which had acquired a sort of mythical halo. Only when the West itself finally came to recognize the value of the Byzantine icon, the profundity of the works of the Fathers, or the beauty of Eastern singing, would the Orthodox begin to show a certain interest in them. Before this happened, Western Europe became the real authority—political, spiritual, and even theological—for the Orthodox East. Traditional Orthodoxy was found only in the villages and the lower classes; the upper classes had begun to measure their faith and traditions by the standards of Oxford or Tübingen.

It is characteristic that after the uprising of 1821, when an independent kingdom of Greece was founded, the Greek bishops themselves did not hesitate to be in schism with Constantinople for almost twenty years in order to obtain their own autocephalous Church; they hardly noticed that its constitution had actually been copied from Lutheran constitutions, and that in general it did not recognize any boundary between Church and state. The same purely nationalistic motives, not at all theological, nourished the schism between Bulgaria and Greece which persisted for sixty years, and similar causes led to the divisions between the Slavic states which are still in force today. How easily the age-old tradition—genuine tradition and not folklore—was sacrificed throughout these decades to pitiful imitations of the West! Konstantin Leontiev frequently and maliciously mocked this fascination with Western petty-bourgeois vulgarity,[11] which he contrasted to the Slavophil interests dominant in Russia; yet in his wrath we often discern a real assertion of the universality of Orthodoxy, so rare at that time, which had been destroyed by the clamorous blossoming of local nationalisms. "He saw," Berdyaev wrote, "that the only reliable protection against the world-wide process of decay and vulgarization, which had involved all the Balkan peoples, lay in faithfulness to the traditions of Byzantinism."

We concede that Leontiev too frequently interpreted Byzantinism esthetically, in the spirit of Western romanticism, but basically he was right; the voice of the Church was almost unheard in the free Orthodox states of the nine-

---

11 K. Leontiev (1831–91), Russian writer and thinker. Cf. V. V. Zenkovsky, *History of Russian Philosophy* (New York, 1953), chap. 12.

teenth and twentieth centuries. Their whole political and state structure and their entire culture somehow "bypassed" Orthodoxy, or in any case were not inspired by it, and the Church, for all its democratic guarantees, found itself held in honored captivity by the state, without being aware of it. The extinction of monasticism; the transformation of the clergy into civil servants and of theology into an applied professional field of knowledge to serve the clergy, or else into a narrow specialization; the decline of the divine services, which became either "showpieces" or performances from incomprehensible books; and finally, the "politicizing" of the state of mind of the Church—all these were characteristic results of the national revivals, to which the Church, incidentally, had contributed so much of its spiritual force. If signs of spiritual awakening are becoming more frequent in the Orthodox world in recent decades, they are linked with reasons outside the framework of this book—with the dawn of new catastrophes, the last and most terrible of all being the collapse of the old world.

6 RUSSIAN ORTHODOXY

Russian Orthodoxy has too frequently been contrasted with another Orthodoxy—Greek or Oriental, while Russian messianism has sometimes simply equated Orthodoxy with Russia, oblivious to its Byzantine origins and the "sleeping East." The late S. L. Frank recently called this national self-infatuation "the chronic disease of the Russian mind."[1] But it would be ridiculous, because of these extremes, the result of ideological disputes, to go to the opposite extreme and simply deny the incomparable significance of Russia for the historical course of Orthodoxy in its earthly forms and wanderings. Here, of course, one can only attempt a brief indication, a mere enumeration of the basic landmarks of what must be called Russian Orthodoxy, despite the ambiguity of the phrase.

Even so modest an attempt immediately runs up against almost insuperable difficulties. The evaluation of Russia's historical development has long been a subject of disputes which even today are not resolved. Whichever of the three basic stages in the dialectic of Russian history one may turn to—the Kievan, Muscovite, or Petersburg period—there are current at least two contradictory and mutually exclusive evaluations of each, arrived at on the basis of sci-

[1] S. L. Frank (1887–1950), Russian philosopher. Cf. V. V. Zenkovsky, *History of Russian Philosophy*, G. L. Kline, trans. (New York, 1953), Vol. II, chap. 5.

entific historical analysis. Yet the history of the Russian
Church cannot be separated from the history of Russia, as
it cannot be separated from its Byzantine origins. Just as
Orthodoxy is one of the major factors in Russian history,
so the destiny of Russia defined the fate of Russian Orthodoxy. Even the simplest delineation of the development of
the Church inevitably includes a definite attitude toward
Russia's past. No complete history of Russian religion yet
exists, since no real history of the Russian Church has yet
been written. Too much is still simply unknown, unstudied.
Some basic questions have only recently been posed. Finally, the agonizing problem of the Church in Russia today
and the importance of Russia itself in the destiny of the
world makes the whole subject infinitely complex. With
the advent of Bolshevism not only was one period in Russian Church history finished, but a whole era in the life of
Orthodoxy itself came to an end. In this light, the Russian
chapter in the history of Orthodoxy inevitably takes on a
universal significance.

Conversion in Kiev—St. Vladimir

The official history of the Orthodox Church in Russia
begins with St. Vladimir, ruler of Kiev, in the latter part
of the tenth century. This does not mean that there had
been no earlier Christianity in Russia. We need only recall
the importance in the Russian Christian memory of St.
Olga, his grandmother—"the dawning light that heralds
the sun," according to the chronicles. Christianity before
the baptism of the Rus (the name of the Scandinavian
tribe that occupied the Slavic territories around Kiev near
the river Dnieper) was already so firmly established and
the bonds witth Byzantium and Byzantinized Bulgaria so
strong, that St. Vladimir's work can only be properly evaluated in the light of these factors. There is even a theory
of the first baptism of the Rus under Patriarch Photius in

the ninth century which has a fair number of adherents in Russian scholarship.

Essentially the work of St. Vladimir was not only a beginning but also the completion of a rather long process, the victory of a certain tendency in the state's conception of itself. However attached to paganism the prince may have been personally, as the chronicle relates, his long hesitation in choosing a new religion, his missions to various countries, and his final choice of Greek Christianity is evidence that the baptism of Russia, like that of Bulgaria before her, was conceived as primarily a state matter and demonstrated Russia's arrival at maturity and readiness to be included in the Christian tradition of the cultured world.

Like Bulgaria, Russia was obliged to choose between the old and the new Rome; we know much more now than we did earlier about her links with Rome both before and after Vladimir. The choice fell on Byzantine Orthodoxy. As with the Bulgars, Christianity in Russia was imposed from above by state authority. Finally, as in Bulgaria, this Byzantine Orthodoxy became established among the Russians in its Slavic aspect, that of Cyril and Methodius. All these factors were to define once for all the development of Russia and the Russian Church. We may leave aside questions recently raised by Russian historians as to whether Greek or Bulgarian influence was first and fundamental; whether the Russian Church in its first years came under the jurisdiction of Constantinople or Bulgaria; and to what extent the tragic fate of the first Bulgarian kingdom in the late tenth and early eleventh centuries was reflected in the early Christian development of Russia. No answer to these questions one way or another would change the basic fact in the history of Russian Orthodoxy: its organic link with Byzantinism, that is, in its Slavic form. In any case, starting with Yaroslav the Wise, the canonical dependence of the Russian Church upon Constantinople cannot be doubted. That this dependence quite early became burdensome in the mind of Church and state—possibly

from the very beginning—we have evidence in the attempts
to install Russian metropolitans (Hilarion under Yaroslav
in 1051 and Ephraim under Iziaslav), and also in the disputes over the same question in connection with the installation of Clement Smoliatich in 1147.

Quality of Kievan Christianity

For a long time the Kievan period was considered no
more than a prologue to the history of the real flowering
of the Russian Church, which was linked in Russian thinking with the Muscovite kingdom. Any spiritual or cultural
achievements were denied it; it was dismissed as possessing
only an elementary piety and moral casuistry and the
schoolboy repetition of Byzantine models. In recent years
these old evaluations have been increasingly shown to
be invalid, and the Kievan period is more and more
acknowledged to have been perhaps the purest and most
versatile of all periods of Russian religion. "Kievan Russia, like the golden days of childhood," writes Professor
Fedotov, "has never gone out of the memory of the Russian
people. Any who wish may quench their spiritual thirst at
the pure spring of its writings; they may find among its
writers guides through the difficulties of the modern world.
Kievan Christianity has the same significance for Russia's
religious way of thinking as Pushkin has for Russia's artistic
consciousness: the significance of a model, a golden mean,
a royal road."[2]

The unquestioned success of Christianity in Kiev—that
is to say, the "Russia" of that period—as soon as it was
imposed cannot be denied, whatever barriers there may
have been. It is apparent, first of all, in the saints of the
period, who reveal how profoundly and purely the evangelical ideal was accepted and the whole rich experience

[2] G. Fedotov, *The Russian Religious Mind* (Cambridge, Mass., 1946),
p. 412.

of Orthodox sanctity adopted there. Among them were Princes Boris and Gleb, who were venerated as bearers of voluntary suffering; St. Theodosius of the Monastery of the Crypt (or caves) and his disciples, whose lives have been preserved in the *Book of the Crypt Fathers*; St. Abraham of Smolensk and St. Cyril of Turov, the sainted bishops who fought paganism and struggled for the moral transformation of their flock. Such souls bear witness to the rapid sprouting of evangelical seed; they also demonstrate the versatility of early Russian sainthood and its unique interpretation of Byzantine classical traditions.

Basically it was of course the same Eastern Christian way to the kingdom of heaven, a sanctity primarily monastic. Its sources lay in the Byzantine literature of saints' lives, partly translated in Bulgaria in the *Menologion*, and partly in Kiev itself in the *Prologue* or the *Books of the Fathers* (*Pateriks*)—one of which had been translated by the Apostle to the Slavs, Constantine (Cyril) himself— and in the examples of the great holy men (*podvizhniki*), in the regulations of St. Theodore the Studite, and elsewhere. But there were new features in it as well: the veneration of the voluntary suffering of Boris and Gleb and the uniquely luminous asceticism of Theodosius of the Caves, which was addressed to the world and particularly devoted to the "humiliated Christ"—that mood or striving which Professor Fedotov has perhaps overemphasized in calling it Russian "kenoticism."

Even during the first century in Kiev a spiritual community was created which left a deep impression not only on the Kievan period but on all subsequent eras of Russian religious development. This was the Kiev Crypt Monastery, begun by St. Antony in 1051 but really organized by St. Theodosius, the true founder of all Russian monasticism. The Crypt Monastery immediately became the example of pure, unadulterated Christianity, and the conscience of the young Christian society. The life of Theodosius shows us his constant participation in the life of the state—by

preaching, exposure, and reminder—at a time when civil
strife between the princes was already beginning to infect it.
This famous *laura* gave the Church as many as fifty bishops,
who disseminated its spirit, traditions, and regulations
everywhere. It was a great center of charitable social action
as well. The monastery was the standard of perfection, and
a throng of saints gave witness to the heavenly kingdom
throughout the land, winning for it the title of "Holy
Russia."

Another proof of the success of Christianity must be
seen in the genuine beginnings of Christian statehood,
whose incarnation was St. Vladimir, the baptizer of Russia.
The chronicler draws a clear distinction between his attitude toward his own authority before accepting Christianity
and afterward, and depicts him as an affectionate prince,
protector of the weak and poor, concerned over the construction of hospitals and almshouses, struggling for justice,
enlightenment, and the ordering of the state. Another
amazing example of a Christian prince is pictured by Vladimir Monomakh in his *Testament*. Although it is bookish
and follows Byzantine models, this work is permeated with
genuine conviction and expresses a personal experience, not
merely a literary one. "Vladimir's religious ethic lies between the Old and New Testaments," Fedotov writes.
"Yet it is always illuminated by a few rays falling from
the Gospel, and in rare, exalted moments it dares to reflect
Christ, the meek Lord, face to face."[3] We must keep in
mind this inspiration of conscience, reconciliation, mercy,
and justice just at the dawn of the Russian state.

In the relations between Church and state we also see
a harmony almost unprecedented in the history of Orthodoxy; at the beginning of the Kievan period the Byzantine
"harmony" operated almost openly through the influence
of the Church, not the state. Although Vladimir had been
responsible for the choice of a religion, the Church in Kiev
was not, in fact, dominated by the state. His Ecclesiastical

[3] *Ibid.*, p. 260.

Regulations significantly broadened the sphere of the ecclesiastical court by comparison to the Byzantine ones: all
family matters, for example, were transferred to it, so that
the Church might carry out the regeneration of society more
successfully. Still more important, the rulers constantly
accepted advice, guidance, and instruction from the
Church, and recognized it as the authority of conscience.

"In the dramatic and even tragic history of relations between the Christian Church and the Christian state,"
Fedotov continues, "the Kievan experience, in spite of its
brevity and fragility, may be regarded as one of the best
Christian achievements."[4] The history of Orthodoxy in
Russia began with Christian perfectionism, a real "transvaluation of values" in the light of evangelical truth.

Kievan Culture

It is equally beyond doubt that there was a real culture
in Kievan Russia; in comparison, the Moscow period may
even be regarded as a decline. Here, too, the initiative came
from above, from the prince and the hierarchy. Although
Vladimir was illiterate, he built schools, and his sons were
examples of fully educated men, especially Yaroslav the
Wise, in whose reign Kiev became one of the centers of
European culture. A whole workshop of translators labored
in his reign, and he selected children for the schools and
himself read day and night, according to tradition. His son
Sviatoslav of Chernigov had "storerooms full of books,"
and the writings of another son, Vladimir Monomakh, bear
witness to the author's undoubted firsthand acquaintance
with Byzantine literature. In Kiev we may sense a deliberate
effort to create a culture and to master completely the
Christian and Hellenic heritage.

Basically, of course, this was a borrowed, translated cul-

[4] *Ibid.*

ture, but original creative work was running dry in Byzantium; moreover, this period of discipleship is inevitable in
the history of any culture. The important thing was that
the Russians were good students. Golubinsky, himself a
wholesale detractor of Russia's past,[5] has called Metropolitan Hilarion of Kiev "not a rhetorician of the worst period
of Greek oratory but a real orator of the period when it
flourished." The sermons of Cyril of Turov retain to this
day their value as literature and not only as historical documents. The early chronicles are filled not only with facts,
but with a whole general outlook. Their authors were "people with a definite and sensitive view of life, not at all
naïve simpletons. In the development of the Russian chronicle we always sense a definite religious and historical
idea."[6] Indeed, the era in which the *Lay of Igor's Campaign*
made its appearance can hardly be termed barely literate.

A certain quintessence of Orthodox Byzantinism was
conveyed to Russia and adopted there; Russian thought
entered into this tradition, and it became the basic source
of Russian culture. The tradition was adopted not only
passively but creatively as well. The first upsurge of Russian
national self-awareness that marks Hilarion's *Word* and
Nestor's *Chronicle* is linked with it. It is no accident that
the prayer to God from the newly-consecrated people with
which Hilarion ends his *Praise to Our Prince Vladimir* was
accepted even into Church usage. His oration, "On the
Law given by Moses, and on the Grace and Truth which
were Jesus Christ, and how the Law departed while Grace
and Truth filled all the earth and the faith spread to all
languages and reached our Russian language, and praise
to our Prince Vladimir, through whom we were baptized,
and a prayer to God from all our lands," composed between
1030 and 1050, during the reign of Yaroslav the Wise, ex-

[5] E. E. Golubinsky, author of a *History of the Russian Church* (1880–81),
famous for its violently critical approach to Kievan Christianity.
[6] G. Florovsky, *The Ways of Russian Theology* (in Russian, Paris, 1937),
page 7.

presses as it were the ecclesiastical and national confession of newly-baptized Russia.

According to D. I. Cizevsky in his *History of Old Russian Literature*, this confession, like all writing of the early Kievan period, is marked by the spirit of majesty and Christian optimism. The Kievan ideologists were inspired by their concept of the unity of Russia and the growth of its idea of statehood, which was beginning in glory. This inspiration was rooted deep in the experience of baptism, in Russia's acceptance of "grace and truth." The Good News came to the Russians at the eleventh hour, but in the person of their prince, Vladimir, they were not diminished in the sight of other Christian peoples. In such Christian hope, in their awareness that God had called them, the Russian sense of nationhood arose, and in the future, at its highest peaks would use this as a standard of measurement and judgment.

Shallows and Hidden Darkness

Of course one must not exaggerate either the success of Kievan Christianity or the depth of the Christianization that had taken place. It remained the sphere of the elite, a group of newborn ecclesiastical and state intellectuals. Certain writings, such as *The Questions of Kirik* for example, show an extremely elementary understanding of the nature of Christianity. One must note at once that Russia had accepted a ready-made Orthodoxy, at a time when conservative attitudes, an effort to refer everything to the past (the perfected model), and a fear of infringing on any of the ancient traditions were expressed with increasing strength in Byzantium itself. Russian psychology was from the first marked by this ritualism and by a somewhat hypertrophied, narrowly liturgical piety.

But it is much more important to note also that here paganism was preserved under Christian cover—a "dual faith," as yet insufficiently studied but undoubtedly one of the keys to Russian religious psychology. Slavic paganism did not offer fanatical opposition to Christianity. It lacked organization, literature, or any developed cult; but this only made it especially vital and dangerous. This was "soft" paganism, based on nature and profoundly bound to natural life. Christianity was long a foreign religion—even doubly foreign, being Greek and coming from the prince as well, which meant its support by the Varangian *druzhina,* the ruling clique in Russia. To receive it required education; it was bookish by its very nature. Its external elements—the divine service, the ritual—were easily accepted; it charmed the people and won their hearts; but there was the danger that they would not see, or even try to see, the meaning or *Logos* behind these externals, without which the Christian rite would in fact become pagan in becoming an end in itself. The soul of the people continued to feed upon the old natural religious experiences and images. "Paganism did not die and was not overpowered immediately," Father Florovsky declares.

In the murky depths of the popular subconsciousness, as in some historical underground, its own concealed life went on, now with double meaning and dual faith . . . The borrowed Byzantine Christian culture did not immediately become generally accepted, but for a long time it was the property and treasure of a literate or cultural minority . . . We must remember, therefore, that the history of this "daytime" Christian culture certainly does not exhaust the fullness of Russia's spiritual destiny . . . One can see that the sickliness of the Old Russian development was due first of all to the fact that the "nighttime" imagination was too long and too stubbornly concealed, avoiding intellectual testing, verification, and refinement.[7]

Later, feeling, imagination, and tenderness would be proclaimed as the basic points of distinction between Russian

[7] *Ibid.,* pp. 2–3.

and Greek Christianity, the latter being considered calcu-
lating and cold. But it would be more correct to see that
the stubborn opposition of the "Russian soul" to the *Logos*
was one of the deepest reasons for many of the fateful crises
in the course of Russian history.

Tatar Conquest—Beginning of Moscow Kingdom

With the Tatar conquest of Russia (1237–40) the
Kievan period in Russian history came to an end. This
catastrophe affected not only the state; the Mongol yoke
began a new stage in the development of the Church
as well, a complex period not easily susceptible of any single
generalization or characterization.

The Tatar invasion did not interrupt Church tradition or
halt the theological or spiritual development that had already begun. But relations between the Church and state
authority gradually changed. If in Kiev harmony between
the Grand Prince and the Church authorities had usually
prevailed, with the collapse of the central power and the
multiplication of small principalities, it became easier to
stifle the voice of the Church. In 1157 Prince Andrew
Bogoliubsky drove Bishop Nestor out of Rostov, and Prince
Sviatoslav of Chernigov expelled Bishop Antony the Greek
in 1168. Monomakh's brother, Rostislav, killed the monk
Gregory for denouncing him, and Grand Prince Sviatopolk
killed the abbot of the Crypt Monastery for the same reason. On the whole, however, the voice of the Church continued to be heard in disputes between the princes and had
a good influence upon them. With the Tatar rule the center
of governmental authority shifted far to the north, to the
region of Suzdal (northeast of Moscow, which was then the
estate of the prince of Suzdal), and the center of the
metropolitan naturally followed.

The thirteenth century marked the flourishing of the
northeastern cities of Vladimir and Suzdal, but as regards

government this was a transitional period. In the fourteenth century the "gathering of the Russian land" around
Moscow began, and a decisive factor in the process was the
alliance of the Church—specifically its hierarchical center
—with Moscow. A new shift of the metropolitan see naturally followed, although the metropolitan long retained the
title "of Kiev," which he had kept throughout the Suzdal
period. The head of the Church could no longer lead an
almost nomadic life, as had the first metropolitans of the
Tatar regime, Cyril and Maxim. The resettlement of Metropolitan Peter and his successors in Moscow resulted from
a natural desire to maintain the unity of the country and
to unite the ecclesiastical center with elements in the state
that, even under Turkish rule, were striving for the consolidation and unity of Russia. But in uniting its fate with
a single policy which it supported in every way, the Church
itself imperceptibly fell under the sway of the state; and
it ceased to be the conscience of the state, gradually becoming a prop and almost an instrument of Muscovite imperialism.

We know by what dubious means Moscow achieved its
hegemony in Russia. The blood of Michael of Tver, tortured by the Horde in 1319 after being slandered by Yuri
of Moscow, was shed at almost the same time as Metropolitan Peter of Moscow was blessing the beginning of that
city's historic rise to power. In addition, the transfer of the
metropolitan to Moscow caused dissatisfaction in southwest
Russia, and the Church's obvious alliance with Moscow
resulted in a large number of disputes, bribery from Constantinople, and competition between metropolitans, which
gradually weakened the moral authority of the metropolitan
who had stood so high in Kiev. While St. Peter, Theognost,
and St. Alexei—the first metropolitans of Moscow—still
maintained this authority, after them we see its gradual
effacement as compared to that of the Grand Prince.

Dimitri Donskoi, who was the first to defeat the Tatars
and to weaken their grip on Russia, simply selected persons

acceptable to himself for positions of Church authority. A characteristic example was his support of Archimandrite Mityai, imprisoning Bishop Dionisi for refusing to ask the blessing of that priest, who had not yet been consecrated bishop. When Metropolitan Cyprian arrived in Moscow from Kiev on the instructions of the patriarch of Constantinople, who wished to restore ecclesiastical unity in Russia, Dimitri simply drove him out, as he drove out Pimen after him, who had managed by bribery to be consecrated in Constantinople.

In the Kievan period and at the beginning of the north Russian period the Church had been independent of the state.

Therefore it could demand of those bearing the princely authority submission to certain principles of idealism in their personal as well as their political lives: faithfulness to their agreements, peacefulness, and justice. St. Theodosius had fearlessly called the prince a usurper, and Metropolitan Nikifor could declare to the princes: "We are installed by God to keep you from bloodshed." This freedom of the Church was possible primarily because the Russian Church was not yet national or "autocephalous," but acknowledged that it was part of the Greek Church. Its supreme hierarch lived in Constantinople, which was inaccessible to the encroachments of the local princes. Even Andrew Bogoliubsky submitted to the ecumenical patriarch.[8]

For all its participation in state affairs, the hierarchy continued to recognize that it represented another, higher whole, the Church Universal, and this made its patriotic contributions weightier and more independent. One sees this awareness even in the first Russian primates. But the stronger Moscow and the power of the Moscow princes became, the weaker became the authority of the metropolitan of Moscow. At a local council held in 1459, the Russian

[8] Fedotov, *op. cit.*, pp. 400–403.

bishops solemnly pledged not to withdraw the metropolitan see from Moscow.

There is no doubt that the nationalization of the Russian Church and its gradual liberation from Constantinople was inevitable. The link had lost its value in the fifteenth century; in impoverished and ruined Byzantium, bribes and deception were frequently stronger than canonical and universal consciousness. Still one must note this narrowing of the horizon of the Russian Church, its gradual subordination to governmental rationale, and its transformation into an "aspect" of the life of the state.

The change in relations between Church and state is connected with the terrible moral collapse that followed upon the Mongol domination. This experience in slavery inevitably brought forth its fruit. The Russian character was completely coarsened and poisoned by "Tatarism."

The princes themselves had to go to the Horde with declarations of their slavish submission and constantly tremble before the might of the Despot and the constant denunciations of spies, even among their own brother princes . . . For the people this school of slavery was even more oppressive; they had to bow down before every passing Tatar, do all that he asked, and get rid of him by deceit and bows . . . Duplicity, slyness, prostration, base displays of the instinct of self-preservation, became the virtues of the era, preached even by the morality of the chronicles.[9]

"Tatarism"—lack of principle and a repulsive combination of prostration before the strong with oppression of everything weak—unfortunately marked the growth of Moscow and the Muscovite culture from the very beginning, and it is incomprehensible, in view of such monstrous aberrations of religious nationalism, why the Moscow period captivated the minds of Russian Churchmen for so long and became for them the standard of Holy Russia.

[9] P. Znamensky, *Manual of Russian Church History* (in Russian, Kazan, 1888), pp. 99–100, 76.

Early Russian Monasticism—St. Sergius

While the general picture of the moral condition of society in the period of the Tatar yoke is undoubtedly a
gloomy one, and the gloom darkened still further with the
passing years, the unquestioned blossoming of Russian acts
of holiness and sainthood gleams against this background.
The ties were not broken with the East or with Mt. Athos,
where a revival and rebirth of spiritual life had come with
the movement of the Hesychasts in the fourteenth century.
Metropolitan Cyprian, for example, a Serb by origin and a
monk of Athos who had zealously pursued liturgical reform
in Russia, was a confirmed Palamite. At Athos whole settle-
ments of Russian monks were created who continued the
work of translation. Through them speculative literature
reached Russia: the works of Basil the Great, Isaac the
Syrian, Maxim the Confessor, and Simeon the New Theologian. Russia was not yet cut off from its blood relations
with universal Orthodoxy. This uninterrupted spiritual
tradition appeared most clearly in Russian monasticism,
of which the fourteenth century was the golden age. This
was the time of St. Sergius of Radonezh and of all that
northern Russian Thebaid—the series of monasteries connected with him—which would remain the true heart of
Russian Orthodoxy forever.

With St. Sergius (1320–92) Orthodox saintliness was
revived in all its brilliance. From his withdrawal into the
desert through physical asceticism, self-crucifixion, and
meekness, to the last rays of the light of Mt. Tabor and the
partaking of the kingdom of heaven, Sergius recapitulated
the journeys of all the great witnesses to Orthodoxy from
the first centuries. The nationalist would emphasize the
support he gave Prince Dimitri Donskoi for his attempt to
liberate Russia from the Tatars. Sociologists and economists
insist upon the colonizing and enlightening significance
of the immense network of monasteries founded by his dis-

ciples and successors; yet these are of course not the most important thing about him—rather, the absolutism of his Christianity, the image of the complete transformation of man by the Holy Spirit and his aspiration to "life in God."

This made St. Sergius the center of Russian Orthodoxy in the dark years of her history and brought many roads to the Trinity Monastery of St. Sergius. All that was genuine and vital in the Russian Church at that time was linked in one way or the other with St. Sergius. He himself wrote nothing, yet nothing expresses so convincingly and forcefully his influence and the content of the doctrine he incarnated than the icons painted by St. Andrei Rublev, discovered rather recently after centuries of oblivion. His "Trinity" is a most perfect work of religious art, an actual "meditation in color." In general, Russian religious experience was expressed and incarnated in those ages less in verbal, theological work than in church architecture and the icon. These bear witness with "a sort of material authenticity to the complexity and genuine refinement of ancient Russian religious experience and to the creative power of the Russian spirit."[10]

The monastery of St. Sergius at Radonezh, near Moscow, soon became the seedplot of monasticism for all northern Russia. Within a century and a half almost one hundred and eighty monasteries were created, providing spiritual formation for a great number of saints. The monastery became the center of spiritual life for the whole society in a period of darkness and barbarism: an extreme of national life in which the people found consolation, instruction, and aid—and, most important, became convinced of the reality of absolute values because they had come into contact with holiness.

As we study the religious life of that time, we see first of all a polarization, a psychological contradiction between the sinful world and the monastery. This is also true of the

[10] Florovsky, *op. cit.*, p. 1.

religious life. There is the crude faith of the illiterate or
semiliterate "white" clergy, who were so exploited by the
bishops that in 1435, in Pskov, the clergy and the people
attacked the bishop's emissaries. There is superstition,
drunkenness, and debauchery; Metropolitan Jonah in a
letter to the citizens of Viatich reproves the inhabitants
because some of them took wives five, seven, or even ten
times, and Yuri of Smolensk brutally killed Princess Juliana
Viazemsky because she refused to satisfy his passion. Yet
amid all this darkness and decay there was the pure air
of the monastery, evidence of the *possibility* of repentance,
renewal, and purification. The monastery is not the crown
of the Christian world, but on the contrary, its inner judgment seat and accuser, the light shining in the darkness.
This must be understood for a comprehension of the origins of the "Russian soul." In the midst of its degradation
it stretches toward this limitless brightness; it contains the
tragic discord between the vision of spiritual beauty and
purity expressed in monasticism and the sense of the hopeless sinfulness of life. Those who see a wholeness in the
Russian religious mind of these ages are deeply mistaken,
for just then, in the centuries after the Tatar invasion, the
dualism which would mark its future course began to enter
into it.

Consolidation of Russian Lands under Moscow

In the middle of the fifteenth century the whole Russian land
consisted of two great state groups of lands: the eastern, under
the administration of the Muscovite autocrats, and the western,
under the authority of the Lithuanian-Polish government. The
Russian Church was also divided into two large provinces, the
Muscovite and the Kievan. The Muscovite metropolitan, under
the protection of the state, flourished within its borders, was
adorned with outward splendor, and revealed from within a remarkable movement of enlightenment. The state, having recovered from misfortunes within and without, began an effort

to assimilate the fruits of Western civilization. By the end of the sixteenth century the Church had reached the point of becoming an independent patriarchate.[11]

So runs an official history at the end of the nineteenth century. Nevertheless, this introduction is in sharp contradiction to the subsequent expositions, from which it is highly apparent that "beneath a pious exterior an Asiatic moral coarseness was revealed." Actually the Muscovite period in Russian Church history is marked by profound spiritual upheavals and is far from showing the organic unity people have so longed to find in it.

Moscow's political triumph in consolidating the country coincided with the first great crisis in the thought of the Russian Church and is deeply marked by it. This was the temptation of the union of Florence and the catastrophe of the fall of Constantinople in 1453. In the Russian mind both events were interpreted as apocalyptic signs and as a terrible break in the history of Orthodoxy. Their Greek teachers and mentors were revealed as traitors to Orthodoxy; perhaps even for this reason subjected by Providence to the Turkish yoke. From the very start the Russian mind, sensitive to grand historical-philosophical themes, had inevitably pondered these signs and drawn new conclusions from them.

True, the way had been prepared. Back in the fourteenth century a dispute had begun between Moscow and Constantinople, and Moscow was gradually liberated from the Byzantine theory of a single empire. This theory, which Greek missionaries had brought into Russia from the very first days of Russian Christianity and which in its essence had been accepted unconditionally at the time, had been shaken by the Greeks themselves—by their "illegal and venal way of dealing with the Russian Church under Metropolitan Alexei, the installation of Cyprian in his place, and

[11] Znamensky, *op. cit.*, pp. 99–100.

especially by the arbitrary installation after his death of
Abbot Pimen, who caused great harm to the Church."[12]

Independence from Byzantium—Messianic Theocracy

Dependence of the Russian Church on Byzantium—
weakened, and corrupted by its weakness—became less and
less justified by the facts and more and more oppressive.
Even at the beginning of the fifteenth century the Grand
Prince Vasili Dmitrievich of Moscow was obliged to listen
to lessons on Byzantine theocratic theory, an example of
which we find in an epistle of Antony, the patriarch of
Constantinople, to the prince.

The Holy Emperor occupies a high place in the Church; he is
not the same as other local princes and lords. The Emperors
in the beginning established and maintained piety throughout
the universe; they summoned the ecumenical councils; by their
laws they established the observance of what the divine and
sacred laws say of right dogmas and the proper ordering of
Christian life, and they took many measures against heresy. And
if with God's permission pagans have surrounded the possessions and lands of the Emperor, still until this day he is
anointed by the great myrrh according the same ceremony and
with the same prayers, and is crowned Emperor of all Christians.
In any place, wherever Christians may be, the name of the
Emperor is mentioned by all patriarchs, metropolitans and
bishops, and no other princes or local rulers have this advantage . . . It is impossible for Christians to have the Church
but not to have the Emperor. For Empire and Church are in
close union and it is impossible to divide them from each other.

We have already learned how profoundly this theory
was reflected in the history of the southern Slavic empires,
literally bewitched by the theocratic dream. Law-abiding
Russia accepted it unconditionally for centuries, although

12 A. Kartashoff, "The Destiny of Holy Russia," *Pravoslavnaya mysl*, Vol.
I (Paris, 1928), p. 143.

it sometimes attempted to weaken its ecclesiastical dependence on Constantinople.

One must add to this that—under the influence of gloomy
reality, Mongol slavery, and general ruin—eschatological
expectations generally increased in Russia toward the end
of the fourteenth century. For example, it was said in
Moscow of the work of St. Stephen of Perm, who translated
Christian literature for his flock: "Before there was no lit-
eracy in Perm—why invent it now, after seven thousand
years, a hundred and twenty years before the end?" Obviously the fall of the empire, the betrayal by the Greeks,
and in particular the place of Moscow in all these events
had acquired a new significance. Before this period Byzantium had been the standard of Orthodoxy; the Russians
could tranquilly build churches and monasteries, pray to
God, and develop their state, for behind it all stood the
guarantee of universal Byzantine Orthodoxy and its in-
fallible authority. But now the standard disappeared and
the authority came crashing down. "At the holy place, in
what has been the Catholic and Apostolic Church of Constantinople, there is now abomination and desolation."

It was now beyond doubt that Byzantium's holy mission
had passed to Moscow and that the theocratic dream of the
East had found a new incarnation. Simeon, a priest-monk
of Suzdal and an eyewitness to the fall of the Greeks at
Florence, had written, "Orthodoxy is at its best in Russia."
And he proclaimed the Prince of Moscow a "reverent,
Christ-loving, and pious, true Orthodox Grand Prince, the
white Tsar of all Russia." The final transfer of metropolitan
power into Russian hands occurred in 1448, when St. Jonah
was elected by a council of Russian bishops and a decree
sent to Greece proclaiming the *de facto* independence of
the Russian Church from the patriarch of Constantinople.
While historically inevitable, this independence became in
fact the basis of the final subordination of the Church to
the Russian state and to its national and political calculations.

It must be recognized that this birth of Russian theocracy

. . . passed for a long time through the crucible of sufferings
and struggles of conscience within the Church. It was not easy
to cross out the historical authority of the Greeks. It was far
more difficult to overcome the canonical authority of the
Mother Church . . . The history of the scrupulous sufferings
of Russia's canonical conscience, over the independent installation of Metropolitan Jonah (1448), which amounted to au-
tocephaly, presents one of the most outstanding pieces of evidence as to Russia's canonical good faith. Grand Prince Vasili
Vasilievich was tormented just as earnestly by the extremely
crucial problem which unexpectedly fell upon him: should he
take up the defense of Orthodoxy, which had faltered in its very
shrine at Constantinople [because of the surrender of the Greeks
to the papacy at Florence in 1439] and threatened in this way to
disappear throughout the world?[13]

Russian religious messianism was indeed born in eschatological tension—in confusion and alarm. But external events
justified it. In 1453 Constantinople fell. In 1472, Ivan III
entered into matrimony with the niece of the last Byzantine emperor, and the two-headed eagle of the empire
legitimately soared over Moscow. Finally, 1480 signalized
the final liberation from the Tatars. Once more the Byzantine idea of a migrating empire was confirmed. Old
Rome had wavered in its orthodoxy, and the empire had
passed to the new Rome. Had not the time arrived for a
new shift, to Moscow? So the theory of Moscow as the
third Rome was conceived, its proponent being Philotheus,
the teaching elder of the Lazarus Monastery in Pskov, an
old city southwest of Novgorod and the future St. Petersburg. According to his letters to the Grand Princes Basil III
and Ivan IV in Moscow, the Orthodox Church, like the
wife in the Apocalypse, had first run from old to new
Rome, "but found no peace there because of the union
with the Latins at the Eighth Council. Then the Church

13 *Ibid.*, p. 149.

of Constantinople fell, and the empire fled again to a third
Rome, which is in New Great Russia . . . All Christian
empires bow down to you alone: for two Romes are fallen,
but the third stands fast; a fourth there cannot be; your
Christian kingdom shall not be given to another . . . You
alone are Emperor over all Christians under the sun."

Muscovite Domination of the Church

Here lay the true tragedy of the Russian Church, for this
victory of the theocratic dream, this upsurge of national and
religious consciousness, turned into a triumph for the Moscow autocracy and contained not only Byzantine but Asian
—Tatar—features as well.

The Tatar element had possessed the soul of Russia, not outwardly but from within, penetrating its flesh and blood. This
spiritual Mongol conquest coincided with the political defeat
of the Horde. In the fifteenth century thousands of baptized and
unbaptized Tatars entered the service of the Prince of Moscow,
merging with the ranks of men in service, the future nobility,
infecting it with their Eastern concepts and the way of life
of the steppe . . . The two centuries of the Tatar yoke did not
yet mark the end of Russian freedom. Freedom perished only
after the liberation from the Tatars . . .[14]

We see this death of freedom first of all in the Church. The
theocratic empire recognizes only one unlimited authority,
the authority of the emperor; beside it the image of metropolitan or patriarch fades away and the voice of the Church
grows weaker. In 1522, at the order of Basil III, Metropolitan Varlaam was removed and secluded in a monastery.
The disgraced boyar Beklemishev wrote of his successor
Daniel, "An instructive word [to the Grand Prince] was
never heard from him and he does not plead on behalf

[14] G. Fedotov, "Russia and Freedom," in his *Novyi Grad* (in Russian,
New York, 1952), p. 145.

of anyone; previously, metropolitans had sat in their seats in their robes and had pleaded to the ruler on behalf of all men." The weakness of the Church was expressed particularly in the matter of the divorce of the Grand Prince from his barren wife Solomonia. This illegitimate divorce was opposed by Maxim the Greek and the Eastern hierarchs who sent their opinions. But Daniel, obeying the prince, made Solomonia a nun by force and married the prince to Elena Glinski, the mother of Ivan the Terrible.

The tragedy of Muscovite Orthodoxy reached its final limit under Ivan, whose reign completed the development of Russian theocracy. In 1547 he was anointed Grand Prince—after the example, he claimed, of the Greek emperors and his ancestor Vladimir Monomakh—and became the first born tsar, "by God's mercy." In 1557 he received confirmation of this rank from the Eastern hierarchs. His reign began with the memorable, promising introduction in which the Church again appeared to have a voice, the voice of conscience, the call to Christian "construction." This was the period of Metropolitan Makari and the Council of the Hundred Chapters, the period when Russian Orthodoxy reached perfection in its own national self-affirmation, although its "well-being" was mostly only external. But even this was broken off when a terrible reaction set in in the decade of the 1560's, covering the whole state with the malevolent shadow of the *oprichnina*.[15] The victory of autocracy was stained with the martyr's blood of Metropolitan Philip (1569); his accusation against Ivan the Terrible was the last general open accusation against the empire by the Church. "I am a stranger upon the earth and am ready to suffer for the truth. Where is my faith if I am silent?"

After him the Church kept silent for a long time. His successors, Cyril and Antony, were mute witnesses to Ivan's acts, "Where are the faces of the prophets, who could accuse the kings of injustice? Where is Ambrose, who re-

15 The bodyguard of Ivan the Terrible, chief executors of his cruelties.

strained Theodosius? Where is John Chrysostom, who exposed the avaricious Empress? Who defends his offended
brother?" To Kurbsky's questions[16] the Russian Church
had no answer. Under the weak Tsar Theodore, Metropolitan Dionisi was cloistered for daring to bring accusations
against the powerful Godunov; it is true that he was criticized not only for an ecclesiastical matter but for a political
alliance with his rival Shuisky as well. But when the patriarch of Constantinople, Jeremiah, solemnly elevated Metropolitan Job to the patriarchate on January 26, 1589, and
two years later a decree reached Moscow of the establishment of a patriarchate in Russia, the Russian Church was
no longer even in captivity to the state. Together they composed a single united world, forged together in a sacral way
of life.

Outwardly, as has already been said, Russian Orthodoxy
reached its peak, its imperial self-affirmation, in the Moscow
empire. It was expressed first of all in the centralization
not only of ecclesiastical life but of the tradition of the
Russian Church itself as well. The subjugation of the appanages to Moscow was accompanied by the unprecedented
subjugation of all local spiritual traditions to the ecclesiastical center in Moscow. Moscow was to be the center of
Russian holiness, and relics from glorious ancient cities
were brought there, often by force. The icon of the Savior
from Novgorod, the icon of the Annunciation from Ustiug,
the Crypt icon from Pskov, the icon of the Mother of God
from Vladimir, and the relics of Prince Michael and his
boyar Theodore from Chernigov were all brought to the
Cathedral of the Assumption.

Along with this appeared a frequently extreme pettiness
of local nationalism: the first Muscovite bishop in Novgorod, Sergius, refused to venerate the relics of his Novgorodian predecessor, St. Moses; Ivan III, after visiting the

[16] Prince Kurbsky (1528–83), one of the most enlightened men in Mus-
covy, deserted to Lithuania. He was the author of famous epistles to Ivan
the Terrible.

Khutyn Monastery, said that the Muscovite relics should be given precedence over those of the local saints.

The chief inspiration and executor of this centralization was Metropolitan Makari. His *Menologion* contained "all the books, combined, which had been found in the Russian lands": the lives of the saints, arranged according to the days on which they are commemorated; the words used in their celebrations; many of their works; whole books of Holy Scripture and interpretations of them. The gathering of all this literary treasure "by many names and many scribes" lasted almost twenty years. Makari is also credited with compiling the *Book of Degrees*, an extensive collection of information on Russian history.

Another document of the period which reflected the final crystallization of Russian Orthodoxy was the *Domostroi* ("Home-Builder") of the priest Sylvester, a contemporary and colleague of Makari. Florovsky calls it "a didactic book, not a descriptive one, and it outlines a theoretical ideal but does not describe daily reality." However, it was clearly conceived out of desire to fix everything, even to the smallest details of domestic life, in a definitive system and actually to convert the whole of life into a ritual. In this rite, along with an unquestionably Christian attitude and asceticism, Asiatic crudeness also breaks out: beatings, for example, become one of the main methods of maintaining Christian life in all its splendor, and also of education. Professor Fedotov writes of this period:

The outlook of the Russian had become extremely simplified. Even in comparison to the Middle Ages the Muscovite was primitive. He did not reason but accepted on faith certain dogmas which sustained his moral and public life. But even in his religion there was something which was more important than dogma. Ritual, periodic repetition of certain gestures, prostrations, and verbal formulas, binds living life together and prevents it from slipping away into chaos, imparting to it even the beauty of formalized existence. For the Muscovite, like all Russians, did not lack an esthetic sense, only now it became oppressive. Beauty became splendor, and fatness was the ideal of feminine beauty. Christianity, when the mystical tendencies of the Trans-Volgans were rooted out, was transformed increasingly into a religion of holy matter. It was ritualism, but a ritualism which was terribly demanding and morally effective. In his ritual, like the Jew in the Law, the Muscovite found support for his feat of sacrifice.[17]

Because the *Domostroi* is not a description but an ideology, its very appearance may be regarded as a sign of the profound spiritual illness, the genuine crisis, concealed under the outward splendor and harmony of Church life in Moscow.

Inner Crisis and Turmoil

The numerous personal defects of Church members— the priesthood, the monks, and laymen—are attested by the Council of the Hundred Chapters, called by Ivan the Terrible. Moreover, in addition to the decline of education, excessive ritualism, remnants of paganism, and so forth, one cannot ignore the straying or irregularities of thought and disturbances within the mind of the Church. Such a straying was evident even in the fourteenth century in the Novgorodian heresy of the Strigolniks, a rationalistic and anticlerical movement. Still more symptomatic in the fifteenth century was the heresy of the Judaizers, a peculiar magical combination of freethinking and dark astrological interests. Afterward began the disputes of the Josephites, followers of Joseph of Volotsk, and the Trans-Volgans,[18] monks of the Trans-Volga hermitages, whose chief leader later became known as St. Nil Sorsky. Outwardly this was a controversy over monastery possessions, the right of the monks to own "villages"—to be a propertied class within the state; and also about the execution of heretics.

Two distinct conceptions of the Christian ideal were, in

17 Fedotov, "Russia and Freedom," p. 151.
18 Name given to the followers of Abbot Nilus of Sora, who opposed Abbot Joseph on the question of monastic properties.

fact, coming into conflict. In his book, *The Ways of Russian Theology*, Father Florovsky writes in this connection of the conflict of "two truths" and defines the truth of Joseph of Volotsk as the "truth of social service." Joseph himself cannot be considered acquisitive.

He can in no way be accused of indifference or inattention to his neighbor. He was a great benefactor, a "helpless fellow-sufferer," and he defended the monastic villages out of philanthropic and social motives alone. Joseph included the Tsar himself in the same system of "God's obligation," the Tsar too is subject to the law, and he holds his power only within the limits of God's law and commandments. One should not submit to an unjust or "obstinate" Tsar.

Yet whatever Joseph's basic truth may have been, his system is fitted too neatly into the totalitarian nature of the Muscovite state and corresponded too obviously to its utilitarian psychology. From this point of view, the defeat of the Trans-Volgan movement, despite the political motives that complicated all these disputes, meant suppression of the spiritual freedom of the Church and of any recognition of its incompatibility with service exclusively to the state or society. The Trans-Volgans lived by the original spiritual tradition of Orthodoxy, "by the process of the spiritual and moral constitution of the Christian personality." Once again, in this experience of genuine spiritual freedom, social conscience also was aroused and entered a protest against the religious use of force—against Moscow's all-devouring system of obligation and the subordination of human personality to the "construction" of it.

Conservatism and Ritualism

Behind all these disputes and irregularities one may perceive very clearly the gradual breaking off of official Russian

Orthodoxy from the creative traditions of its universal past. Liberation from canonical dependence upon the Greeks came to mean distrust of everything Greek in general and the opposition of Russian Orthodoxy and Russian antiquity to Greek Orthodoxy. This was the meaning behind the famous Council of the Hundred Chapters of 1551, summoned on the initiative of Ivan the Terrible but expressing the attitudes of Makari and Sylvester in particular. The council was to cure the scandalous defects in ecclesiastical society; Ivan's plan was apparently a profound and many-sided reform. Yet it is characteristic that neither Ivan nor the participants in the council conceived of these corrections as a self-examination in terms of the sure criteria of the universal tradition of the Church, or the creative renewal of them under new conditions. Ivan was inspired by the West and did not like the "Greek faith." The council responded to his "liberal" questions with the experience of olden times—what had prevailed under their ancestors—and not by affirming the truth. Even the correction of Church books, a problem that had already arisen even then, was a complete failure, reflecting the lack of any genuine perspective in the thinking of the pillars of Russian Orthodoxy. The semiliterate, unjustified translations accepted, and the helplessness in defining criteria, in themselves sowed the poison of schism.

For the first time, here, we see very clearly the distrust of thought and creativity. Salvation lay only in the strict preservation of antiquity; this helpless conservatism reveals all the tragedy and depth of Moscow's break with living Orthodox culture. The road to salvation became observance of regulations and the performance of ritual. Because people did not understand it, the ritual became an end in itself, so that even obvious mistakes in the text were inviolable because hallowed by antiquity—it would be dangerous to the soul to correct them.

Finally there developed a simple fear of books and knowledge. The teachers themselves, according to Kurbsky, "would lure away boys who were diligent and wished to gain knowledge of the Scriptures, saying: 'Do not read many books,' and would point to one who has lost his mind, saying, he wandered astray in books and fell into heresy." The printing press in Moscow was closed down and the first Russian printers, Ivan Fedorov and Peter Timofeev, were accused of heresy; then "because of the growing hatred of many leaders and priests and teachers," they left for southern Russia. The tsar himself finally intervened on behalf of book publishing and reopened the printing press in 1568.

Only in the light of this break in the creative theological tradition can we understand all the fateful significance of the first "encounter with the West," which coincided with the triumph of the Moscow kingdom. It was fateful because it was not a free encounter or argument; it was a case of either replacing Byzantinism by Western influence or indiscriminately rejecting everything Western, as the plague. Russia's national self-assertion had been roused in opposition to Byzantium, but the latter's universal Orthodox heritage had also been rejected.

Western Leanings and Resistance to Them

Beginning with Ivan III, a real fascination with the West made its appearance in court circles. His marriage to Sophia Paleologos, which made Moscow officially the heir of Byzantium, actually opened the door to the Italian Renaissance and to complex and contradictory Western influences. His successor Basil III was also a Westernizer, whose doctor, Nikolai Nemchin, even conducted a correspondence concerning the union of the churches. It is characteristic that when a new translation of the Bible into Church Slavonic was begun in Novgorod under the enlightened Metropolitan Gennadi, the deciding textual influence was not the Greek text (which was not consulted at all) but the Latin

Vulgate. In general, "under Gennadi a whole movement of Latin style can be observed in Novgorod." It is just as evident in the case of Deacon Viskovaty, who did not accept the new style of the Moscow icons, which were beginning to show the influence of Western models and the predominance of allegory over the symbolic, hieratic style of the Byzantine and Old Russian canon. Particularly tragic was the condemnation of St. Maxim the Greek in 1521. Maxim himself had spent a long time in the West and had undergone a long spiritual development. But in Russia he defended a purely patristic tradition and the creative work of the Christian East.

It was not the encounter with Europe that was so fateful, but the unfree conditions of it. Moscow had defended herself from Byzantium by her own ancient past; she used the same instrument to oppose the West as well. To the fascination with the West on the upper levels, the Church responded with anathemas, not against Western heresies but against the West itself, simply because it was the West.

By confusing the existing with the nonexistent, the ritualistic religious outlook was extended to ordinary objects and customs of everyday life as well: everything native and Russian seemed Orthodox and everything alien was heretical and "heathen." Russians wore beards, and the beard became an essential symbol of being Orthodox, while the clean-shaven face was a sign of belonging to the Latin heresy. The Council of the Hundred Chapters forbade the celebration of funeral services for those without beards, as well as the offering of communion bread or candles on his behalf; he should be counted with the unbelievers.

Under such psychological conditions free encounter or discussion were impossible. These two extremes in Russia's attitude toward the West, mortal fear or blind worship, persisted for a long time. When a few young men were sent abroad under Godunov for study, they did not return

home but remained in the West and betrayed their Orthodoxy.

True Holiness

As in ossified Byzantium in its later years, so in the
Moscow kingdom, too, holiness—the breath of the Spirit,
which breathes where it wills—gradually withdrew to the
forests, the outskirts, the periphery. This was the era of the
saints of the north, who achieved inner freedom in their
struggle against wild and merciless nature: St. Alexander of
Svir, Korneli of Komel, Makari of Koliazin, Savvati, Zosima,
German of Solovetsk, Antony of Sii, and Nil of Stolbensk.
The list could be prolonged. Sanctity was not scarce, and
"Holy Russia" continued to grow alongside the "great
power"; but they must not be confused.

Nor was the real thirst for sanctity dying out among the
people. Perhaps just at this time, or very near it, when the
moral level was falling and growing coarser, and outward
piety and splendor were becoming divorced from their
moral and theological inspiration, the only perceptible ideal
within the whole of society became that of absolute holiness. The outward appearance of Christianity could be
maintained, preserved, and fixed in the world, but it was
obvious that "the world abides in evil" and that its Christian covering—all the splendor of life, rite, and form—
could be brought to fulfillment only by complete withdrawal to some freedom beyond the limits—to the search
for a new heaven and a new earth, where the truth lives.
In this era of state "obligation," fixed pattern of life, and
static, oppressive "sacralness" there matured in Russia the
type of the wanderer, the tramp, the eternal searcher after
the Spirit and the truth, free with the freedom of complete
abnegation, but achieving unity with nature and men.
Behind the ceremonial, self-satisfied Russia of daily life was
born another, unpatterned, "light" Russia, illumined by the

vision of an ideal world, one that was loving, just, and joyous. This spiritual perfectionism did not rise up against the Church, and denied nothing in it, but on the contrary lived by the grace received from it. There developed a dangerous habit of distinguishing the "objective" element in the Church—the grace itself—from its bearers, the Church community. The Russian believed in the necessity for the priest as the performer of sacraments, but he had ceased to expect from him anything else—as for instance, instruction, leadership, or a moral example. What could be expected of the priesthood, in view of the complete lack of schools and the priests' growing dependence on their parish; their poverty, oppression, and crudeness? It is enough to read the rules of the Council of the Hundred Chapters about the secular clergy to become convinced of their decline in the Moscow period. The priest ceased to be the head, the father, the pastor of the community, to become a performer of services. Living souls did not seek to slake their spiritual thirst or to find spiritual leadership in the official hierarchy, but turned to elders, saints, and hermits. Indeed, the Church community disappeared from the thought of the Church itself. There remained the sinful world; within it were sources of grace, certain centers contact with which became a treasured dream. Spiritual life withdrew deeper and deeper into an underlying world; it became a mysterious underground river that never dried up in Russia, but had less and less influence on the life of the state, of society, and (in the end) of the Church itself.

The Moscow period was not an organically unified era but marks a profound break, a crisis, and a division in the history of Russian Orthodoxy.

The Seventeenth Century

The seventeenth century, the last century of pre-Petrine Russia, must be interpreted in the light of this crisis. It began with the time of troubles and ended with Peter. It is frequently contrasted with the following era as the "dark background for great transformations, a stagnant century." There is very little truth in the characterization. Certainly many were still living in the old ways and customs; many felt an increased need to fix their whole lives in a sort of solemn ritual, sanctified if not sacred. But it is precisely when their way of life is breaking down that men begin to be upset by the indestructibility of their fathers' principles and traditions. So in the intensity of the seventeenth-century search for a definite pattern of life we sense rather a delayed self-defense against the decay of the old pattern, a depressive "flight into ritual, rather than the immediate integrity and strength of their way of life."[19] In the seventeenth century the crisis in Muscovite Orthodoxy was revealed and exposed, and Moscow's way became the dead end that made Peter's breakthrough inevitable.

Two main themes defined the life of the Russian Church in the 1600's. These were its encounter with the West by way of Kievan Orthodoxy, on the one hand, and the schism of the Old Believers, on the other. Both were of immense historical significance.

Encounter with the West

The first theme brings us back to the Kievan metropolitanate which in the fourteenth century had remained outside the borders of Muscovite Orthodoxy, just as the Russian lands began to be gathered around Moscow. This division of the Russian Church into two metropolitanates may be explained in the first place by the rivalry between Moscow and Lithuania for a central position in pulling the state together. In the fourteenth century Lithuania was in fact a Russian land and had claims as good as Moscow's to draw together the appanages. Hence the Lithuanian princes strove

19 Florovsky, *op. cit.*, p. 58.

to acquire their own metropolitan, who would be independent of Moscow, and by the fifteenth century they were successful. Even earlier, through the marriage of Yagailo to
Jadwiga of Poland in 1386, the Lithuanian kingdom was at
first in personal union with Poland, and later, after the last
upsurge of Lithuanian independence under Vitovt (1398), in
political union. After the middle of the fifteenth century
the southwest metropolitanate was under the authority of
Roman Catholic kings and in direct contact, first with Catholicism and later with Protestantism—that is, under the
constant and very strong impact of alien forms of faith. That
bitter struggle cannot be described here; it is difficult to
imagine anything more remote from genuine unity of the
Church than the campaigns—conducted by fire and sword,
and with falsehood and violence—that broke the spirit of
the people and poisoned Christianity with hatred, all in the
name of *unia*, or unification! The union of Brest-Litovsk of
1596, which started a period of bloody persecution of Orthodoxy in Galicia, Lithuania, and Volynia, was a fitting end
to the Byzantine "unions," with the sole distinction that
the latter, thanks to the Turkish yoke, proved ephemeral
whereas Brest-Litovsk poisoned the southwestern Slavs
with hatred, divisions, and discord for many centuries to
come. Real persecutions of Orthodoxy have flared up here
even in the twentieth century.

But this history has another distinguishing mark. When
almost all the Orthodox hierarchy at the end of the sixteenth century seemed drawn to union (or rather, that is,
to the rights and estates of Polish Catholic bishops), the
defense of Orthodoxy was undertaken in the first place by
Orthodox intellectuals, and secondly by the people of the
Church themselves. Among the followers of the influential
Prince Ostrozhsky the first cultural center was formed, a
college was founded, and Orthodoxy defended by pen and
book. Prince Kurbsky and the first Russian printer, Ivan
Fedorov, took refuge in Ostrog, and here the famous Ostrozhsky Bible was printed (1580–81).

It is true that there was even sharper controversy here with Protestantism, which was gaining strength in Poland and Lithuania, but the important thing was this conception of cultural action in Orthodoxy—this first refuge of the "Greek-Slavic" tradition. In the face of terrible pressure from the Jesuits sent to Poland to combat Protestantism, beginning in the 1580's, the decisive factor was the opposition of the people, which found expression in brotherhoods. Patriarch Joachim of Antioch, as he was passing through Russia in 1586, gave a charter to the most ancient brotherhood of Lvov; it could expose those opposed to the law of Christ, even excommunicate them from the Church, and bring accusations even against bishops. After Lvov, brotherhoods arose in Vilno, Mogilev, Polotsk, and other cities. After the Council of Brest, the brotherhoods are the centers of resistance, using literary polemics and theological work. The brotherhoods organized schools, opened printing presses, and published books. In 1615 the famous Kievan Brotherhood was founded, and the Brotherhood school was opened with the co-operation of the Cossacks. Here in Kiev the main center of southwestern Orthodoxy was created.

While the first influences here were those of Byzantine tradition, this began to be more and more mixed with Western influence. In struggling against the Latins, "by necessity they turned to Western books. The new generation passed through entirely Western schools. The Western, Latin example attracted them."[20] The whole significance of this Kievan chapter in the history of Orthodoxy lay in the fact that at this time Orthodox theology, in defending Orthodoxy from aggressive *unia*, armed itself gradually with Western weapons, and Orthodox tradition slowly shifted into Latin scholastic categories. The influence of the famous Kievan metropolitan, Peter Mogila (1633–47), proved decisive. "He was a convinced Westernizer, a Westernizer by tastes and habits." In Kiev, to counterbalance the Slavic-Greek school of the Brotherhood, he founded a completely Latin-Polish institute which soon

20 *Ibid.*, p. 43.

engulfed that of the Brotherhood. Its program was taken from Jesuit schools, and teachers who had graduated from Polish Jesuit colleges taught there. Here the question of Orthodoxy and Catholicism was transformed into a purely "jurisdictional" one; these Westernizers did not sense any difference in faith, or rather the pattern of their own minds was by now wholly Latin. The main theological document of this movement, the "Orthodox Confession," usually ascribed to Mogila, was essentially Latin, and was written in Latin. True, it rejected papal primacy, but its whole spirit was Latin. After Mogila, Latin formulas and theories also began to penetrate Orthodox theology.

The injection into Russian Orthodoxy of this "Ukrainian baroque"—even before the time of Peter the Great and his "window into Europe"—which made all Russian theology and the whole Russian theological school dependent upon the West, was extraordinarily important in the history of Russian Orthodoxy. "The Western Russian monk, taught in the Latin or the Russian school, molded according to its example, was also the first who brought Western science to Moscow." The fathers of the new Russian school theology were two obvious Latinists, Simeon of Polotsk and Paissy Ligarid. Jesuits appeared even in Moscow, and the dispute "over the time of the transformation of the Holy Gifts," which arose in the 1670's in Moscow was a typically Western dispute by its theme alone. The first schools opened in Moscow followed the model of those in Kiev, and when the time of Peter's reforms arrived, Russian theology would be already "Westernized"! The Church did not oppose these influences. There was no free encounter of Orthodox tradition with the West; it was the conquest of unarmed Orthodoxy by Latinism.

Schism of the Old Believers

The tragic history of the Old Believers bears witness to this crisis in tradition. The main reason for it was the question of correcting the Church books, but behind that in the thinking of the Church stood profounder questions and doubts. The isolation of the Moscow kingdom ended with the time of troubles, and it stood at the crossroads or even at a parting of the ways. Meetings with foreigners and the ties with Kiev, the East, and the West, which were increasingly frequent and growing stronger, made direct and persistent demands on it to put its own ecclesiastical affairs in order, and aroused thought in Church circles, showing up the one-sidedness, inadequacy, and indefensibility of Muscovite traditions.

Particularly acute, in connection with book printing, was the question of the service books. There were too many variants in the manuscripts. Which copies should be used for printing? The books of the Lithuanian press raised doubts about Orthodoxy, while the Russian ones were defective and contradictory. Under Michael, the first Romanov to be elected (1613), the disputes concerning the liturgical books several times reached the point of sharp rupture and condemnations. One of these was the condemnation by the hierarchy in 1618 of the Abbot Dionisi, of Trinity Monastery outside Moscow, for correcting the *Book of Needs*. The passion of these disputes indicates the uneasiness and disturbance in the thinking of the Church. With the accession to power of Tsar Alexey Mikhailovich reform tendencies at court increased. This was the period when Kievan influence was growing stronger in Moscow and Westerners were pouring into Russia. We must particularly note the restoration of close bonds with the Orthodox East, however; under Alexey Mikhailovich we see Eastern patriarchs several times in Moscow. An active correspondence was conducted with them, and Russians in turn were sent to Greece. However strange it may seem, these new bonds with the Greeks were one of the causes of new troubles.

At last it was decided to correct the books according to the Greek models. This Greek theme stemmed from the tsar and a circle of "zealots" close to him. But unfortu-

nately in accepting the Greek model those in Moscow did
not specify or distinguish the quality of it, which was often
no less defective than the Russian, and the whole correction took place in the complete absence of cultural and
theological perspectives. Too frequently the authorities
were questionable migrants from Greece seeking charity or
profit in Moscow, who became teachers by chance. The correction of the books was inspired not so much by a return
to the spirit and truth of Orthodox worship as by a drive
for uniformity, and often by thoughtless Grecophilia.

The role of Patriarch Nikon was particularly crucial. He
had "an almost morbid tendency to remake and shift everything in the Greek way, as Peter later on had a passion to
remake everything in the German or Dutch way. They also
shared this strange readiness to break with the past, this
unexpected lack of an established pattern of life, this pre-
meditation and artificiality."[21] Too many anathemas and
curses were immediately imposed, too much carried out by
order and decree. But what was worse, the Greek liturgical
books printed in Venice were frequently suspected by Russians to be Latinizing, like the Kievan editions of Peter
Mogila. This does not mean that the adherents of the
"Old Belief" were right—Avvakum and those like him—
but they were indignant at this "wholesale denial of every
old Russian ceremony and rite," this general leveling according to the dubious Kievans and the no less dubious
Greeks, many of whom had indeed studied in Rome and
in order to do so had temporarily even accepted the Latin
faith. Hence the schism acquired unfortunate depth as a
dispute over history, and especially over the meaning of
Russian Orthodoxy in it.

The anxiety of the schismatics may be expressed as follows: if all this consecrated and holy past of Moscow, the
third Rome, the last bulwark and hope of Orthodoxy, is
guilty of so many errors and distortions, as the innovators
claim—does this not mean that history is coming to an end

[21] *Ibid.*, p. 64.

and that the Antichrist is near? "It was not at all the 'rite' but the 'Antichrist' which was the theme and secret of the schism . . . The whole significance and inspiration of the first schismatic opposition did not lie in 'blind' adherence to separate ritualistic details of daily life, but in this apocalyptic riddle."[22] The schism was nothing but the price paid for Moscow's dream of a consecrated pattern of life and of a complete incarnation in history and on earth of the last Kingdom. At a deeper level, it was the price paid for the radical antihistoricism of Byzantine theocracy, which had rejected Christianity as a way and a creative process, and had wanted to stop history by "eternal repetition" of a single all-embracing mystery.

Both the perfectionism and the limitations of this theory are revealed here: the whole of Orthodoxy was measured externally, according to rituals and words; the dispute never once went beyond a stifling ritualistic casuistry. In a certain sense the schism did draw away from the Church its best forces—those for whom the outward tenor and pattern of life were not self-sufficient values, but only the outer form of the inner high ideal in their conception of Christianity and its adaptation to history. These people lived by an integral concept of the Christian world; it was not their fault that this concept, both in later Byzantium and especially in Moscow, was cut off from its vital sources—from the creative inspiration of the early Church, which had narrowed down to the *Typicon* and the *Domostroi*.

But their opponents did not use tradition or truth to nourish their reform. The new books were better than the old, more correct, more sensible; but the hierarchy, which accepted the reform so easily, without reaching back to the sources of the faith and teaching of the Church, now too easily accepted other reforms so long as they came from the authorities and were made "by the will of His Majesty." The schismatics were not so opposed to the Church as they were to the empire; but in the name of that other theory

22 *Ibid.*, p. 67.

of empire which—no matter how trivial it was made or narrowed down—saw and wanted to see itself as the Kingdom serving Christ. Their opponents were almost unaware of this purpose: the metamorphosis of Christian theocracy into the ideal of the Kingdom.

Thus in the seventeenth century relations between Church and empire again became strained. From the patriotic services of Patriarch Germogen and the Trinity Monastery of St. Sergei in the time of troubles, through the peculiar "papocaesarism" of Patriarch Philaret, we come to Nikon and the schism. One feels that a transformation of the state has started, that its self-awareness has begun to change. Even the "Most Pacific" Tsar Alexei Mikhailovich, offering repentance in the name of the empire before the relics of St. Philip, was essentially already remote in psychology from the Byzantine and Old Russian theocratic self-conception. The atmosphere of Western absolutism was more and more obviously coming into Moscow. Nikon's break with the tsar in a certain sense repeated in Russia the Western dispute over relations between empire and priesthood; it was first of all a dispute over authority. But perhaps the schism made inevitable the triumph of state absolutism under Peter the Great.

Reforms of Peter the Great

The dispute over the significance and the evaluation of the Petrine reforms may be called the basic dispute in Russian Orthodoxy. It is a sharp and painful theme in the thinking of the Russian Church. True enough, no one will defend the spirit of Peter's ecclesiastical reforms—the synodal structure of the Russian Church, the procurator, and the *de facto* transformation of the Church into the "Department of the Orthodox Confession."[23] But there remains a far-reaching question, frequently concealed be-

[23] Official name given to the Church in imperial terminology.

hind the others, about the general meaning of the synodal period in the history of Orthodoxy. It can be answered
within the framework of this book only if reduced to an
inevitably simplified form. The time has not yet come for
a scholarly answer, and the answer in terms of life can be
given by the future alone.

Hardly anyone will argue against the proposition that
Peter's reform was first of all a sharp break in a theocratic
tradition, a deliberate passage along many lines toward a
Western system of thinking. It represented the reign of
Western state absolutism in Russia. Usually Peter and his
successors and the whole Petersburg period are accused of
depriving the Church of its freedom and independence.
But the Church had not been free, in the modern sense of
the term, since the time of Constantine the Great—neither
in Byzantium nor in Moscow. Yet without being free, it
was still distinct from the state and had not been dependent on it for its very existence, structure, and life. However far the departures from "symphony," they were always departures and sooner or later recognized as such—as,
for example, when the state itself venerated its own victims.
This occurred because the state recognized a law higher
than itself, Christian truth, of which the Church was the
preserver. Western absolutism, born out of struggle against
the Church, denied that it had any right to be the conscience of the state and squeezed it within the narrow
framework of "ministering to spiritual needs," which the
state itself defined, as it defined how they should be min-
istered to.

In its caretaking inspiration the "police state" inevitably turned
against the Church. The state not only is its guardian; it takes
its own tasks from the Church, takes them away and under-
takes them itself. It assumes responsibility for the indivisible
task of caring for the religious and spiritual well-being of the
people. If it subsequently again entrusts this concern to the
clergy, it does so by governmental delegation of power, and only

within the limits of this delegation of power to the Church is it alloted its place in the structure of the life of the people and the state, and only to the extent and with the motivation of its usefulness and need to the State.[24]

The "Synodal Period"

Canonically the synod was recognized by the Eastern patriarchs, and the sacramental and hierarchical structure of the Church was not harmed. Therefore the abruptness of the reform did not lie in its canonical aspects but in the psychology that produced it. Through the institution of the synod the Church became a governmental department, and until 1901 its members in their oath called the emperor "the high judge of this Sacred College," and all its decisions were adopted "by its authority, granted by His Imperial Majesty." This way of thinking is best expressed in the *Spiritual Rule* of Bishop Theofan Prokopovich, the chief assistant of Peter in his ecclesiastical reforms; he brought into Russia all the basic principles of the Protestant territorial Church, its concept of the relations between Church and state, according to which the visible or earthly Church was conceived as also a religious projection of the state itself.

This radical, fundamental falsehood of Peter's reforms was not recognized by the Russian authorities and was not repudiated, in fact, until the Revolution of 1917. There was a basic ambiguity in the relations between Church and state which infected the thinking of both state and Church alike. It must be emphasized that the Russian Church in essence and in good conscience did not accept Peter's reform. For it the emperor remained God's Anointed, and it continued to accept this anointment in the terms of Byzantine or Muscovite theocracy. Therefore state and Church

[24] Florovsky, *op. cit.*, p. 83.

interpreted the imperial authority in different ways, proceeding from almost contradictory presuppositions. The Russian Church was now anointing Western absolutism with the Byzantine anointment to the throne, meaning the consecration of the earthly emperor to serve as Christian basileus. From this point of view, Byzantine anointing with oil is theocratically a *limitation*, not the absolutizing of imperial authority. And for one day the splendid Western officer, by "divine" right of blood and inheritance the unrestricted master of millions of people, seemed indeed to be the Byzantine basileus or the Moscow tsar. In his sacred robes, with the Cross on his head, he seemed again an icon of the sanctified Christian empire. The Church and the people always regarded him as an icon, but beginning with Peter the state itself was not aware of it; on the contrary, it was constructed wholly on the principles of Western absolutism. This difference between the relations of the state to the Church ("the Department of the Orthodox Confession") and the relations of the Church to the state ("God's Anointed") composed the main falsehood and discrepancy of the synodal period.

In Byzantium and Moscow Church and state had spoken a single language and had lived within the same dimensions of consciousness. Therefore, despite all the subordination of Church to the state, the Church maintained an immense authority in the life of the state from top to bottom. Now, due to the difference in language and the incompatibility of their outlooks, the Church acquired a slightly anachronistic tinge as a remnant of antiquity, not only outwardly but psychologically, from within. For a long time its theocratic ideology prevented it from simply becoming aware of its captivity in an alien world; and from recognizing all the falseness of its subordination to an empire which was not Orthodox in any of its roots, or from wishing for freedom and recognition of the already accomplished fact of the separation of the Church from the state. There remained silent fright and obedience to the law.

The clergy in Russia after Peter's era became the "frightened
class." Frequently they dropped down or were pushed back
into the depths of society. At the higher levels an ambiguous
silence was maintained. The best were locked within themselves and withdrew "into the inward desert of the heart." This
frightened constraint of the clergy was one of the most undeniable results of Peter's reform. In the future the thinking
of the Russian Church developed under this dual restraint, administrative decree and inward fright.[25]

Culture Under Peter the Great

Yet under this state pressure, which had become utterly
alien, the life of the Church did not perish, and the synodal
period, despite the very widespread conviction to the contrary, can in no way be considered a time of decay or impoverishment of spiritual forces, or any sort of degenera-
tion. The great and profound culture that was gradually
created within the Church at this time, unlike the Moscow
period, is too frequently forgotten. True, it was started by
a powerful injection of Western influences and traditions.
Peter himself, in his ecclesiastical transformations, had relied on the Kievans and had used them to replace the
native Russian bishops. Therefore the Russian divinity
school (twenty-six seminaries were opened before 1750)
was a Latin school in language and in the spirit of its teaching. There is no doubt that "this transferral of the Latin
school onto Russian soil marked a rupture in the way of
thinking of the Church, a dichotomy between theological
'learning' and ecclesiastical experience; people still prayed
in Slavic but theologized in Latin."[26] In the ecclesiastical
and theological experience of the Russian Church, this theological Westernizing of course played a fateful role which

25 *Ibid.*, p. 89.
26 *Ibid.*, p. 101.

must not be underestimated. Yet still, after centuries of Muscovite darkness, after the break with all scholarly and cultural traditions, mental discipline returned for the first time to the Church, and education and the inspiration of creative work returned as well. Father George Florovsky has made a whole study of the development of Russian theology; there is no space here to list even its major names.

Even though it came through the West, from Latin or German books, the great forgotten tradition of thought, that of disinterested search for truth and ascetic service to it, were revived again in Orthodoxy. In cultural circles our divinity schools have had a bad reputation; they have been judged by *Sketches of a Seminary* by Pomialovsky, and such characters as Barnabas Prepotensky or Rakitin. "Seminarism" became a term of scorn.[27] Yet in the obscurantism engulfing them on all sides, the lowering of all standards and the coarsening of all traditions, this divinity school, poor and downtrodden, despised and frequently helpless, comes to life as one of the glorious bulwarks of Russian culture, and in the history of Orthodoxy its contributions are great. The academic level and freedom of the professors of the Russian graduate seminaries—"holy academies," as they were called by one Russian religious writer—were in no respect inferior to Western European or Russian secular scholars, and frequently surpassed them. This theology remained "scholastic"; its contributions were more in history and philosophy, or rather in preparing for a genuine theological renaissance. But it produced the Metropolitans Philaret and Nesmelov.[28] At the beginning of the twentieth century Russian theology was on the threshold of a genuine cultural

[27] Prepotensky was a seminarian who became an atheist in Leskov's *Cathedral People*; Rakitin, the seminarian in Dostoevski's *Brothers Karamazov*.
[28] Metropolitan Philaret of Moscow (1782–1867) was one of the greatest Russian hierarchs and theologians; V. I. Nesmelov (1863–1918) was professor at Kazan Theological Academy and author of the remarkable *Science of Man* (1903).

flowering, a renaissance in all strength of the universal tradition of Orthodoxy. But the Revolution came.

There was also an obvious rebirth of monasticism in Russia and a new, unforgettable resurgence of holiness in the synodal period. The eighteenth century was illumined by St. Tihon of Zadonsk (1724–82), and the early nineteenth century by the wonderful light of St. Serafim of Sarov, the elders of Optina Pustyn, and many other centers of spiritual life.[29] Here the ancient but eternally youthful traditions of Orthodoxy were very clearly restored, and the full force of the never-silent summons to "do honor to the heavenly calling" appeared once more. Behind the complex and tragic official history of Petersburg Russia we glimpse again and again another history which never ceased to develop, that of the slow summoning of the spirit, the "acquisition of grace," the enlightenment of the blackened human image by the ineffable glory of the First Model. One cannot reduce the history of Russia to the history of her culture, political struggle, social movements, or economic development, and forget this dimension of holiness, which drew so many to it (and not only the common people by any means)—this gradual but inspiring inward liberation of Orthodoxy from its bureaucratic destiny. To ignore this process would mean to overlook something most essential in the spiritual progress of Russia and of all Orthodoxy, in that crucial nineteenth century when the curtain was already rising on the "accomplishments" of the twentieth.

Bridge and Unifier

One must indeed admit that the history of Russia has been a tragedy, and it is this tragedy that makes it so important in the history of Orthodoxy. When we think of the

[29] Cf. G. Fedotov, *Treasury of Russian Spirituality* (New York, 1948).

great Russian literature, we have to acknowledge that it was not only inevitable for Peter to turn to the West, but essential. Only in free encounter with the world could Russia become herself, grow to her full height, and find her true calling, which was to overcome the terrible gulf between East and West which had been the chief sin of the Christian world since the Middle Ages. There was much dispute about East and West in Russia, but Russia herself revealed a truth that had dropped out of sight in Europe long before: that this contrast was in itself false and even sinful, for it was a falsehood against the original unity of the Christian world, whose spiritual history goes back to the miracle of Pentecost. All the best that Russia has created is the result of the inward reconciliation of "Eastern" and "Western," of all that was true and immortal that sprouted from Byzantine seed, but could grow only by identifying itself once more with the general history of Christian humanity.

"Europe is a mother to us, as is Russia, she is our second mother; we have taken much from her and shall do so again, and we do not wish to be ungrateful to her." No Westernizer said this; it is beyond Westernizers, as it is beyond Slavophiles. Dostoevsky wrote it at the height of his wisdom, on the threshold of death . . . His last hope was Messianism, but a Messianism which was essentially European, which developed out of his perception of Russia as a sort of better Europe, which was called upon to save and renew Europe. This hope may have been unjustified, but those who maintained such a faith were not turning their "faces toward the East," they were turning to Europe, believing that the "Eastern," meaning the Russian, light, or the light of Europe renewed, would shine over Europe. They did not yet know that their prophecy, to the extent that it was fulfilled, was fulfilled by them themselves.[30]

Russian literature was born from the "Western injection" and began as an imitation of Western literature; but it became a great world literature, and more than just a litera-

[30] V. Weidle, *The Task of Russia* (in Russian, New York, 1956), pp. 47–50.

ture of modern Christian thinking, only when it ceased to be either Western or Eastern. The more clearly its Christian root was revealed, the more it became simply Russian.

In some mysterious way, not yet thoroughly explored, Russia's primitive Christian Orthodox inspiration turned out to be the soul, the conscience, the profundity of this upper-class Western culture. More than that, what Eastern Orthodoxy alone revealed, sensed, and perceived in the world, in man, and in life became the source of new depths and discoveries in Russian literature. The man of whom this literature speaks and to whom it is addressed is the Christian man, not in the sense of moral perfection but in the sense of the depth and illumination used to perceive and describe him. Thus G. P. Fedotov calls *The Captain's Daughter* by the lucid, classical Pushkin the most Christian of all literary works. It was not by chance that for Russians themselves, in the nineteenth century, literature gradually became more than mere literature. In no other country did the writer pay so frequently for his art by his blood and his life as in Russia.

Russian thought, also, was born from Western roots. It has long been known that in Russia not only the Westernizers but the Slavophiles, too, were the fruit of German idealism, of Hegel and Schelling. But here again it was transformed into something more than merely imitative philosophy by what came out of the depths of Orthodox memory, and the Western patterns were suddenly filled with new content and new force. From Khomiakov, whom Samarin called "a teacher of the Church," to the Russian philosophers and theologians of the twentieth century, its themes more and more clearly emerged as the universal truth of Orthodoxy—not of Byzantinism, not of the East, but of an all-embracing, final Christian synthesis. These were not only mental patterns; behind them the light of spiritual resurgence in the Church itself glows more and more brightly—the return within the Church's own consciousness to the vital and eternal sources of its faith.

Tragic Halt

Thus, in Russia, Orthodoxy began to emerge from its Eastern isolation and to regain the universal spirit without which it is not Orthodoxy, not an eternal answer to the longings, hopes, and strivings of the world, but a withdrawal from this world into comfortable, intimate little dead ends.

The tragedy is that this development in Russia was not the only one, but in fact, century by century and year by year, there grew as well that terrible divarication which ended in the triumph of Bolshevism. Again there have been many disputes over the Western or the Eastern sources of this evil. Any oversimplification is inappropriate here. Never has the connectedness of everything in history, the interweaving of freedom and determination, of good and evil, seemed so clearly revealed as in the growth of the Russian catastrophe. The final rootedness of everything lies in those same depths in which the spiritual choice is made. Simultaneously with the growth of light in Russia there was a growth of darkness as well, and it is a terrible warning, judgment, and reminder that the darkness proved the stronger.

On the historic road of Orthodoxy the Russian chapter is now of course the final one, the last. Here Orthodoxy once more became history and was recognized as a way and a task, a creative inspiration for life. The way seems cut off, and in persecution and the blood of martyrs a new chapter in the history of the Orthodox Church is beginning. The past as well must be judged by them; they bear witness to the fact that what is eternally living and victorious over "the world abiding in evil" can only be rooted in whole-hearted faithfulness to Christ.

As we end this brief outline of the historic way of Orthodoxy, I do not intend to draw conclusions. The way is not finished, history goes on, and while it continues there can be no final conclusion for the Christian. I would like to add only that too many people regard the history of the Church as a temptation and avoid it for fear of "disillusionment." I am afraid that in this book, too, they have found both temptations and disillusionment. In the record of Orthodoxy, as in the story of Christianity in general, there is no lack of defects and human sins. I have not wished to hide them, for I believe that the whole strength of Orthodoxy lies in the truth; moreover, "discerning the spirits" of the past is a condition for any real action within the Church in the present.

In modern Church thinking, the past frequently oppresses and enchains rather than being creatively transformed into faithfulness to genuine tradition. This reveals an inability to evaluate the past, to distinguish the truth in it from mere bygone history and custom. Unless a distinction is made, true tradition becomes confused with all sorts of traditions that should themselves be judged in the light of the eternal truth of the Church. What is partial, one-sided, and even distorted is frequently proclaimed as the essence of Orthodoxy. And there is a sin of absolutizing the past which inevitably leads to the reverse extreme— to "modernism," meaning essentially rejection of the past and acceptance of "modernity," "science," or "needs of the current moment" as the sole criterion.

But just as the maintenance of Orthodox externals alone is incapable of concealing the profound crisis in modern Orthodoxy, so modernism is incapable of healing it. The only way out always lies in a return to the truth of the Church itself, and through it to a mastery of the past. In it we find the eternal tradition of the Church, as well as innumerable betrayals of it. The true Orthodox way of thought has always been historical, has always included the past, but has never been enslaved by it. Christ is "yesterday and today and forever the same," and the strength of the Church is not in the past, present, or future, but in Christ.

SHORT BIBLIOGRAPHY

History

ATTWATER, D. *The Christian Churches of the East.* 2 vols. Milwaukee, Wis., vol. 1, 1948; vol. 2, 1947.

BENZ, ERNST. *The Eastern Orthodox Church: Its Thought and Life.* New York, 1963.

Cambridge Medieval History, vol. 4, The Byzantine Empire. Ed. J. M. Hussey. 2 parts. Cambridge, 1967.

CHADWICK, H. *The Early Church.* Baltimore, Md., 1967.

DVORNIK, F. *The Slavs in European History and Civilization.* New Brunswick, N.J., 1962.

EVERY, G. *The Byzantine Patriarchate.* London, 1947.

HUSSEY, J. M. *The Byzantine World.* New York, 1961.

KIDD, B. J. *The Churches of Eastern Christendom.* London, 1927.

MEYENDORFF, J. *The Orthodox Church: Its Past and Its Role in the World Today.* New York, 1962.

MOURAVIEFF, A. N. *A History of the Church of Russia.* Oxford, 1842.

NEALE, J. M. *A History of the Holy Eastern Church.* London, 1850. Part I, General Introduction.

OBOLENSKY, D. *The Byzantine Commonwealth: Eastern Europe 500-1453.* London, 1971.

OSTROGORSKY, G. *History of the Byzantine State.* New Brunswick, N.J., 1957.

PALANQUE, J. R., BARDY, G., and DE LABRIOLLE, P. *The Church in the Christian Roman Empire.* 2 vols. London and New York, 1949-52.

RUNCIMAN, S. *The Great Church in Captivity: A Study of the*

Patriarchate of Constantinople from the Eve of the Turkish Turkish Conquest to the Greek War of Independence. Cambridge, 1968.

SPINKA, M. *A History of Christianity in the Balkans.* Chicago, 1933.

SUMNER, B. H. *A Survey of Russian History.* London, 1948.

VASILIEV, A. *A History of the Byzantine Empire.* 2 vols. Madison, Wis., 1958.

WARE, T. *The Orthodox Church.* Baltimore, 1963.

ZERNOV, N. *The Russians and Their Church.* London, 1945.

Doctrine, Spirituality, Liturgy

ARSENIEV, N. *Mysticism and the Eastern Church.* London, 1926.

BRIGHTMAN, F. E. *Liturgies, Eastern and Western.* Oxford, 1896. Vol. 1.

BULGAKOV, S. *The Orthodox Church.* London, 1935.

FEDOTOV, G. *The Russian Religious Mind.* 2 vols. Cambridge, Mass., vol. 1, 1946; vol. 2, 1966.

GAVIN, F. *Some Aspects of Contemporary Greek Orthodox Thought.* Milwaukee, Wis., 1923.

GRABAR, A. *Byzantine Painting.* New York, 1953.

HAPGOOD, I. F. *A Service Book of the Holy Orthodox Catholic Apostolic Church.* New York, 1906.

KADLUBOVSKY, E. and PALMER, G. E. M. *Writings from the Philokalia.* London, 1951.

_____ *Early Fathers from the Philokalia.* London, 1954.

KONDAKOV, N. P. *The Russian Icon.* Oxford, 1927.

LOSSKY, V. *The Mystical Theology of the Eastern Church.* London, 1957.

MEYENDORFF, J. *Christ in Eastern Christian Thought.* New York, 1969.

_____. *St. Gregory Palamas and Orthodox Spirituality.* Crestwood, N.Y., 1974.

OUSPENSKY, L., and LOSSKY, V. *The Meaning of Icons.* London, 1938.

RICE, D. T. *Byzantine Art.* Oxford, 1935.

SALAVILLE, S. *An Introduction to the Study of Eastern Liturgies.* London, 1938.

SCHMEMANN, A. *Introduction to Liturgical Theology.* London, 1966.